an overview of...

Broken Strings, Missing Notes

We live in a nation that is out of tune. The gap between the rich and poor grows ever larger, our critical energy and environmental problems receive little attention, and our country no longer plays a leadership role in seeking global peace and justice. An oligarchy of ideological extremists and religious legalists, operating behind closed doors, threatens our fundamental democratic rights and individual liberties. Exploiting fear and religious differences, it embraces militarism and global capitalism in its pursuit of power and money. Its agenda is inconsistent with the views of not only most Democrats, but also many Republicans.

Broken Strings, Missing Notes challenges this oligarchy and its underlying premises of privatization, deregulation, and legalistic moralism. This book presents a vision for the renewal of our nation based on the continued strength and broad acceptance of its guiding principles. It speaks to those seeking to build a more just, humane, and sustainable society, to religious communities concerned about distortions of their traditions, to conservatives concerned about fiscal irresponsibility and our costly mistakes in Iraq, and to liberals searching for new ways to express their ideals. It emphasizes cooperation rather than legalism, pluralism rather than exclusivity, and consensus decision-making rather than tyranny by the majority.

As suggested by its title, *Broken Strings, Missing Notes* uses the violin as a metaphorical model for our democracy and its goal of ensuring that there are no longer any "broken strings" or "missing notes" in our society.

Reactions of readers...

"...much enjoyed..."

"...a desperately needed vision..."

"...one of the most engaging books of nonfiction I've read this year..."

Broken Strings, Missing Notes

About the author

Larry J. Eriksson is a consultant and writer residing with his wife, Karen, in Madison, Wisconsin. He has served as an engineer, manager, officer, and director at various corporations and is the author of *Business Decisions: the impact of corporate mergers and global capitalism on our lives.* He received a B.S.E.E. from Northwestern University, an M.S.E.E. from the University of Minnesota, and a Ph.D. from the University of Wisconsin at Madison. Dr. Eriksson is a member of Madison Area Business Consultants, Advent Lutheran Church, and the Wisconsin Network for Peace and Justice. In addition to practicing his violin, he enjoys swimming, biking, and golfing.

About the publisher

Quarter Section Press, a unit of Eriksson Research, LLC, publishes books with a special emphasis on themes related to building a more sustainable, just, and humane world. Its name recalls the 160 acres or quarter section that comprised the typical small, family farm in the years following the Homestead Act of 1862.

Broken Strings, Missing Notes

...strengthening democracy and seeking justice
in a nation out of tune

♫ ♫ ♫

Larry J. Eriksson

QUARTER SECTION PRESS
Madison, Wisconsin, USA

The statements in this book are the opinions of the author based on his personal research and experiences.

Printed on acid free paper.
The text is set in 11-point Times New Roman font.

First edition, first printing

ISBN 0-9721875-1-0

Library of Congress Control Number: 2005905345

QUARTER SECTION PRESS
a unit of Eriksson Research, LLC
6105 Fairfax Lane
Madison, WI 53718-8262 U.S.A.

608.222.2689
erikssonresearch@execpc.com
www.execpc.com/~erikres www.madisonconsultants.com

Please contact Quarter Section Press for information on quantity discounts.

Contents

Quick look glossary

absentee managers:	nonresident corporate decision makers
bimodal society:	more rich and poor than in a normal distribution
checks and balances:	dividing authority, power, oversight
communism:	organizing society without private property
comparative advantage:	where you are most competitive relative to others
corporate governance:	processes to monitor corporate behavior
democracy:	government of, by, and for the people
deregulation:	eliminating governmental regulations
economic diversity:	measure of variety in an economy or business
fascism:	extreme nationalism and regimented industry under repressive dictatorship
fiduciary responsibility:	obligation to protect the owner's interests
fiscal austerity:	paying off debts, borrowing less
free trade:	trade without barriers such as tariffs
globalization:	the transformation to a global economy
hedonics:	adjusting product prices to account for features
legalism:	obsessive focus on rules and laws
market liberalization:	dropping trade barriers
nationalism:	emphasis on nation over other values
oligarchy:	government by the elite few
outsourcing:	moving jobs to alternate suppliers
plutocracy:	government by the wealthy
privatization:	moving functions from public to private sector
productivity:	measure of economic output for a given input
separation of powers:	dividing power between branches of government
socialism:	extensive public involvement in the economy
totalitarianism:	government by repressive regime or dictator

Contents

Quick look glossary

absentee managers:	nonresident corporate decision makers
bimodal society:	more rich and poor than in a normal distribution
checks and balances:	dividing authority, power, oversight
communism:	organizing society without private property
comparative advantage:	where you are most competitive relative to others
corporate governance:	processes to monitor corporate behavior
democracy:	government of, by, and for the people
deregulation:	eliminating governmental regulations
economic diversity:	measure of variety in an economy or business
fascism:	extreme nationalism and regimented industry under repressive dictatorship
fiduciary responsibility:	obligation to protect the owner's interests
fiscal austerity:	paying off debts, borrowing less
free trade:	trade without barriers such as tariffs
globalization:	the transformation to a global economy
hedonics:	adjusting product prices to account for features
legalism:	obsessive focus on rules and laws
market liberalization:	dropping trade barriers
nationalism:	emphasis on nation over other values
oligarchy:	government by the elite few
outsourcing:	moving jobs to alternate suppliers
plutocracy:	government by the wealthy
privatization:	moving functions from public to private sector
productivity:	measure of economic output for a given input
separation of powers:	dividing power between branches of government
socialism:	extensive public involvement in the economy
totalitarianism:	government by repressive regime or dictator

To Karen

♬ ♬ ♬

Prelude

Playing the violin is an intimate musical experience. You embrace a violin with your cheek. You coax the music out of the instrument with your bow. You feel the music through the bow, the strings, and the vibrating body of the instrument. The movie The Red Violin *describes the fictional journey of a single violin through generations of owners. It beautifully portrays the music, heritage, romance, and broad appeal of the violin. The story of the violin is the story of a fragile instrument that has endured to become the leader of the symphonic orchestra. Its story parallels the story of the United States in many ways -- a nation that survived an unlikely birth to become a world leader with its robust but still fragile democracy.*

♫ ♫ ♫

We live in a nation that is out of tune. Our collective political, economic, and social lives are no longer proceeding in a harmonious fashion. A general unease appears to have taken hold among many Americans reminiscent of the national malaise described by President Carter more than 25 years ago. An AP-Ipsos poll of adults in 2005 found that only 35 percent thought our country was headed in the right direction. Joan Chittister, in her 1998 book on spirituality, *Heart of Flesh,* speaks of the violence, militarism, and economic exploitation that permeate our society.

Many Americans no longer look to the future with confidence. Equal opportunity for all is giving way to more money and control for the already rich and powerful. Members of the middle class, the historic core of our national prosperity and strength, are slowly, but inexorably, slipping down the economic ladder. Their wages have not seen any real growth in 25 years. Their ability to find and keep suitable jobs continues to decline. Obtaining and paying for proper health care becomes ever more difficult. Their future and that of their children grows more uncertain.

Political discord is on the rise. Partisan disagreements are ever more strident. In late 2000, for the first time in our history, a judicial decision effectively determined the results of a presidential election. The investigations that followed exposed problems with our election processes that caused embarrassment and disillusionment throughout the nation. Neal Gabler suggested in *The New York Times* that the 2000 presidential election shattered our collective illusion concerning the sanctity of voting in our democracy.

Following the controversial results of the 2000 presidential election, a conservative oligarchy of the rich and powerful took control of the White House supported by an unlikely coalition of ideological extremists and religious legalists. Members of this oligarchy in the White House and Congress used the subsequent 9/11 attacks and the fight against terrorism to justify unilateral militarism, repressive legislation, and economic exploitation.

A nation that once barely maintained a peacetime army now finds its national leadership declaring and waging virtually endless, and even preemptive, war while its military budget remains by far the largest in the world. New laws endanger our personal liberties, threaten the separation of church and state, and exploit the fears of American citizens. Meanwhile, the gap between the rich and poor grows ever larger, and our critical energy and environmental problems receive little attention.

The United States' reputation for freedom, justice, and fair play is fading as its friends and foes alike complain about its irresponsible and reckless actions. Our country no longer plays a leadership role in seeking global peace and justice. As a result, the United States, a founding member and host of the United Nations, finds itself at odds with many of its members. In 2005, when the Senate Judiciary Committee interviewed a Bush nominee for Attorney General with seemingly ambiguous views of torture and the Geneva Convention, even a Republican senator suggested that "we have lost our way."

Legalistic moralism divides our nation, threatening our personal freedoms, and discriminating against minorities. From a government founded on the principle of the separation of church and state, we are slowly, but seemingly inexorably, taking on the characteristics of a fundamentalist Christian state.

A nation that once encouraged the trustbusters now allows global corporations to apply undue influence on both its economy and government. Global trade agreements cede political power to anonymous groups beyond the reach of the people and their elected officials. Powerful moneyed interests apply excessive influence on elections. Despite conspicuous failures, conservative politicians continue to push for economic deregulation and privatization. Paul Krugman in an essay in *The New York Times* suggests that rather than calling support for Social Security "class warfare" and concern for inequality the "politics of envy," we should do something about the "politics of greed."

Many of the same political forces that have long served desires of the wealthy and global corporations now have almost complete control of the three branches of our federal government. The agenda of these extremists, operating behind closed doors, is often inconsistent with the views of not only most Democrats, but also many Republicans, both past and present. At a time when books on the so-called "founding fathers" appear regularly on best seller lists, our nation is ignoring lessons from its own history.

♫ ♫ ♫

This book describes the need for transformative change in our economic, political, and religious lives. It proposes a vision for the future based on cooperation rather than legalism, pluralism rather than exclusivity, and consensus decision-making rather than tyranny by the majority. It challenges the direction that political conservatism and religious fundamentalism are taking our nation.

Arundhati Roy writes eloquently and powerfully, in her book *War Talk,* on the interconnected nature of militaristic nationalism, religious fundamentalism, and global capitalism. *Broken Strings, Missing Notes* emphasizes these interconnected issues as it discusses the actions of the Bush administration since the 2000 election.

The recurring themes of this book include the importance of memory in creating a better future, the dangers of totalitarian government, and the need for checks and balances in a democracy. It draws on our nation's founding documents, speeches, and writings to identify the guiding principles that unite us as a people. It explores how the continued strength and broad acceptance of these guiding principles provide a strong foundation for the renewal our nation.

Broken Strings, Missing Notes takes seriously the great spiritual traditions of our country including the stories and parables found in the New Testament Gospels of the Bible. Among the questions that it considers are the source of authority in our lives, the connection between peace and justice, the relationship between law and grace, and the tension between the community and the individual.

This book speaks to those concerned about the erosion of our individual rights and liberties, to those seeking to build a more just, humane, and sustainable society, to religious communities concerned about distortions of their traditions, to conservatives concerned about fiscal irresponsibility and our costly mistakes in Iraq, and to liberals searching for new ways to express their ideals.

This book is not a memoir, but it does draw on my personal experiences to introduce or illuminate some of its primary themes. In December of 2002, I was recovering from colon surgery for removal of a cancerous tumor. At the same time, my mother was entering a more advanced stage of memory loss associated with Alzheimer's disease. Along with many other Americans, I worried about the state of our nation. I began to see parallels between our political discord, my malignant tumor, and my mother's memory problems.

In addition, some years after my father died, I decided to begin taking violin lessons using the violin that my father had played as a young man. There are no frets on a violin to guide the position of the violinist's left hand. Consequently, a degree of ambiguity and uncertainty characterize the music of a violin.

Broken Strings, Missing Notes uses the violin as a musical metaphor for our democracy. The broken strings of the title are the lives broken by our ill-advised economic, political, and military decisions as well as the damaged democratic processes of our nation. The missing notes of the title are the lost memories of our people as well as inability of many citizens to participate fully in our nation's economic, political, and social life. The book focuses on the need to heal the brokenness and emptiness in our country by strengthening our democratic processes and seeking justice for all citizens. A brief vignette at the beginning of each chapter explores the relationship between the violin and the topic in that section.

This book begins with the 2000 presidential election in which George W. Bush became president. It concludes with the defeat of the proposed constitution for the European Union by voters in France and the Netherlands in May and June of 2005. It appears that the failure of EU supporters to develop and communicate an adequate set of guiding principles for the proposed union prior to these votes contributed to these startling defeats.

A nation grows out of its guiding principles, not hundreds of pages of constitutional legalese. The future success or failure of the United States depends upon our ability to unite around the ideals that have inspired our people throughout our history. The resolution of many of the stories in this book remains uncertain. Nonetheless, regardless of their final outcome, these stories will continue to provide valuable lessons for the future.

♫ ♫ ♫

Broken Strings, Missing Notes contains four major parts. Part I discusses two major themes. The first theme is the emergence in our government following the 2000 election of a conservative oligarchy of the rich and powerful supported by an unlikely coalition of ideological extremists and religious legalists. The second theme is the continued strength and broad acceptance of our nation's guiding principles. The hopefulness of the second theme counterbalances the darkness of the first theme.

Chapter 1 discusses the role of guiding principles for a nation and uses Argentina to illustrate the consequences of failing to develop a constructive set of shared ideals. Chapter 2 reviews the narrow and controversial victory of the Bush administration in the 2000 presidential election and its divisive actions following the election. Chapter 3 describes the impact of corporate power and globalization on the national economy. Chapter 4 reviews the impact of global capitalism on the local economy.

Interlude One considers of the importance of memory for a society. Beginning with a brief discussion of Alzheimer's disease, it describes the ways in which the conservative oligarchy and global corporations are systematically ignoring or destroying our collective memories. It concludes with a description of efforts by various groups to recover their memories and cultural identity -- some of the "missing notes" of the book's title.

Part II discusses the divisive and often deceptive actions of the Bush administration following the 9/11 attacks and their impact on our national immune system of checks and balances. Part II is often dark and at times can seem never ending. Nonetheless, it prepares the way for the discussion of reform and renewal contained in Parts III and IV of this book.

Chapter 5 discusses the preemptive and "endless" war on terrorism, the repressive Patriot Act, and the Bush administration's self-serving domestic agenda. Chapter 6 reviews the scandals and frauds that resulted from aggressive capitalism, conflicts of interest, and the blurring of the boundaries between the corporate world and the government. Chapter 7 reviews the administration's deceptive justifications of its premature, ill-advised, and poorly managed war in Iraq. Chapter 8 describes how these deceptions have undermined our societal immune system including the media, the political opposition, and the judiciary. Chapter 9 reviews how an oligarchy of the powerful and wealthy restricts political protest, structures the electoral process to its unfair advantage, and controls the free flow of information.

Interlude Two presents a brief discussion of my personal encounter with cancer and expands to consider ways in which malignant growth can also endanger the health of societies. It discusses the ways in which totalitarian governments use lies, deception, and censorship to damage or destroy democratic institutions and processes -- some of the "broken strings" of the book's title.

Part III discusses the revival of our national immune system of checks and balances. It reviews specific actions people are taking to regain control of their personal, political, and economic lives.

Chapter 10 explores the ways in which people are beginning to regain control of their economic lives. It discusses efforts to control the impact of global corporations on communities, to protect investors from unscrupulous corporations, and to regain control of local economies. Chapter 11 extends this discussion into political life and reviews how the political opposition regained its voice during the 2004 presidential election campaign. It concludes with a description of how conservative extremists struck back at efforts of moderates and liberals to regain power. Chapter 12 discusses the results of the 2004 election and concludes with reflections on how a political minority can play a more active role in our nation.

Interlude Three uses my personal experience with transformative change to introduce the need for our society, both individually and collectively, to let go of its misconceptions and faulty assumptions.

Part IV presents the need for broader and deeper transformative change in our society. It presents a pluralistic approach to religious issues that is consistent with the teachings of the Gospels as well as the founding principles of our nation. It endorses a return to

America's long standing heritage of pluralism, consensus, and balance.

Chapter 13 discusses transformative change in the way in which we view our religious beliefs. It calls for inclusive approaches rather than exclusive, cooperation rather than legalism. Chapter 14 discusses the need for transformative change in how we implement our democratic ideals. In order to avoid tyranny by the majority, it calls for greater use of consensus decision-making techniques. Chapter 15 discusses the unique strengths that the political left brings to our political system, the importance of investing in our social capital, and the need to recommit ourselves to the guiding principles of our nation.

At the conclusion of the book, a brief Coda reflects on the unfinished nature of this story, summarizes some of its major themes, and discusses our personal roles in influencing the way in which the future may unfold. Appendix I presents additional information on the violin, and Appendix II presents an analysis of numerical results from recent presidential elections and public opinion polls.

♬ ♬ ♬

I am grateful for the contributions of all those who helped me find my way along the multiple paths that run through this book: my family, friends, and medical team that enabled me to return to good health following my colon cancer surgery with a minimum of difficulty and discomfort; my extended family who helped my mother through her various transitions as her memory problems deepened; my violin teacher, Kelly Nelson, who welcomed an older adult as a new violin student and also reviewed the portions of this book discussing music and the violin.

I also appreciate the contributions of those who read part or all of various drafts of this book including Jeff Boldt, Doug Crews-Nelson, Marily Crews-Nelson, John Rowe, and Char Thompson, as well as my son, Mark Eriksson, and my daughter, Jodi

Eriksson Wollack. Needless to say, they do not necessarily share the opinions that I have expressed in this book, but they have helped improve this book in many ways.

Most importantly, I want to express my appreciation for the continuing love and support of my wife, Karen. She encouraged me to study the violin, supported me during my illness, and helped in countless ways with this book. These include discussing numerous ideas and issues, providing suggestions on both the form and content, and carefully reviewing numerous drafts. Without her help and encouragement, this book would not exist.

June, 2005

Larry J. Eriksson
Madison, Wisconsin

Part I

Loss of harmony

...of, by, and for the people...

We hold these Truths to be self-evident; that all men are created equal, that they are endowed by their Creator with certain unalienable Rights, that among these are Life, Liberty, and the Pursuit of Happiness...

The Declaration of Independence
July 4, 1776

We the People of the United States, in Order to form a more perfect Union, establish Justice, insure domestic Tranquility, provide for the common defense, promote the general Welfare, and secure the Blessings of Liberty to ourselves and our Posterity, do ordain and establish this Constitution for the United States of America.

The Preamble to the Constitution, 1787

Four score and seven years ago our fathers brought forth...a new nation, conceived in liberty and dedicated to the proposition that all men are created equal...we here highly resolve...that this nation, under God, shall have a new birth of freedom -- and that government of the people, by the people, and for the people, shall not perish from the earth.

Abraham Lincoln
Address at Gettysburg, 1863

Chapter I

The role of guiding fictions

...we hold these truths to be self-evident...

♫ ♫ ♫

I walked slowly with my mother up the stairs of her house. We opened the door to a closet and removed an old violin case from the shelf. The black leather case mirrored the shape of the violin that it protected. On the front was a small clasp and lock. Anxious to inspect the violin, I tried to open the case, but the clasp refused to budge. My mother had no idea where the key might be. Disappointed, we stared in frustration at the sealed case. I told my mother that I would take it to a music shop, and perhaps they would be able to open the lock. Sometimes, it is not easy to enter the past.

The curious case of Argentina

Argentina is a South American country about one-third the size of the United States bounded on the west by the Andes Mountains, on the east by the Atlantic Ocean, and extending about 1500 miles from its northern border with Bolivia to the tip of Cape Horn. Its capital and largest city is the vast metropolis of Buenos Aires. In the 1950s, Argentina was a strong, prosperous nation, comparable in many ways to the wealthiest nations of North America and Europe.

Over the past 50 years, Argentina has suffered through military coups, ill-advised wars, and economic reversals. It has struggled to regain its footing in a world that seems to have passed it by. Despite its former economic wealth, rich agricultural lands, high level of literacy, and strong ties to European markets and technology, Argentina appears to be a nation that has failed to fulfill its potential.

Nicholas Shumway, in his book *The Invention of Argentina,* draws on the work of Edmund S. Morgan, and his book *Inventing the People,* to suggest that a nation's success often depends on its ability to formulate broadly accepted set of aphorisms he describes as "guiding fictions." They are fictional in the sense that they are not literally true, although there must be some truth behind them. Despite its pejorative connotation, guiding fictions represent what the nation values and hopes to achieve; for this reason, this book will sometimes use the parallel term, "guiding principles."

Success and health on an individual or collective basis depends on the creation of guiding fictions that provide strength for the present as well as inspiration for the future. For the present, they encourage compliance with societal norms and structures. For the future, they encourage a spirit of reform and renewal as we strive to move closer to achieving the ideal expressed by the guiding fiction.

Shumway emphasizes the role of these "guiding fictions" in the political development of nations. He maintains that Argentina's failure to formulate and accept a suitable set of guiding fictions played a primary role in limiting its future success.

Argentina achieved independence through a rebellion against Spanish colonial rule in the early 19th century, not long after the formation of the United States. Following independence, the urban residents of Buenos Aires, the largest city and province, fought with the outlying, more rural provinces over political and economic power. The so-called porteños of Buenos Aires wanted a strong central government, looked to Europe as their ideal, and believed in the superiority of an elite oligarchy in Buenos Aires. The populists in the provinces exhibited national pride in "La Gran Argentina," believed that the gaucho represented the spirit of the true Argentinean, and felt that the elitists and oligarchs exploited the provinces for the benefit of Buenos Aires. Shumway suggests that these factions developed competing sets of guiding fictions that prevented the nation from unifying around a common set of core values.

Unfortunately each group also developed a set of negative guiding fictions that have served to reinforce the differences between the two groups. Many of the porteños of Buenos Aires embraced the myth that the political opposition is evil and deserves elimination. This has led to an atmosphere of periodic violence and killings rather than mutual cooperation. For their part, the populists in the provinces have embraced a belief in the need for a strong man, a caudillo, to lead them in their search for justice and recognition. This has led to the election of leaders that sometimes more closely resembled fascist dictators than democratically elected politicians.

A broadly accepted set of suitable guiding fictions would have helped unify Argentina and strengthen its democratic processes. These guiding fictions may also have inspired the nation to create a more authentic Argentine identity rather than focusing on European models. This would have provided a basis to develop solutions to the problems that Argentina and virtually every nation must face.

Stories, guiding fictions, and slogans

People tell stories to make sense out of an often confusing and seemingly senseless world. Although these stories may sometimes be incomplete or inaccurate, they nonetheless help us to better understand their lives. Guiding fictions or principles often emerge from these stories and find expression in memorable phrases, sayings, maxims, aphorisms, mottoes, or slogans. They capture the core values of a society and provide inspiration for the future.

Unhealthy and often destructive maxims create divisions rather than unify and move us away from our core values. Sometimes they unify without providing much sense of inspiration for the future. Most middle aged Americans remember a time when leaders of the Soviet Union proclaimed "we will bury you." As it turned out this maxim was more fiction than truth. But even ignoring the eventual failure of the Soviet Union, the phrase seems inadequate as a useful guiding fiction. It may have unified the Soviet people around increasing production, but it did not provide much inspiration for renewal and progress towards a better society.

Garrison Keillor, in his morning feature on National Public Radio *The Writer's Almanac,* presented a story about Mary Gordon and her book *The Shadow Man: A Daughter's Search for Her Father.* As an adult, Gordon learned that the stories her father told her about his life were very different from the truth. In fact, he was not the Harvard graduate and writer as he had claimed. However, despite her resentment, Gordon believes that the myth that emerged from the apocryphal stories that her father told her became a guiding fiction that inspired her to become a successful author.

Individuals, governments, businesses, and organizations develop aphorism, slogans, and mottoes that summarize their goals, ideals, or historical experiences and inspire action. They are often capsule summaries of their underlying guiding principles. State mottoes can be as simple and direct as Wisconsin's "Forward" or as rich with historical content as New Hampshire's "Live free or die" or as descriptive as Indiana's "The Crossroads of America." Corporations adopt a variety of slogans. Some are short-lived and last only as long as the current advertising campaign. Others reflect the overall corporate mission and remain for many years. Many organizations have simple mottoes such as the Boy Scouts' "Be prepared." Some years ago, our church adopted the slogan, "Growing together" for its building fund campaign.

Many individuals also use short slogans or phrases to express their own personal values or interests. Automobiles are a favorite place to display these slogans either on bumper stickers or on license plates. All political views are in evidence. From the aggressive "These colors don't run," to the reflective "Peace is patriotic." Some Americans protesting the war in Iraq placed yard signs in front of their homes declaring "War is not the path to peace."

Without consideration of the appropriateness or value of these specific mottoes and slogans, they generally have several characteristics in common. First, they attempt to unite people around a common ideal or value, and second, they provide guidance for the future. However, the most striking feature about most of these slogans is that they are literal fictions. Our colors may not retreat in the eyes of some, but they certainly have retreated from battles and in the case of Vietnam from entire countries and wars. War may not be the path to peace, but some wars, such as World War II, seem to be unavoidable and have led to an extended period of relative peace. Our church may have wanted to grow together, but the slogan itself implies some concern about moving apart.

Nonetheless, guiding fictions provide a useful framework for analyzing the health and vitality of nations, businesses, organizations, and individuals. Despite their idealistic nature, they can be powerful tools for inspiring and guiding societies and individuals towards greatness. At its founding, the United States benefited from the wisdom of those involved in creating a rich array of positive guiding fictions for our nation.

Guiding fictions in the United States

The original colonists sought new opportunities in America for themselves and their families as they fled religious and political oppression in Europe. Initially, they maintained many of their bonds with their homelands. However, as the colonies grew stronger, they came to resent the burdens and restrictions that Great Britain placed on their lives and work. After much discussion and debate, they made the difficult decision to form a new country.

The United States of America, formed out of an extended and violent war of independence, saw itself as a great experiment in self-government free from the trappings of monarchy and grounded on democratic ideals. It struggled for some years to find a suitable form for its government. After a frustrating effort under the Articles of Confederation, the United States Constitution established a balance between a strong central government and the governments of the constituent states. Almost as an afterthought, the Constitution included a Bill of Rights to articulate and protect the basic human rights of all Americans.

By most standards, the United States has been a highly successful nation. Blessed with abundant natural resources, dedicated workers, and enlightened democratic government, it began a long and steady path to material prosperity in the 19th century and global leadership in the 20th century. Most of its citizens enjoy the benefits of great economic wealth, democratic government, constitutionally protected rights and freedoms, a strong military, and a land rich with natural resources.

Its early leaders were innovative, courageous, and generous as they invented a new form of government for the nation that they created. Following its uncertain beginning and lengthy Revolutionary War, the United States has faced many severe problems including among others slavery, the Civil War, the Great Depression, World Wars I and II, and attacks by terrorists. Although it has made mistakes, its history for well over 200 years is a remarkable example of success and progress on many fronts.

One of the reasons for our nation's success has been its ability to develop powerful guiding principles. These principles unite us around a set of important core values and inspire us to fulfill their promise. We find them in our founding documents, great speeches, songs, stories, and legends. They provide a capsule summary of our collective ideals as well as our dreams and aspirations for the future.

Walter Isaacson has noted that the United States won its independence due to the ability of its leaders to win the war of ideas. Our Declaration of Independence affirms the basic, though certainly idealistic, equality of all people, certain unalienable rights such as life, liberty, and the pursuit of happiness, and the necessity of the government to have the consent of the governed. A few years later, our Constitution codified the functions of government and preserved through the Bill of Rights the basic human rights that continue to guide us today. The genius of the Constitution is in the way in which it formulated a government that united diverse factions and beliefs around a few central principles that stress tolerance, justice, and liberty. Although the United States has often fallen short of its highest ideals, perhaps most notably in its long tolerance of slavery, its founding documents ultimately enabled it to move closer to these ideals as it developed as a nation.

We express what it means to be an American through a collection of guiding fictions that express our shared ideals and governing principles. They take many forms and include phrases such as "all men are created equal" and "America is the land of opportunity," metaphors such as "the United States is like a melting pot," and simple maxims such as "a penny saved is a penny earned." They grew out of the experiences of the founders and builders of our nation including their desire for freedom, the challenges of forming a new nation, and the need to be a good neighbor in a sparsely settled and often difficult wilderness.

At face value, the statements that "all men are created equal" and that "America is the land of opportunity" are demonstrably false. They are fictions that were never literally true and probably never will be. Although, in many ways, our country has been and remains a land of opportunity for many people, the opportunities often come at great sacrifice and are not equally available to all newcomers. Many immigrants found more difficult conditions than they expected and, in some cases, returned to their home countries.

However, despite its lack of literal accuracy, there is some truth in the statement. Our Constitution contains legal protections that apply, at least in theory, to all members of society regardless of their social rank or wealth. Over time, our pursuit of this ideal has evolved into efforts to create "equal opportunities" for all Americans. In fact, "equal opportunities for all Americans" has become a new guiding fiction. Unfortunately, we still fall far short of fulfilling even this weakened version.

The melting pot concept has a similarly mixed story. My own children and grandchildren have grandparents and great-grandparents whose ethnic heritage represents at least nine European countries -- a classic example of the melting pot. However, despite the broad range of ethnic groups in our country, these groups have not always worked and lived together as well as the melting pot concept might suggest. In some cases, the desires of immigrants for the freedom to retain their native culture and old ways have come into conflict with the guiding fiction of America as a melting pot. As with many guiding fictions, there is some truth and some fiction in each of these broadly accepted, but less than fully accurate phrases.

Nonetheless, our country has usually endorsed central myths and guiding fictions that serve to unify rather than divide, to endorse fundamental human rights, and to support our democratic processes. Some examples include "every vote counts," "equal rights for all," and "the American Dream." They have united and inspired our nation towards greatness. Their simplicity and appeal have also captured the imagination of many others throughout the world.

David Hackett Fischer, in his book *Liberty and Freedom,* portrays and discusses the iconography of our nation such as flags and coins. Sayings such as "Don't tread on me" or "Liberty or death," that early Americans used on their flags, reflected their strong beliefs in liberty and independence. The Stars and Stripes contains a field of stars representing the individual states forming our nation and thirteen red and white stripes to remind us of the cost of freedom. Among the recurring images on our coins are eagles, olive branches, and arrows -- symbols of strength, peace, and freedom.

The book *American Virtues, Values, and Triumphs* suggests that American values include freedom, ingenuity, friendship, faith, humor, perseverance, loyalty, courage, honesty, and compassion. It offers many speeches, writings, poems, songs, and slogans that illustrate these various ideals throughout our history. In many ways, they are guiding fictions. Although it is easy to find many counterexamples of how our country and its people failed to practice these virtues, they are nonetheless inspiring values for many Americans. Most of us learn them at home as small children, and our schools reinforce them throughout our formal education. For most of us, these principles are so central to our national character that we rarely give them a second thought.

New guiding fictions

New guiding fictions evolve even as older aphorisms fade away. Many have their origin in times of crisis. From the Civil War era, we have the guiding fiction that "Lincoln freed the slaves." Actually the Emancipation Proclamation only freed the slaves held in the rebellious states. It was not until the passage of the 13th Amendment to the Constitution that the country outlawed slavery across the land. Nonetheless, many people use the aphorism that "Lincoln freed the slaves" as shorthand for the end of slavery in this country.

Over the years, others have expanded and enhanced our collection of positive guiding fictions. Abraham Lincoln may not have heard of "guiding fictions," but he certainly articulated many of our country's most powerful examples in his Gettysburg Address. A number of the chapter titles in this book come from that speech. He also understood the dangers inherent in destructive and divisive guiding fictions. For example, in his opposition to slavery and the revocation of the Missouri Compromise, Lincoln quipped that we have gone from "declaring that all men are created equal," to declaring that allowing "some men to enslave others is a 'sacred right of self-government.'" The latter is hardly a statement designed to unite and inspire a nation.

From Abraham Lincoln's *Gettysburg Address* to Martin Luther King's *I Have a Dream* speech, our leaders have continued to enunciate basic human values and ideals through widely accepted guiding fictions. During the Great Depression, Franklin Roosevelt told the nation that the "only thing we fear, is fear itself." Later, in the aftermath of the attack on Pearl Harbor, he stated that the day of the attack would live on as "a day of infamy." Both aphorisms have evolved into guiding fictions of the United States. Once again, they have that kernel of truth even though perhaps not literally true. Today, we still fear many things more than "fear itself," and the shock of Pearl Harbor and even the meaning of "infamy" has receded in our collective consciousness. However, in times of great trauma and crises, these phrases both serve to unify us as well as enable us to move forward in a positive manner -- the dual values of all useful guiding fictions.

In 1944, Roosevelt's state of the union message noted that in addition to the Bill of Rights in the Constitution, we now have a second Bill of Rights that includes the rights of workers "to a useful and remunerative job," of farmers "to raise and sell...products" at a decent return, of businesses to trade free from "unfair competition and domination by monopolies," of every family "to a decent home," and of all people "to adequate medical care," "protection from economic fears of old age, sickness, accident, and unemployment," and "a good education." This extraordinary summary of basic human rights built on Roosevelt's Four Freedoms -- freedom of speech and religion, freedom from want and fear. Many have reached guiding fiction status while others still create controversy.

David Shipler, in his book *The Working Poor,* contrasts the "American Myth" that "hard work cures poverty" with the "American Anti-Myth" that "society is responsible for poverty." He calls for an amalgam that attempts to create a new synthesis of these two positions. Although this is certainly a reasonable approach, it may be more helpful to look at both the myth and anti-myth from the perspective of their potential roles as guiding fictions.

Both statements have some truth behind them, but also fall short of being fully accurate. However, Shipler's "myth" tends to divide Americans between those who work hard and those who don't. It may inspire some individuals to work harder, but it fails to inspire society to do anything. In fact, it suggests society has little to do with poverty. On the other hand, Shipler's so-called "anti-myth" tends to unify society in opposition to poverty and to inspire society to take those steps necessary to alleviate poverty through education, training, job creation, employment services, social services, and so on. It suggests that together we can create a society where everyone can live a better life.

We are living at a time in our history when some are attempting to impose new guiding principles on our country. In evaluating their rhetoric, we need to ask ourselves several questions. Will these principles lead to a healthier, more just and sustainable society? Will they unite or divide? Will the future be more open or closed?

Many aphorisms are less than inspiring. These include "do what I tell you," "father knows best," "it's for your own good," "might makes right," and "God is on our side" -- although some of our current leaders often seem to believe that the latter is indeed true. It may be no coincidence that these statements are very similar to the beliefs of totalitarian dictators as well as abusive parents as discussed by Alice Miller in her book *For Your Own Good.*

What does it take for a new and positive guiding fiction to emerge? Some examples, such as "one man (person), one vote," have a balance between truth and inspiration. Statements of the naked truth are often uninspiring pessimism; successful guiding fictions include a degree of inspiring overstatement. An example might be the title of the book *It Takes a Village* (to Raise a Child) by Hillary Clinton. On the other hand, statements that only inspire are often too idealistic to be achievable. Promotions that promise "everyone's a winner" fall into that category. Efforts to created utopian societies in the 1800s virtually all failed due to too much inspiration and too little attention to the shortcomings of human nature.

A land of opportunity

Lost in the xenophobia that has taken control of many of our leaders in the name of homeland security is the reality that we remain a nation of immigrants. Despite the rhetoric concerning the need for stringent controls over immigration, even many native born Americans are only one or two generations removed from the immigrant experience themselves. For many of them, one of our central guiding fictions, that the United States is a "land of opportunity," was and remains an inspiration.

In its early years, this country attracted successive waves of immigrants from Europe who took the long and sometimes difficult voyage across the Atlantic Ocean to build new lives. In the early years of the 20th century, many of them passed through Ellis Island in the shadow of the Statue of Liberty. Millions waited in long queues to learn whether officials would allow them to enter the country or force them to turn back and return to Europe.

My own family provides a typical example of the process. My mother was born in 1920 in Slovenia, the northernmost region of the newly formed republic of Yugoslavia, adjoining Italy and formerly part of the Austro-Hungarian Empire. Shortly after World War I, when my mother was only two years old, my grandmother departed with her from Novo Mesto, Slovenia, never to return. They soon arrived, presumably by rail, at the great French port of Le Havre and boarded the ocean liner *Paris* to cross the Atlantic.

My father was the fourth child of his Swedish immigrant parents. His mother was seventeen years old when she left Sweden in 1904, to travel to the United States. Two years later, she married my grandfather who had also emigrated from Sweden. They were both from southern Sweden, a rural, agricultural part of the country that, much like Slovenia, had limited economic opportunities.

Immigrants often emigrated to this country seeking better opportunities and fleeing societies torn apart by class divisions and militarism. After they arrived, they soon found themselves struggling with an unfamiliar language in a strange new land. They worked long hours at difficult jobs as they learned a new language and a culture different in so many ways from the one they had left behind. They sacrificed to create better lives both for themselves as well as their children and grandchildren.

Those who came to this country during the great wave of immigration at the start of the 20th century soon found their problems compounded by the Great Depression. After a decade of economic struggle, World War II brought an era of horrifying headlines, frantic production, domestic shortages, and personal loss. Many served in the armed forces along with friends and relatives. Thousands never returned. This cascade of trials and tribulations had a profound effect on the lives of those who survived these turbulent years.

Eva Hoffman, in her book *After Such Knowledge,* considers the holocaust during World War II from the perspective of its impact on her generation, the generation that followed the actual victims of this horrific event. She notes that her parents' generation, the survivors of the holocaust, often minimized the problems of her generation when compared to the hunger, pain, and suffering that the survivors had endured. The survivors also hoped and expected that the younger generation -- the second generation -- would live the perfect lives that the holocaust had denied them. The second generation would have every advantage, would solve every problem, would save the world -- and be happy while they were doing it.

Not surprisingly, Hoffman views these attitudes of her parents' generation as the source of various dysfunctions in the lives of the children of the second generation. They grew to in some sense envy the status that their parents achieved as survivors of a great event, the holocaust. Despite the hardships and many lives lost in the holocaust, the second generation often viewed their parents as the beneficiaries of an historical accident that gave them the opportunity to achieve what their children could never match. The accomplishments of the second generation could never meet their parents' expectations, and more importantly, their own. Too often, they saw their own lives as second rate compared to the heroic experiences of their parents. Their efforts to overachieve and meet their parents demands for perfection led to feelings of failure, guilt, and disillusionment.

Without diminishing the unique scope and impact of the holocaust, there are some parallels between the lives of the first generation holocaust survivors that Hoffman describes in her book and the lives of many American immigrants. After experiencing in rapid succession the trauma of emigration, the Great Depression, and World War II, they too considered themselves survivors of great difficulties.

After decades of struggle, many looked to their children, the "baby boomers," to achieve the successes that war and depression had denied them. Their children would have a head start since they knew the language and had grown up as Americans. They would go to college and build a new and better world.

Many immigrant parents expressed these feelings about life in stories, i.e. guiding fictions, that they created for their children. They tended to fall into two quite different groups. One group created stories that went something like this: "Life is good. Your family has achieved success over great odds through hard work. If you work hard, you can also succeed." As with all guiding fictions, this story is not literally true -- life is a mixture of good and bad, hard work does not guarantee success. However, it does unite the family around its past successes and inspires the next generation to enter the future with a certain degree of confidence, partners with those who have succeeded in the past.

The other group created stories that went something like this: "Life is a struggle. Your family has achieved success by making great sacrifices. To show your appreciation for these sacrifices, you must succeed." Again, this story is not literally true. Life is not all struggle. Sacrifices do not guarantee success. However, in contrast to the first story, this story does not unite. It divides the family between those who made the sacrifices and those who will benefit. It does not inspire the next generation, it threatens them with a mantle of guilt.

Although these two approaches illustrate the differences between healthy and unhealthy guiding fictions, they both contain a clear expectation of success. For this reason, the baby boomers, whose parents too often expected the impossible, have strengthened our nation with their efforts to meet the very high standards that their parents' expected. Many succeeded. As adults, some celebrated their achievements with parents whose positive guiding fiction had united and inspired their family. Others, from families whose negative guiding fiction emphasized separation and guilt, found less joy in their accomplishments.

Despite their many successes, as Hoffman notes, it is impossible for any generation to meet all the expectations that parents sometimes place on them. As we will see in the next chapter, this clash between parental expectations and historical reality for the baby boomers created a generational divide over the Vietnam War with continuing repercussions to the present day.

♫ ♫ ♫

Nations formulate a great variety of guiding fictions. Some are more important than others. Some are more constructive Some receive broader acceptance. The Declaration of Independence begins with the statement that "we hold these truths to be self-evident." In fact, it is one of our guiding fictions. However, at that time, and perhaps even now, these "truths" were not at all "self-evident." In fact, there was considerable debate over the source of these "basic truths" or guiding fictions. During our Civil War, hundreds of thousands lost their lives when some Americans chose to once again "institute new government" and formed the Confederacy because they believed, much like the founders of our nation, that the existing government had become "destructive" to their rights. Those who remained in the Union certainly did not find the right of the Confederacy to revolt in 1861 self-evident anymore than the King of England found the right of the United States to revolt in 1775 self-evident. Nonetheless, many of our guiding fictions encompass values that are shared by many Americans. They continue to serve as our collective insurance against attempts by the few to twist our nation into their own distorted vision of the future.

♬ ♬ ♬

Chapter 2

The 2000 presidential election

...the consent of the governed...

♫ ♫ ♫

A few days after finding the violin, I was waiting for service at the repair counter of our local music shop. As I fiddled with the lock one final time, the case suddenly opened. Its resistance to being opened was not due to the lock, but was simply the stubborn behavior of an eighty year old clasp. As I opened the case on the counter, the condition of the violin astonished and dismayed me. The violin itself looked to be in beautiful condition. The highly polished wood had a reddish tone with few scratches or marks. However, the strings were lying in a loose tangle. The bridge that supported the strings was lying on top of the violin. I had no idea how difficult or expensive it would be to repair the instrument. The violin technician soon came over and looked at the mess in the old case. To my surprise and relief, it was an easy matter and not very expensive to replace the strings and to reset the fallen bridge that supports them. In my ignorance, I hadn't realized that the tension of the strings on a violin is all that holds the bridge in place. When the ancient strings failed, the bridge simply fell over. Similarly, in our society, it is the creative tension between opposing forces that holds our nation together.

Vietnam and discord

The United States is one of the most powerful and prosperous nations on the face of the earth. It enjoys the benefits of rich farmlands and abundant natural resources. It takes pride in its support of basic human rights and democratic freedoms. It has made important contributions in business, technology, medical science, art, entertainment, and many other areas. And yet, we seem to have lost our way as a people. We find ourselves living in a country sharply divided and virtually unable to even discuss the problems that we face, much less constructively deal with them.

This loss of harmony has been underway for some time. By the early 1960s, life was good for many youthful baby boomers. Most had grown up in comparative prosperity and did not have to endure the economic poverty that their parents had experienced in the Great Depression. The oldest were beginning to enter higher education.

Sadly, as many baby boomers came of age, an ill-conceived and poorly executed war in southeast Asia cast a dark shadow over our nation. Many baby boomers had to interrupt their personal lives and educational plans either because they were drafted or because they pursued alternatives that allowed them to avoid Vietnam duty. In either case, the focus was on survival rather than achievement.

More than 8.7 million Americans served in Vietnam suffering about 210,000 casualties including over 58,000 deaths, more than our casualties in the Korean War and about one-fifth our total casualties in World War II. Millions avoided the military draft through often capricious deferments and exemptions. Some avoided service in Vietnam by joining guard or reserve units. Some fled the country, often to Canada. Many others avoided service due to their good fortune when the draft resorted to a lottery.

The draft, unpredictable and unfair in the view of many, generated considerable hostility, particularly among younger Americans. This hostility combined with the destructive futility of what many saw as an unnecessary, unjust, and unwinnable war created a large and vocal antiwar movement. As a result of these war protests, people became aware of the lies and deceptions that our government had used to justify and sustain the war. These deceptions created a distrust of the government and our leaders that have not yet fully healed for many Americans.

In contrast, many of those who supported the Vietnam War even today are unable to accept that it was a war that we shouldn't have fought and that we couldn't win. Shrouded in denial, they continue to blame our defeat on the antiwar movement and still maintain that we could have somehow won the war if we had only given adequate support to our forces -- despite the millions of soldiers and huge amounts of equipment sent to Vietnam.

The massive cost of the war in lives and money, coupled with the fact that we ultimately lost, created divisions across our nation that were deep and long lasting. Thirty years later, politicians on both sides must still explain why they were or were not in favor of the war and what they were or were not doing at that time and why.

In 1968, the Vietnam War drove one president, Lyndon Johnson, out of office and brought another, Richard Nixon, to power, at least partially due to his "secret plan" to end the war. Although Nixon continued to pursue the war for a number of years, by the time of his reelection in 1972, all American ground troops had left Vietnam and he was anticipating an investigation related to the burglary of Democratic Party offices in the Watergate Building.

The specific charges against Nixon revolved around the cover-up of this burglary including obstruction of justice, failure to uphold laws, and refusal to produce material subpoenaed by a house committee. However, subsequent investigations revealed an extensive misuse of power that went well beyond politics as usual. In 1974, President Nixon resigned rather than face what most felt was his probable removal from office under the articles of impeachment recommended by the House Judiciary Committee.

As the war came to its ignoble conclusion with the collapse of South Vietnam in 1975, the nation remained sharply divided, often along generational lines. Not only were many baby boomers unable to live the great lives that their parents and grandparents had visualized for them, their generation hadn't even duplicated the successes of their parents' generation. There was considerable irony in this view, since it was primarily the World War II generation that had begun and directed the war in Vietnam, while boomers paid the price. Nonetheless, in the years that followed, the baby boomers remained identified with losing their war in Vietnam as their parents became known as the "greatest generation."

In the 1970s, the economy went through a series of recessions, several oil embargoes led to long lines at the gas pumps during the Nixon and Carter administrations, and the overthrow of the Shah of Iran led to the Iran hostage crisis. These consecutive crises generated a widespread desire for change that led to the election of Ronald Reagan. He brought with him a conservative perspective that ironically combined patriotic gusto with a deep distrust of government. The years that followed saw a broad embrace of deregulation, privatization, and globalization as the answer to virtually every problem facing the nation.

After twelve years of the Republican administrations of Reagan and George H. W. Bush, Democrat Bill Clinton won election to the presidency in 1992. The conservative right quickly denounced Clinton and his administration for their liberal policies and actions. Despite the fervor of their opposition, it is difficult to make the case that his administration was especially liberal. Its polices for the most part were a mixture of progressive views on social questions, rather traditional positions on business and international trade, and more liberal views on environmental protection.

In addition to their dislike of his political rhetoric, conservatives did not like his avoidance of military service during the Vietnam War, his activist wife, Hillary Clinton, and the shortcomings in his personal behavior. Perhaps they also envied the way in which his education, intelligence, and attractive personality got him elected president -- the first member of the baby boomer generation to have reached the White House.

Despite Clinton being in many ways a rather moderate Democrat, conservatives in Congress fought endless battles to remove him from office. They appointed a Republican in 1994 to serve as an independent counsel to investigate the Clintons' involvement with the real estate transactions known as Whitewater. This lengthy and expensive investigation soon evolved into a far reaching investigation of all aspects of Bill Clinton's public and personal life. Moving far beyond its original focus on Whitewater, it soon investigated topics as far afield as the death of a White House lawyer, the management of the White House travel office, and several allegations of personal misconduct.

In the midst of these investigations, Clinton won reelection in 1996 by a large margin to a second term in office. The country was in an extended period of economic prosperity, the Cold War had just ended, and Clinton was a charismatic politician who remained very popular. Nonetheless, the ongoing investigations were a distraction throughout most of his second term. Ultimately, the years of investigations, the expenditure of many millions of dollars, and the ongoing distractions from more important issues facing the nation culminated in impeachment charges in 1998 related to Clinton's personal impropriety in an incident involving a White House intern during his second term. Following intense debate, the Senate acquitted him of the impeachment charges in 1999.

The hostility directed at Clinton may be easier to understand in light of the Vietnam War. For some of his opponents, Clinton personified the baby boomer generation's failure in Vietnam. In addition, some still resented the fact that many baby boomers managed to avoid service in Vietnam through the lottery, draft deferments, or service in various guard or reserve units. Neither Clinton nor his successor, George W. Bush, served in Vietnam.

In contrast, Senator John Kerry, Bush's opponent in the 2004 presidential election, was a baby boomer with a distinguished combat record in Vietnam. Curiously, but tellingly, this fine record brought him little but criticism and ridicule from many of his opponents in the 2004 campaign. Seeing the baby boomer generation as responsible for America's first defeat in war, they couldn't bring themselves to acknowledge honorable military service by a baby boomer, even one with as distinguished a military record as John Kerry, particularly since Kerry subsequently became a leading opponent of the war.

Despite its huge size, the baby boomer generation has often had difficulty in achieving positions of power in politics and business. Even as the oldest baby boomers are beginning to retire, the World War II generation, reluctant to step aside for the next generation, continues to dominate many political and business circles. President George W. Bush, a baby boomer in age if not in temperament, surrounded himself with cabinet officials and advisors drawn from the previous administrations of his father, George H. W. Bush, as well as Ronald Reagan and even as far back as Richard Nixon.

The political clash over the Vietnam War was partially due to different views of authority. Supporters of the war tended to respect authority. They trusted leaders who insisted that the war was strategically important for the United States; they believed reports that suggested victory was just around the corner. Opponents of the war tended to question authority. They decided, despite the claims of our leaders, that the war was not critical to the future of our country and that we were unlikely to achieve victory. This conflict between differing views of authority foreshadowed the conflicts that would develop following the 2000 presidential election and the 9/11 attacks.

The 2000 presidential election

The deep political divisions that emerged from the controversies surrounding the Clinton presidency set the stage for the unprecedented 2000 presidential contest between Vice President Al Gore and George W. Bush, governor of Texas. At the national level, there have been occasional disputes regarding some presidential elections, but the hotly disputed results of the 2000 presidential election were by far the most controversial since the 19th century.

As has happened before, the debate centered on the Electoral College. This system, established in the Constitution, places the final election of the president in the hands of electors representing each of the states. Each state receives one vote for each of its Representatives to Congress as well as two additional votes for its Senators. When the public votes for president, they are really electing representatives to the Electoral College to vote for a candidate on their behalf. In 2000, there were a total of 538 votes in the Electoral College. A candidate needed a majority of 270 votes to become president.

The results of the election were ambiguous and highly controversial. A number of voting irregularities in Florida, where Bush's brother was governor, contributed to the confusion as to who actually won the right to the Florida representatives to the Electoral College. Election officials denied some legitimate voters the right to vote with inaccurate charges of being convicted felons. Poll workers turned some black voters away from the polls because they didn't have I.D. cards even though they didn't require I.D. cards from white voters. Election workers closed polls early in black districts and changed the location of polling places without notice. One commentator reported that election officials dismissed more than 187,000 votes in Florida, the majority of which were from black precincts. Undoubtedly these types of abuses have occurred before in Florida as well as other states, but this was the first election in many years where they would clearly make a decisive difference.

In Palm Beach County, a so-called butterfly ballot confused some voters and cost Gore critical votes. *The Palm Beach Post,* following its investigation of the election, reported that Gore would have gained a net increase of 784 votes over Bush if election officials had counted every "hanging chad, pinhole, ding or dimple." This alone was more than enough to overcome the 537 vote official statewide margin of victory for Bush. Gore also lost votes that voters erroneously cast for Pat Buchanan due to the confusing ballot design.

There was confusion concerning paper ballots throughout the state. Although the butterfly ballot probably attracted the most publicity, many other voters lost their votes for a variety of reasons including the failure of election officials to review ballots that optical scanning machines had rejected. In some cases, voters requesting replacement ballots instead received stickers from election officials to cover their mistaken votes. Unfortunately, the scanning machines still rejected these ballots as containing overvotes.

Despite election officials turning away many legitimate votes and failing to adequately count properly completed ballots, a post election statewide examination of 171,908 punch-card and optical scan ballots by the *USA Today, The Miami Herald,* and *Knight Ridder* newspapers concluded that even with these various abuses in the voting system, Gore would have won the election, but for mistakes made by voters. The newspapers estimated that voter errors probably cost Gore statewide from 15,000 to 25,000 votes -- far more than necessary to put Gore in the White House.

In the days and weeks following the election, there were endless legal arguments attempting to resolve the controversy concerning the presidential election results in Florida. There was disagreement ranging from the scope of proposed recounts to the analysis of punch cards with "hanging" chads, dimpled chads, and pinholed chads. Rather than performing a complete review of the election, attorneys for the opposing candidates resorted to battles in courts from the Florida Supreme Court to the United States Supreme Court. Ultimately, the U.S. Supreme Court effectively selected the next president for the first time in our nation's history.

As a result of the court's decision, for the first time in 112 years, the winner of the popular vote failed to win a majority of votes in the Electoral College. Bush won the presidency with 271 electoral votes, one more than a majority, Gore received 266 electoral votes, and there was one abstention protesting the District of Columbia's lack of voting power in Congress. Al Gore won the overall popular vote with about 500,000 more votes than George W. Bush.

A number of factors contributed to the frustration and bitterness that followed this decision. Many Democrats felt that the Republicans had stolen the election. The early decisions by various news sources to declare Gore the winner in Florida only to change their reports as the election night dragged on helped create a climate of suspicion. The revelation of numerous voting irregularities tainted the Florida election results and further compounded the problem. In addition, the resolution of the conflict was virtually without precedent, since Congress had resolved all previous controversies regarding the selection of a president. However, in this case, a Supreme Court, with 7 of its 9 justices appointed by Republican presidents, made the final decision rather than a democratically elected Congress.

There was also considerable hostility between Democrats and members of the Green Party along with their nominee, Ralph Nader. Although their third party campaign undoubtedly brought out some new money, campaign workers, and voters, most Democrats suspected that the majority of these resources would probably have gone to the Democrats and Al Gore in the absence of the Green Party candidate. Most telling, the Supreme Court decision led to Bush winning Florida by less than 600 votes. Nader received over 97,000 votes in Florida. Even if you presume that many of Nader's supporters would not have voted if Nader was not on the ballot, almost certainly a sufficient number would have voted and favored Gore to carry Florida for Gore and elect him president.

The need for fair and open elections is a fundamental guiding fiction of our democracy. During the civil rights protests, the concept became abbreviated to the simple, if sexist, aphorism of "one man, one vote." As with all guiding fictions, this one is not strictly speaking true. Our elections are never perfectly fair, nor are they completely open. Running for political office requires resources and support that are difficult for most citizens to obtain. However, in principle, we try to make our elections as fair as possible, and many people can with some effort get on the ballot for many lower level political offices.

At the founding of the country, "one man" meant literally one "free man." Women, slaves, and certain ethnic groups found themselves unable to cast their vote. Over time, the right to vote has expanded to include all adults, but still excludes youth, children, and felons. And so, despite its limited accuracy today and in the past, it captures a basic truth -- a broad swath of society should collectively and equally share in the right to determine the course of the nation. As such, this guiding fiction helps ensure acceptance of decisions made by the government and provides a standard by which to judge whether or not we are moving in the right direction.

Democratic processes do not eliminate disagreement and discord following elections. Controversy is not unusual whenever and wherever people come together. We often have legitimate differences of opinion on most any question. Through our democratically elected government, our political representatives must make decisions on a multitude of important questions. They must strike a balance between representing the views of those who elected them while not forgetting the views of the minority who did not.

Over the years, this political process has served us well. Despite highly contentious campaigns, we have a tradition that those we elect should work together cooperatively in our representative assemblies. Although the majority generally made the final decisions, they usually gave the concerns of the minority serious consideration and often crafted compromises that were more broadly acceptable.

Tax cuts and social divisions

Unfortunately, political discord escalated dramatically after the 2000 presidential election. The close and controversial nature of the election results, the sharp differences in views of the two candidates, and, perhaps most importantly, the willingness of the Bush administration to aggressively pursue a highly partisan agenda with little regard for the desires of the majority of voters who voted for Al Gore all contributed to a divisive and hostile political atmosphere.

Despite the virtual dead heat in the election, the Bush administration responded as if the nation had given it a mandate for change. As a result, the divisions present in the country, exacerbated by the controversial election result, failed to heal for many voters.

Instead of uniting the country, Bush seemed content to ignore if not exploit the conflicts that existed between various political factions and interest groups. The Democratic opposition, stunned by the election results, struggled to find ways to articulate its vision and provide a voice for the popular vote majority that the new administration had reduced to irrelevance.

At the top of the Bush agenda, and continuing down a path forged by the Reagan administration, was a budget that featured extensive tax cuts for the wealthy as well as privatization and deregulation initiatives for business interests. Presented to Congress by Bush in February of 2001, it included a 10 year, $1.35 trillion dollar tax reduction plan. Under his proposed plan, which Congress soon passed with only minor revisions, taxpayers in the top 1% income group (with annual incomes in excess of $319,000) would receive more than 42% of the total tax reductions. On the other hand, the bottom 60% of taxpayers (with annual incomes less than $39,300) would receive only 12.6% of the proposed tax reductions.

By 2004, the combined effect of three consecutive tax cuts in 2001, 2002, and 2003 resulted in the middle class paying a substantially greater share of federal taxes than they had been paying before the 2000 election. In addition, most of the middle class had seen little or no increase in their wages after inflation for the past 25 years. Many workers had lost manufacturing jobs that paid attractive wages and provided health insurance benefits.

My own field of electrical engineering, a middle class profession formerly in great demand that offered premium salaries, experienced levels of unemployment not seen in many years due to weaknesses in the U.S. economy and the outsourcing of engineering work to foreign suppliers. Those workers who were able to find new jobs often settled for a much lower salary and in some cases no longer had access to health insurance. Most disturbingly, according to Department of Labor statistics, the number of employed electrical engineers declined from 444,000 in 2000 to 363,000 in 2003, a drop of 81,000 or about 20% in just 3 years.

Economists like Paul Krugman noted that we have entered a new Gilded Age where the gap between the rich and the rest of us has grown into a chasm. Globalization, technology, changes in taxation policies, and aggressive capitalism have contributed to a growing concentration of wealth in our nation. Variations of "trickle down" economics, generally discredited even by those who initially supported it during the early years of the Reagan administration, have reemerged to justify a wide variety of policies that favor the wealthiest members of our society.

Godfrey Hodgson, in his book *More Equal than Other: America from Nixon to the New Century,* discusses the growing income inequality that has been the dominant social theme in the United States since the shift to the right in the 1970s. By 1999, real average wages were lower than they had been in 1973, the United States had the highest poverty level of the 16 most developed nations, and many Americans lacked adequate health insurance. Along with many others, Hodgson questioned our reliance on a kind of "casino capitalism" in which there are few winners and many losers.

Debts and deregulation

Due to the continuing series of huge tax cuts, articles soon began to appear asking where the federal budget surplus had gone. By August of 2001, the non-social security surplus for the federal government in the 2001 fiscal year declined from $124 billion to only $1 billion. Although $46 billion of the decline was due to decreased tax receipts, the remainder of the decline was due to tax rebates, corporate tax payments shifted into 2002, and increased spending. In 2003, Senator Ernest Hollings noted that a $5.6 trillion, 10 year budget surplus had become a $4 trillion deficit.

By 2004, due to additional tax cuts, an economic slowdown, and increased military spending, the federal budget was still generating huge deficits. Rather than continuing to reduce the national debt, as begun during the Clinton administration, the national debt expanded dramatically while allegedly conservative Republicans controlled all three branches of the federal government. The Congressional Budget Office reported that for the ten year period beginning in 2005, the cumulative deficit would be $2.75 trillion. The estimated costs of making the Bush administration's tax cuts permanent and funding its 2005 Social Security proposals would result in a deficit through 2015 of approximately $4 trillion with much of the cost not occurring until after Bush leaves office. Although the projected budget deficits varied somewhat from year to year, it was clear that elimination of the federal debt had become as unimaginable as ever, and the consequences would create major problems for our future leaders.

Along with efforts to reduce the tax burden on the wealthiest taxpayers, the Bush administration consistently turned to the right on domestic environmental and regulatory issues. It pursued repealing or delaying many of governmental regulations designed to enhance public health and safety, protect the environment, and preserve our natural resources. By April of 2001, the administration had already proposed the withdrawal, delay, or reversal of numerous regulations including those reducing the levels of arsenic in our drinking water, setting more protective standards for the removal of lead-based paints, establishing improved efficiency standards for various home appliances, protecting wetlands, preserving national forests, and protecting endangered species.

In addition to the Bush administration's regressive policies on regulations and environmental matters, it took highly divisive positions on a variety of other domestic issues. These included cutting funds for reproductive health programs, supporting increased restrictions on abortions, mandating changes in the public school system, and supporting restrictions on class action and malpractice lawsuits. In an ironic twist, Republicans, who formerly supported states rights and local decision-making, increasingly expanded the power of the federal government to restrict the ability of local officials to govern their own communities.

Abandoned treaties

On the international scene, the actions of the administration were, if anything, even more controversial. In one of its early and very controversial actions, the administration reversed the decisions of previous administrations on controlling carbon dioxide emissions and abandoned the nation's commitment to the Kyoto Protocol, the international agreement on global warming.

A March, 2001, editorial in *Science* magazine noted that a Bush spokesperson called Bush's campaign pledge to regulate carbon dioxide emissions a "mistake" despite growing evidence that the climate is indeed changing and that fossil fuel emissions are at least a significant contributor to these changes. A subsequent letter from Bush to four Republican senators used the California power crisis as a convenient excuse to justify his reversal, i.e., a foreshadowing "flip-flop" by the president The reversal was not only another example of the close bonds between the Bush administration and corporate board rooms, but it also was an early demonstration of how the president's actions were often inconsistent with his rhetoric.

If this seems too strong, Carol Williams, in a *Los Angeles Times* article in March of 2001, described the reactions of other leaders throughout the world to Bush's decision on global warming as ranging from "mildly reproving to venomous." She quoted Britain's *Guardian* as describing the U.S. as "the unrepentant outlaw," the *Tokyo Shimbun* as denouncing the administration for "great-power greed," and the Portuguese newspaper *Publico* as describing Bush as acting with "the arrogance of someone who thinks he owns the world." Williams also quoted political leaders in Britain and Germany criticizing the global warming decision, the *World Council of Churches* describing the decision as a "betrayal of ...responsibility," and China denouncing it as "irresponsible."

It is important to remember that the decision on global warming as well as the harsh reactions that followed occurred in just the first few months of the new administration, well before the attacks of

9/11, the war in Afghanistan, and the war in Iraq. In fact, in a chilling foreshadowing of what was to come, Williams quotes a *Guardian* editorial stating that the global warming decision, along with other military and diplomatic actions of the Bush administration, is a "Taliban-style act of wanton destruction" that sends an appalling message to the rest of the world. The editorial further notes that Bush seems intent on confronting the world rather than leading it. After the 9/11 attacks, many people forgot the controversies created by the actions of the Bush administration in the spring of 2001.

Global warming is far from the only area where the White House was out of step with the international community, including many of our closest friends and allies. For example, it withdrew U.S. support for an International Criminal Court and abandoned efforts to enforce the 1972 Biological Weapons Treaty. It refused to sign or support the Comprehensive Test Ban Treaty, a proposed ban on anti-personal mines, or a treaty limiting the export of small arms.

The administration also unilaterally withdrew from the Antiballistic Missile Treaty and moved ahead with its plans for an anti-missile system, despite serious doubts over its practicality as well as grave concerns over its potential destabilizing effects. In early 2005, Canada announced that it would not participate in the anti-missile system, either in its construction or operation. In response, the departing U.S. ambassador to Canada said that Canada was in effect giving up its sovereignty with this decision. Needless to say, Canadian Prime Minister Paul Martin took exception to this observation and insisted that the United States still must get permission from Canada to fire it missiles over Canadian airspace. The controversy reflected the deterioration in our country's relationship under the Bush administration with even our closest ally.

In one of the administration's major breaks with the past, it adopted a much more passive posture regarding the problems between the Israelis and Palestinians in the Middle East. This was in stark contrast to the efforts of previous administrations to lead the search for peace in that region. During his administration, President

Jimmy Carter hosted meetings between Prime Minister Rabin of Israel and President Sadat of Egypt that led to the much heralded Camp David Peace Accords. Late in his second term, President Clinton hosted meetings between Israeli Prime Minister Barak and Chairman Arafat of the Palestinians in efforts to reach a new peace agreement. Despite coming very close to a potentially far reaching solution to this endless problem, these negotiations failed, reportedly because Chairman Arafat may have felt that he could obtain a better deal with a new American administration in the White House.

Unfortunately for all concerned, the new administration was much less interested in taking an active role in the Middle East and adopted a passive stance towards the conflict between the Palestinians and Israel. However, following the 9/11 attacks, the Bush administration took an extremely militant stance towards its opponents and pursued a policy of preemptive warfare for the first time in the history of the nation. In what some could argue was no coincidence, Israeli leaders soon began an aggressive program to suppress, divide, and control the Palestinians.

In early 2005, after the death of Yassar Arafat, there was some indication of possible progress between Israel and the new Palestinian leadership. In a belated comment during Bush's tour of Europe following his reelection, called by some his "charm offensive," he stated that "we would not stand by as another generation in the Holy Land grows up in an atmosphere of violence and hopelessness." Of course, we had been essentially doing just that for the past four years. The comment seemed much like a leader running to catch up with the parade. During the same tour, he also suggested that the Iraq War was "the major issue" that irritated the Europeans. While Iraq certainly continued to be a problem in 2005, many Europeans still objected to many other positions and actions of the Bush administration. It is easy to forget that most of these predated the 9/11 attacks and the Iraq War.

The administration also marginalized our international relationships through such institutions as the United Nations. In addition to its decision in 2003 to wage war in Iraq without U.N. authorization or support, the Bush administration had earlier withdrawn funding from the U.N. Population Fund, a move that U.N. Secretary-General Kofi Annan and many others criticized due to its negative impact on women's and children's health. A few years later, in early 2005, the Bush administration nominated a harsh critic of the United Nations to be our new representative to that body.

Our actions regarding these various international treaties and organizations caused continuing damage to our relationships with our allies. As a consequence, our friends and allies increasingly saw the United States as isolationist and prone to unpredictable and unilateral action. Many believed that the U.S. would work cooperatively with other countries only when it suited our country's immediate interests. The Bush administration arrogantly presumed that it had the wisdom, the power, and the right to restructure the world into the image that it desired. One commentator suggested that the United States, called the "indispensable nation" by Madelyn Albright, had become the "irresponsible nation."

The wrong path

Following the 2000 election, people argued endlessly over the results. Some had complained about the disenfranchisement of voters due to flaws in election technology and procedures. Others had objected to the way in which the Supreme Court unilaterally, and perhaps prematurely and unnecessarily, ended the controversy with a decision in which confidence in the impartiality of the judiciary was the loser according to Justice John Paul Stevens' summary.

Nonetheless, at least one analyst suggested that if the 2000 presidential election created a constitutional crisis, it was a good time to have one since Gore and Bush varied little on most substantive issues. Similarly, throughout the campaign, Ralph Nader, the Green Party's candidate, claimed that there was no real difference between the candidates of the two major parties. Unfortunately, the first seven months of the Bush presidency demonstrated that these statements were simply not true.

The coming months would soon illustrate the chasm separating Al Gore and his principles from George W. Bush and the actions of his administration. Our nation was about to endure horrific events and make many momentous decisions. Many people would soon overlook the fact that the president making these decisions gained office through a deeply flawed election and unprecedented interference by the Supreme Court sharply divided along highly ideological and partisan lines.

By the end of July, 2001, the administration's senior officials were hard at work practicing damage control and resisting accusations of isolationism. The stock market was in steep decline following the collapse of the Internet bubble. California was staggering under electrical power shortages and skyrocketing rates. The administration had begun a series of tax cuts that primarily benefited the rich and powerful, rolled back regulations and reduced environmental constraints for the benefit of corporations, and withdrawn from a number of global treaties with our allies.

It crafted many of its policies and actions, such as its energy policy, behind closed doors without even revealing who attended the meetings much less what they discussed. Between practicing favoritism for the few, taking unilateral action whenever it wished, and ignoring global allies and issues, an administration established by a Supreme Court decision acted as if it had a mandate to change the direction of the country on virtually every issue.

It's perhaps not surprising that many Americans felt that we were moving down a new and dangerous path. Even some Republicans began to recognize that the agenda of the Bush administration was not only at odds in many ways with the principles of the Democratic Party, but also with the traditional values of the Republican Party. Unjustified tax cuts and ballooning deficits were inconsistent with Republican fiscal conservatism. Its embrace of unbridled corporate power and wealth, including its close relationships with corporations such as Enron and Halliburton that would soon make headlines for their financial misdeeds, confirmed the accuracy of Republican President Dwight D. Eisenhower's warnings about the perils of the military-industrial complex.

On the national scene, the administration sowed discord through its use of divisive religious rhetoric, a subject that both Democratic and Republican political leaders have long recognized as outside the purview of government in a land proud of its separation of church and state. On the international scene, its isolationism was inconsistent with the accomplishments of previous Republican presidents in foreign affairs, perhaps best exemplified by Richard Nixon's opening up our relationship with China in 1972. Whether you were a liberal Democrat or traditional Republican, it was becoming clear that the Bush administration was moving our country away from some of its great political and democratic traditions.

Meanwhile, President Bush spent the month of August at his ranch in Texas, just 6 months after taking office and despite widespread criticism that he was already spending much less time on the job than his predecessors. On September 4, 2001, the administration finally found time to hold a meeting of the so-called Principals Committee. The purpose of this meeting was to finally review the anti-terrorism plans brought forward from the Clinton administration by Richard Clarke. He had been attempting to convene such a meeting since the new administration took office in January. September 11 was one week away.

♬ ♬ ♬

"The consent of the governed" is a phrase found in the Declaration of Independence. According to this document, it is the source of the "just powers" of the government which is to secure "certain unalienable rights." As such, it is at the foundation of our system of democratic government. For this reason, elections hold a special place in the hearts of most Americans. They are perhaps the most important way in which every citizen has an opportunity to directly influence the direction of our government. Whenever the results of an election fail to reflect the will of the people for whatever reason -- mistake, malfunction, or malfeasance -- it is a tragedy. In some cases, we try to rectify the error through recounts and sometimes through new elections. If this is not possible, those elected have a responsibility to conduct themselves with special sensitivity to the views of the opposition. Following the deeply flawed 2000 presidential election, the Bush administration failed in its responsibility to honor the views and desires of not just those who voted for Bush, but also of those who voted for Gore. Fortunately, this failure would ultimately make it much more difficult for the administration to achieve its goals.

Chapter 3

The power of corporations

...regulate commerce...

♫ ♫ ♫

In the foreword to her recording of four Bach concertos, concert violinist Hilary Hahn describes the way in which Bach's music evokes a sense of community for her. As people perform and listen to Bach, they continue a three century old tradition of appreciating his creative genius and gain new perspectives on their life together. They appreciate anew the contributions from the past as they face the future. Unfortunately, as global capitalism and corporate mergers destroy the local businesses that once provided jobs, products, and services in our communities, we are losing practices, cultures, and experiences that took years to develop -- rather than preserving our business heritage, we are too often simply throwing it away.

The growth of corporations

Two of the centerpieces of the conservative agenda are to privatize and deregulate as much of the economy as possible. The Bush administration and many of its supporters want to create a world free from government interference and public oversight. The primary beneficiaries of their policies are the giant corporations that dominate much of our economy and the wealthy executives who control them.

The modern corporation is a relatively recent invention. It evolved during and after the Civil War driven by the need for huge industrial enterprises for such activities as making steel, building ships, and manufacturing armaments. These enterprises required more capital than any single entrepreneur could typically provide. The corporation provided a means through which multiple investors could pool their investments, elect a board of directors to represent their interests, and hire corporate officers to manage a business. Although the corporate model presumes that the officers are accountable to the directors who in turn are accountable to the investors, the global corporations of today have grown so large and most investors are so unfamiliar with the business that it is often difficult to locate corporate accountability and authority.

According to David C. Korten, in his book *The Post-Corporate World,* the U.S. Supreme Court extended the protections of the 14th Amendment to private corporations in 1886. This momentous change was the result of a brief declaration by one justice, accepted without debate, that gave private corporations, legal creations of the state, the same protections provided to freed slaves. As a result, the legal system considers corporations to be persons for many purposes.

The unique status of corporations has resulted in a number of strange contradictions. Korten suggests, perhaps with some hyperbole, that if shareholders own the corporation and corporations are legal persons, then their ownership becomes a form of slavery forbidden by the 13th Amendment. On perhaps a more realistic level, the law grants corporations rights such as free speech and due process, while they have no obligations to serve on juries, to perform military service, or to serve within the community. They also do not face prison for violating the law. In some ways, the courts have granted corporations a more privileged status than human beings.

With their legal status enhanced, corporations began their seemingly inexorable growth into the dominant business form in our society. Driven by corporate demands for greater efficiency and profitability, Frederick Winslow Taylor soon developed his principles of scientific management to manage and control workers. Industrialists like Henry Ford perfected mass production and assembly line techniques in the manufacture of automobiles. In order to protect workers rights in this era of corporate growth, labor unions began their lengthy struggle for recognition. The government made its first tentative steps towards regulations to protect both workers and consumers. Through it all, corporations grew ever larger and more powerful.

During World War I, the industrial and military strength of the United States made its first major impact on the world stage as it contributed to the final victory by allied forces. Following rapid economic growth and unregulated financial speculation in the 1920s, the world entered the Great Depression that lasted until the start of World War II. During this war, the scientific and technological strength of the United States, enhanced by many immigrants, resulted in the development of a variety of new military technologies including radar and the atomic bomb. An unprecedented production effort built planes, ships, tanks, trucks, and guns of every description in unfathomable quantities. During the war, my father, a toolmaker still in his twenties, served as a foreman at a Milwaukee defense plant that produced superchargers for aircraft engines.

As a result of our success in developing and producing massive quantities of armaments of every description, the United States gained a reputation as the "arsenal of democracy," a new guiding fiction for our nation. Historically, the United States had prided itself on its civilian control of the military and the diminished role of its military during peacetime. However, following World War II, we retained our extensive armed forces as well as a huge defense industry to produce their weapons. As mentioned earlier, our nation soon became dominated by the military-industrial complex that President Dwight D. Eisenhower had warned against as he left office.

By the end of the war, the United States occupied a unique position of strength in the world. It was one of the few nations at war that suffered relatively little damage on its own soil. Its industrial capabilities and financial resources were unrivaled by any other nation. It emerged as the dominant player on the world scene. As the war ended, the allies led by the United States formed the United

Nations to provide a forum for conflict resolution without resorting to war and to alleviate hunger and disease. They also created a number of international economic organizations, including the World Bank and the International Monetary Fund (IMF), whose goals were to reduce poverty in lesser developed nations and to enhance the stability of the world financial system, respectively.

In the years that followed, the developed nations rebuilt their economies and continued on a path to growing prosperity for most of their citizens. Progress was more difficult in the developing nations, many of which lagged far behind in economic development. Though poverty remained a problem in the United States, it was intractable for many countries in Africa, South America, and Asia. Many saw a world roughly divided between the developed northern hemisphere and the impoverished southern hemisphere.

Global capitalism

In post-World War II America, manufacturers worked hard to meet pent-up consumer demand. Returning soldiers went to school under the G.I. Bill of Rights and soon bought houses for their new families. After years of strong demand and a sellers market, competition gradually increased among manufacturers. By the 1960s, many began to search for ways to reduce costs, boost sales, and increase profits.

At one of my early jobs, as a student engineer, I helped evaluate the performance of automated equipment that my employer had installed to reduce costs. In addition to more efficient equipment, this firm, along with many others, also sought new locations for its plants that offered lower costs, fewer regulations, nonunion labor, improved access to customers, and, in some cases, financial incentives from local communities. At first, these locations tended to be in the southern United States, but foreign locations soon followed. Businesses began closing excellent facilities with highly skilled work forces that had received strong support from local communities for many years, but that they now considered too costly to operate.

Cost reductions grew from being one goal to being virtually the only goal. During my career, I saw the business world change from emphasizing quality products, good jobs, and long term relationships to focusing almost exclusively on short term profitability.

Noël Mostert, in his book *Supership,* describes the problems created by the huge increase in the size of crude oil carriers in the 1970s. Desires to reduce costs through so-called economies of scale drove the creation of ever larger, underpowered ships operated by smaller crews. With single hulls and only one engine, the new ships had little redundancy in case of trouble. The core values of professionalism and concern for safety in the maritime industry faded as demands for corporate profitability increased. Some owners began to pay less attention to training or maintenance. The result was a series of major accidents and colossal oil spills. Similar problems emerged in other industries as the corporate world too often sought quantity over quality, profits over people, and today over tomorrow.

By the 1970s, a new conservative prescription emerged to allegedly improve economic growth and prosperity in our nation as well as developing third world countries. Nobel winning economist Joseph Stiglitz, in his book *Globalization and Its Discontents,* notes that by the 1980s, many political and economic leaders embraced the so-called Washington Consensus of fiscal austerity (minimize debt), privatization (reduce government), and market liberalization (open markets) as the path to economic success.

Stiglitz suggests that despite the positives aspects of these principles, they too often became ends in themselves in support of powerful financial interests in developed nations. Many believe that the middle class in our country would not exist without easy access to credit to purchase cars and homes. Similarly, demand for debt repayment can cripple developing economies. Privatization cedes the responsibilities of government to profit-oriented corporations outside a nation's democratic processes. Open markets often lead to job losses due to pressures on domestic suppliers from outside competitors. Stiglitz points out that without appropriate institutions and regulations, liberalization of markets can lead to exploitation of workers and consumers rather than real economic progress.

The effects of the North American Free Trade Agreement (NAFTA) of 1994 illustrated many of the problems with the current approach to globalization. Prior to this agreement, imports and exports between the United States and Mexico were approximately equal. During the ten years after NAFTA, U.S. imports from Mexico grew much more rapidly than our exports. In 2002, our imports totaled $134B versus exports of $97B, a deficit of nearly $40B. Many of these new imports were products formerly produced in U.S. plants.

As a consequence, many workers in the United States lost their jobs as corporations closed facilities and moved production to Mexico. However, despite the rapid growth of imports from Mexico, most Mexican workers did not benefit from NAFTA either. Mexican wages have actually declined. In addition, cheap agricultural imports decimated the local Mexican farm economy. Many Mexicans migrated to the U.S. for work.

More ominously, the growth of trade between the two countries leveled off as companies began to move production from Mexico to China and other Asian countries. Mexico faced the dual problems of the loss of older locally owned businesses that were no longer competitive as well as the closure of more modern foreign owned plants as their owners sought lower cost labor elsewhere.

Under NAFTA, the United States lost jobs, Mexico saw a temporary increase in jobs, though at lower wages, and ultimately lost many of these jobs as well to countries with even lower wage structures -- a classic “race to the bottom.” The proposed Central American Free Trade Agreement (CAFTA) would create many of the same problems for Central American countries.

At the end of 2004, a new trade pact, the Agreement on Textiles and Clothing, brought an end to a system of quotas that had regulated the global textile industry since 1974. As a result, a *Time* magazine report projected that textile production will become concentrated in a small number of nations, with the primary beneficiaries being China (from a 16% share of the U.S. market for manufactured clothing to 50%) and India (from a 4% share to 15%). Mexico may see its share of the U.S. market decline from 10% to 3%.

The results for Mexico and many other Third World economies in Asia will be devastating. An article in January of 2005 on the country of Lesotho in southern Africa reported that since November of 2004, six textile factories had already closed with the loss of 5,600 jobs, while others were working fewer hours. Many believe that thousands of the remaining textile jobs in the United States will also soon disappear. It is not in our nation's best interests to lose entire key industries to foreign competitors.

The writers of the U.S. Constitution directed Congress to "regulate commerce" in Section 8 of the Constitution. Congress cannot carry out this constitutional directive when it surrenders its regulatory authority to international tribunals and trade agreements negotiated behind closed doors beyond easy reach of our democratic processes. Unfortunately, recent administrations have not only endorsed such agreements, but the Bush administration has allowed the separation between the responsibilities of government and the desires of global corporations to virtually disappear.

In addition to the problems that globalization creates for the United States, Clyde Prestowitz argues, in his *Chicago Tribune* essay, that it is also unsustainable at the global level. The global economy revolves around the United States as the prime consumer of goods and borrower of money. As with all borrowers, at some point, our country will reach its debt limit and the world economy will come crashing to a halt.

Economic diversity

My book, *Business Decisions,* describes how aggressive capitalism and corporate consolidations also damage our economy by reducing economic diversity. A diversity of species in a natural ecosystem provides sustainability and stability. Our society receives similar benefits from economic diversity. Economic diversity grows with an increase in the number, location, and variety of businesses, distribution channels, purchasing options, employment opportunities, management styles, business cultures, and so on.

Corporate mergers continue to concentrate economic power in our country and throughout the world. Many of the companies where I once worked either no longer exist or have changed beyond recognition due to corporate mergers and reorganizations. Family-owned or closely held businesses have either closed or vanished into huge, impersonal corporations driven almost entirely by a desire to maximize growth and profits. The business culture of acquired firms changes dramatically as new corporate owners seek often elusive synergies and economies of scale.

The dominance of mega-stores and growth of global corporations have reduced the economic space available for smaller businesses. A few giant companies dominate retail sales in most communities and a few major manufacturers dominate production in most industries. We increasingly find ourselves living in an "economic desert" in which there are few niches remaining where one can earn a living. Some economic "species," such as many specialty stores and smaller manufacturers, have already become virtually extinct while the future of many others remains uncertain.

The decline of economic diversity results in a world economy that is less stable, and ultimately less sustainable. With fewer independent companies, other businesses find that there are fewer independent customers to buy their goods and services. They also become dependent on a smaller number of suppliers for their own businesses. The destruction of the manufacturing plant of a single large supplier can have global repercussions. The quarterly results of a single large corporation can have a profound impact on hiring decisions in many communities throughout the world. There are fewer independent employers for job seekers.

Ironically, corporate mergers also create major problems for the merging corporations. The costs and complexities of reconciling two different systems for accounting, marketing, and production are often much larger than anticipated. Different computer hardware and software as well as contrasting corporate cultures further compound the problems. The new, larger organization is more unwieldy and difficult to manage. Rather than producing the synergistic savings promoted to gain support for a proposed merger, the new organization is less able to serve the combined customer base.

At least the problems of a corporation following a merger are due to its own decisions. The problems experienced by individuals and communities as a result of the merger, such as job losses and layoffs, are not of their doing. Nonetheless, they still must deal with the aftermath of these economic dislocations.

Flawed data

Unfortunately, our society and its businesses often makes their economic decisions using flawed and incomplete information. The primary measure used to determine economic growth and prosperity is the Gross Domestic Product (GDP). The GDP measures total economic activity or gross income of our economic markets.

As noted by Robert Constanza, the GDP fails to consider the total costs and benefits of this economic activity. All economic activity, both good or bad, adds to the GDP. It increases even when we produce more weapons, create more pollution, or experience more crime. Furthermore, the GDP ignores the contributions of volunteer workers, stay-at-home parents, or other activities that do not occur within the market economy. Finally, Costanza notes that the GDP ignores the fact that an increase in the GDP that enriches the wealthy is less beneficial for our society than one that rewards the poor.

One of the ways that the government uses the GDP is to determine overall economic productivity by dividing the GDP by total hours of labor worked. The general belief is that increases in productivity reflect increasingly efficient workers; gross revenues are increasing faster than the number of hours used to produce that revenue. Workers continually hear that wage increases are dependent on productivity gains.

However, the productivity measure is suspect for several reasons. In addition to the inadequacies in the determination of the GDP described above, determining the hours worked to produce the flawed GDP is notoriously difficult. Underestimating the actual hours worked causes productivity to increase. Productivity also increases when prices increase (increasing revenues without any increase in labor) or when companies cut jobs and simply ask the remaining workers to work harder (often with a decrease in quality of the goods or services being produced).

Although productivity can increase when companies invest in new equipment, software, or procedures (some analysts use Total Factor Productivity to subtract gains due to such investments), the impact varies widely. In some cases, these investments actually decrease worker productivity. Their overall impact is often difficult to determine. We do know that many of the most costly defense systems purchased by the military have rarely performed as advertised. Similarly, virtually all businesses make investments that fail to fulfill their promises.

As with GDP itself, productivity reports fail to consider any impact, good or bad, on the productivity of volunteer or non-paid workers. In addition, in this era of laptop computers and the Internet, they also ignore the impact of companies transferring work and costs to workers who must finish work at home that they could not complete at the office.

Similar problems also affect such measures as unemployment rates. Unemployment is a politically sensitive topic that is easily subject to manipulation regarding who is actually unemployed. Many workers have stopped looking for a job, not because they do not want one, but because they are unable to find a position with work, location, and wages that reasonably meets their expectations and needs. The government does not include these discouraged job seekers when computing the unemployment rate.

More subtly, Austan Goolsbee has reported on the impact of more generous disability standards on decreasing unemployment. Rather than unemployed, the government now considers many workers as disabled. He believes that including these disabled workers as unemployed would have increased the actual unemployment rate during the 2001 recession from about 6% to about 8% (as high or higher than the 1982 and 1992 recessions).

Statistical distortions in the basic information that the government and businesses use to make their decisions are also present in inflation rates. The problem revolves around the mix of products used to determine the inflation rate. The costs of many manufactured goods have declined due to the outsourcing of jobs to China and other less developed nations. However, many goods and services that people buy on a regular basis have seen rather dramatic increases. In recent years, medical costs, tuition payments, gasoline prices, and insurance premiums have increased at rates far higher than the reported rates of inflation.

Much like other economic indices, the devil is in the details. The costs of some important goods and services have increased at a much higher rate than average inflation, but the widely quoted Consumer Price Index (CPI) in many cases does not reflect their impact. For example, Daniel Kadlec noted in a *Time* magazine article that the housing component of the CPI only reflects the cost of rent which has been quite stable in most areas. It ignores increases in home prices and borrowing costs. The CPI also fails to reflect the explosive growth in the cost of medical insurance premiums since it only considers total health care expenditures. Cost shifting from employers to employees through increased insurance premiums has no direct impact on the CPI. For many Americans, their mortgage payments and medical premiums are among their largest monthly expenses, and increases in either have no effect on the CPI.

Another hotly contested aspect of the CPI is the use of hedonics, a term adopted by a General Motors economist, Andrew Court, for studies of auto prices in the 1930s and discussed in a *Wall Street*

Journal article by Timothy Aeppel. Hedonics, a term stemming from "doctrine of pleasure," attempts to use statistical techniques to account for changes in features when comparing the prices of succeeding models of the same product. This approach lowers the price of the new model based on the presumed value of new features that it contains in order to calculate price inflation relative to the older model. However, hedonic analysis may or may not provide an accurate representation of the value of new features, resulting in further distortions of the CPI.

In addition, this type of analysis, as noted in Aeppel's article by Ron Blackwell, chief economist of the AFL-CIO, is more responsive to increases in value due to new features and less responsive to decreases in value due to declining product quality. These shortcoming in the CPI cause it to underestimate inflation. As a result, inflation based increases in Social Security payments and wages under labor contracts are lower than they should be.

It is not just the large scale economic data generated by the government that paint a highly misleading picture of the economy. Many corporations have adopted accounting schemes that are so complex that few, if any, of their managers and directors fully understand their consequences, as in the Enron debacle. Investors find it almost impossible to determine the true condition of a business from financial reports peppered with nonrecurring charges, special charges, charges for discontinued operations, and so on. And perhaps most importantly, voters have a hard time deciding between candidates with differing economic policies amidst a flurry of confusing claims and inaccurate or distorted data.

The government and the economy

The rise of global capitalism is reducing the ability of the government to control economic activity. In response to proposed legislation or regulations that may restrict their businesses, corporations sometimes move or threaten to move their businesses to those states or countries where labor is cheaper, environmental controls are less restrictive, or there is less government interference.

Increasingly, corporations may also use various trade treaties to restrict the ability of people to regulate businesses in their own countries through their representative governments. Some of these treaties allow foreign corporations to recover damages for lost profits due to local regulations such as environmental controls. Other provisions enable corporations to demand full access to markets even for services traditionally provided by the government whenever some degree of private participation exists. Thus, demands for "modest" levels of privatization of such critical public services such as Social Security, Medicare, and public education could easily open the door for private corporations. Privatization of such critical social services may make it difficult to maintain the quality and accessibility that the local community desires. Community leaders may find themselves obligated politically and legally to accept the lowest bid even when it may not be the best long term solution.

Global capitalism also undermines the ability of the local community to respond to the challenges of open markets. The theory of comparative advantage suggests that less productive economies, even including those that are deficient in all areas, will naturally gravitate to producing those goods in which their relative disadvantage in productivity is the smallest. This will enable more productive countries to focus their efforts on those areas in which their comparative advantage in productivity is the greatest. In theory, overall global production will increase, and all nations will benefit.

Unfortunately, it is difficult for countries or local economies to redirect the use of their productive resources when absentee owners own these facilities. Rather than following the logic of comparative advantage and maintaining the operation of a plant that may not be quite as competitive as those in other countries, these absentee owners will more often simply close the facility. These problems are not only occurring in developing nations. They are also spreading to developed nations and across all economic classes and industries.

For this reason, the loss of a corporate headquarters has a disproportionately large negative impact on the overall economic health of a community. In addition, to providing more direct access to decision makers, the presence of the headquarters tends to enhance prospects for the retention and expansion of existing facilities and to provide community support in other ways.

Consequently, nations and communities throughout the world are offering substantial incentives in the form of favorable tax treatment or outright grants to attract or retain corporate headquarters or major production facilities. However, incentives given to businesses result in substantial financial and social costs for the community. Corporate managers hint at these hidden costs in announcing their selection of locations for their new facilities when they cite the availability of low cost labor, lack of unions, and reduced governmental interference -- all of which result in costs absorbed by the workers and the local community.

Perhaps counter-intuitively and despite their intense efforts, virtually all communities are losers in the global competition for corporate headquarters and new plant locations. As global consolidations continue, the number of communities that are home to the headquarters of a major corporation or a major production facility grows ever smaller. Following the acquisition of Chicago-based Bank One Corp. by J. P. Morgan Chase, some analysts began to ask whether the Second City was beginning to move to second tier status. Since 1995, the number of Fortune 500 companies with headquarters in Chicago has declined from 35 to 28 companies. If a megalopolis like Chicago is regressing to second tier status, what does that say for other cities? It is unlikely that any city is immune; in the global economy, there are only losers.

An article by Robert Manor in the *Chicago Tribune* describes how the problem is by no means limited to the United States. Just as the American steel industry has consolidated into a few giant companies, similar trends are occurring throughout the world. Manor reported that the merger of three giant steel makers created the world's largest steel company, Arcelor, with headquarters in Luxembourg. As a result, a few large holding companies now control much of the world's steel production.

The few communities that manage to retain or acquire a significant corporate presence must still confront the reality that absentee owners in distant locations still control much of their local economic activity. And despite their incentives and concessions, there is no guarantee that the corporate headquarters, new plant, or mega-store will be more than a temporary presence in the community. Globalization is turning the entire world into a colony governed by the seemingly omnipotent, but often transitory power of the mega-corporation.

The modern corporation has made many beneficial contributions to our lives. We need to develop innovative ways to maintain its strengths while increasing its accountability to society. In order for democracy and free markets to survive, we must regain control of our economy from those who would prefer the concentration of political and economic power in the hands of the few.

Strengthening government oversight and regulation of global corporations would be a good start. Many conservatives present this issue as a false dichotomy between governmental control and socialist thinking on the one hand versus private ownership and free market capitalism on the other. The market economy is a highly successful invention. It has shown great effectiveness and robustness in meeting the needs of our complex society in an efficient manner. However, it is far from perfect. The market narrowly focuses on the short term desires of a single buyer. There is no past; there is no future. There is only the present. The market does not take a long range perspective, is highly risk averse, and does not consider justice, morality, or ethics in making its decisions.

The market assumes that there are a large number of buyers and sellers of comparable knowledge and power. Today, the economic marketplace includes parties of greatly disparate power, wealth, and knowledge. Whatever the theoretical advantages of free and open markets, it is clear that in the real world, market consolidations and corporate mergers continue to move us ever further from this theoretical ideal. In the name of free market capitalism, we are allowing global corporations to drive many smaller companies out of business. Ironically, the relationships of these smaller companies with their customers, suppliers, and competitors more closely resembles the free market ideal that our nation claims to embrace.

♫ ♫ ♫

Long before corporations became "people" and grew into the dominant form of business organization, the founders of our nation saw the necessity for the active involvement of Congress in the economy. The requirement to "regulate commerce" is only one of many duties that the Constitution assigns to Congress related to our economy. Through the Constitution, Congress gained the authority to establish duties and taxes, regulate business activities, borrow money, coin money, standardize weights and measures, establish post offices, and secure rights for authors and inventors. Supporters of deregulation and privatization initiatives want to erase memories of the past and create the illusion that governmental oversight of the economy is a 20th century idea. In an era of aggressive capitalism, the government needs to play a more active role in the economy than ever before.

Chapter 4

The decline of the middle class

...promote the general welfare...

♫ ♫ ♫

Although a small number of global corporations dominate the production and distribution of mass market entertainment, live music remains primarily a local activity. Corporate resources are largely irrelevant. Small music shops and independent teachers offer music lessons. Children perform in school bands and orchestras. Local musicians perform to small, but appreciative crowds. Congregations regularly sing hymns in worship services and listen to choirs, organists, pianists, and other instrumentalists. Most local musicians perform for little or no compensation. Perhaps this helps explain why the arts including music often struggle for support in our schools -- they are indifferent to the corporate world's "bottom line."

The local economy

Global corporations compete across national boundaries subject only to a patchwork of national regulations. They are free to relocate their operations wherever they wish in a never-ending search for lower cost labor and laissez-faire, business-friendly governments in nations with fewer regulations, the so-called "race to the bottom." In their ongoing efforts to control markets and achieve ever greater economies of scale, these giant corporations aggressively seek to eliminate or absorb their competition. As a result, a small number mega-corporations increasingly dominate the global economy.

Senior executives direct the operations of these global giants from their corporate headquarters. They impose their corporate culture, core values, and management style on distant operations owned by their corporations. Throughout the world, virtually all communities, from small cities to large metropolises, are finding that decisions made by absentee managers in distant board rooms can create serious long term local problems.

Absentee corporate owners can exploit local natural resources through large scale farming, mining, logging, or drilling activities. The aggressive use of fertilizers and herbicides can contaminate water supplies. Improper manure handling from large corporate farms can pollute the air and water. Run-off from mining activities can contaminate streams and damage local fisheries. Aggressive logging can lead to erosion that mars the land and muddies local streams. Deep wells for irrigation or for the bottling of drinking water can lower the water table and cause local wells to go dry.

Absentee owners can also exploit the human resources of a community through aggressive management practices. These include suppressing wages, reducing benefits, imposing harsh working conditions, eliminating labor unions, and ignoring procedures to protect worker health and safety.

It is increasingly difficult for residents to exert local control over business activities that can profoundly affect their lives and communities. International trade agreements, such as NAFTA, often place restrictions on the ability of local citizens to seek restrictions on corporate behavior by local, state, or national governments. Moreover, in the global economy, competition between communities to obtain and retain a decreasing number of jobs is fierce. Global corporations are ready and willing to abandon a local facility if the local community or labor force does not cooperate.

After reaping years of profits from local businesses, many absentee owners close facilities or eliminate jobs with little or no advance notice to the workers or the community. The investments made by the workers, other local businesses, and the community over many years to support the local plant for the benefit of its distant owners usually receive minimal consideration.

Workers made investments of time and money in their education, experience, homes, and families. Locally owned companies invested in their businesses to support the operations of the absentee owners and the needs of its workers. The community made investments in infrastructure ranging from streets, highways, and water systems to police departments, fire departments, schools, and churches. While operating its facilities, corporations externalized the costs of these benefits to their workers, the owners of local businesses, and the local community. When absentee managers decide to close these facilities, the community often struggles to survive in a radically changed economic landscape without any consideration for years of direct and indirect support.

Unfortunately, current rules for fiduciary responsibility allow corporate managers to justify decisions to eliminate hundreds or even thousands of jobs based on as little as one additional dollar of profit for the corporation. There is no need to obtain input from those in the community most affected by their decisions. Strictly speaking, they need not, and indeed must not, consider the effects of their decisions on anyone other than the shareholders of their corporation. Ironically, although these shareholders nominally own the corporation, they rarely have much connection to its activities and are often shareholders for only a short period of time. For the modern corporation, their primary purpose is to justify the pursuit of short term profits by corporate executives.

Today, we hear a great deal about the importance of productivity and efficiency in our economy as discussed in the previous chapter. However, our system allows corporate executives to tear apart communities and marginalize the investments made by these communities, their workers, and other businesses simply to improve the short term profitability of a single corporation. We are all losers in a system that can so wantonly destroy wealth for the benefit of a single corporation, its owners, and executives.

When closing a facility or reducing the number of local jobs, corporations often announce that they will be outsourcing the work to some distant location to lower costs. Although they usually claim that they had no other choice in order to remain competitive, they rarely decide to outsource high cost senior management positions. If the goal is to replace more costly local employees with less expensive workers elsewhere, why not outsource the management functions as well? Surely, there are capable managers in India who would jump at the opportunity to be the president of a global corporation and would be willing to work at a small fraction of the cost of a chief executive officer in this country. In fact, why not complete the process and also outsource the supply of capital by selling the entire business to foreign investors?

In fact, this is exactly what has happened. Foreign interests now own or control many major U.S. businesses. In a startling example, IBM completed the sale of its personal computer business in May of 2005 to the Lenovo Group in China. This was followed by news, in June of 2005, that Maytag, a major producer of household appliances founded in Newton, Iowa, in 1893, was considering a takeover bid from a unit of China's Haier Group. There is a competing offer from an American-based investor group, but according to an article by David Greising in the *Chicago Tribune,* the Haier bid is higher and offers a good strategic fit with the Maytag product line. However a successful takeover by Haier would likely result in much of Maytag's production and many of its jobs moving to China. The lonely Maytag service personnel might find themselves among the few workers keeping their jobs.

The logical result of these trends is that workers in the United States and most other highly developed countries would only make products and deliver services that require a local presence, albeit under the auspices of a foreign corporation. Aside from the seeming absurdity of such a world, our country would have no way to pay for the products and services that it wishes to obtain from others. For reasons of economic need as well as lifestyle considerations, we need to retain a variety of economic activities in this country. Although some costs may incrementally increase, we will gain the benefit of improved employment opportunities, economic stability, and national security. Unfortunately, it is not clear that this is possible as long as global corporations continue their "race to the bottom" driven by demands that they maximize short term, bottom line profitability.

A bimodal society

After the dot-com crash of 2000, the overall economy and the stock market began a long and gradual decline. The economic situation in this country, particularly for middle and lower income Americans has gotten significantly worse. The 9/11 attacks brought a sharp drop and quick recovery, but the general decline continued in 2002. Many corporate employees who thought they had secure financial futures woke up one day to find that they no longer had a job, their company stock had no value, their retirement savings had disappeared, and they had no medical insurance coverage. Others continued to work for corporations whose stock had fallen by half or more. The decline forced many employees to put their plans for retirement on hold.

The collapse of the dot-com industry, the steep decline in broader based technology companies, and the subsequent economic recession resulted in the loss of millions of jobs. Even as corporate profits and the market staged a modest recovery in 2003, the national unemployment rate stayed around 6%. Low interest rates made mortgages attractive for home buyers, but devastated the income of retirees.

During the Christmas shopping season of 2003, upscale retailers reported the greatest sales gains. Discount stores and wholesale clubs also did well. Those retailers focusing on middle income consumers, such as traditional department stores and other midrange retailers, saw little or no increase in sales. Continuing into 2004, manufacturers reported strong growth in demand for expensive yachts as well as luxury automobiles. By Christmas of 2004, even the discount stores were struggling. Once again, reports indicated that only upscale stores catering to wealthier consumers were prospering.

In many urban centers, the wealthy continued purchasing $250-300,000 homes as "teardowns" and replaced them with new $1,000,000+ houses. At the same time, many full-time workers found "affordable" housing harder than ever to find. Families with only a single wage earner working as a civil servant, teacher, or clerical worker and making perhaps $35,000 per year could only qualify for $125,000 houses. In many larger cities, such houses virtually no longer exist. As a consequence, middle income workers must often commute great distances to work due to the lack of affordable housing closer to their place of employment. Expensive condominiums that many middle and lower income workers cannot afford dominate our revitalized downtowns.

Local companies continued to suffer as the economic slowdown combined with the effects of the global economy to hurt their businesses. Main street shopping declined as big box superstores captured ever more customers due to low prices and huge selection, despite sometimes mediocre products and service. Smaller and medium sized parts manufacturers and job shops saw their customer base evaporate as large manufacturers moved their plants offshore.

Salaries for senior executives skyrocketed even as professionals often found good jobs hard to find. Many engineering jobs went to cheaper offshore design facilities thanks, in part, to the Internet; lower cost Asian radiologists replaced local radiologists for the analysis of x-rays for U.S. clinics. Pharmacies in large discount stores drove many independent pharmacies out of business. Even classical musicians found their wages stagnate as executive directors and conductors at non-profit orchestras earned six and seven figure incomes. Anonymous, poorly paid bands or even computer generated music accompanied wealthy pop stars.

Members of the middle class struggled to maintain their economic position. With incomes that have seen little growth after inflation since 1980, many middle class families restructured their lives in order to maintain or improve their lifestyle. Two income families became much more common. Mortgage debt, home equity loans, and consumer debt continue to grow along with our national debt as we borrow from tomorrow on both an individual and collective basis.

"Winner takes all" continued to be the theme and the gap between the wealthy and the rest of society continued to grow. The distribution of wealth and income in the United States is moving towards a bimodal distribution with a small percentage of high income, wealthy Americans and a large percentage of low income, high debt Americans living at the margins of society. Stephen Brobeck of the Consumer Federation of America, in an article by Will Lester, noted that it appears to him that although, overall, fewer people have debt problems, more people have severe debt problems.

One report suggested that automakers now viewed the auto market as a hourglass with sales of high and low end cars growing at the expense of the middle -- reflecting the decline of the middle class. Following its decision to drop its midrange Oldsmobile car line, the vice chairman of General Motors reported in 2005 that he hoped GM would not have to drop one of its other weaker brands, such as Buick or Pontiac. Both brands seek primarily mid-market customers, an endangered species in our bimodal society.

A small and decreasing number of individuals and corporations now control a disproportionate share of economic wealth and power. There are a relatively small number of big winners, most often younger, urban, and educated, and a much larger number of losers. The vast majority of the latter, including many of the older, rural, less well educated members of our society, struggle to survive.

Members of this large and growing underclass find it difficult to support themselves with full time jobs paying minimal wages. Often unemployed or underemployed at low wage jobs with limited, if any, insurance benefits, many visit overburdened local food pantries to put food on the table. It remains difficult for them to find affordable housing in most cities. They meet their medical and dental needs and those of their children on a haphazard basis.

The elderly, often dependent on Social Security and fixed income investments, have seen their monthly income plummet as interest rates remain low. The drop in interest rates has reduced the annual interest income for many retired Americans to half of what they had expected. Meanwhile, skyrocketing costs of prescription drugs, insurance premiums, and energy have placed additional and unexpected financial burdens on older Americans.

The trend towards giant stores owned by huge corporations has particularly made grocery shopping more difficult for the poor and the elderly. Many either do not drive or do not have easy access to a car. Mass transit continues to become less available and more expensive. When the neighborhood store closes, they must choose between taking a long and inconvenient bus ride to a more distant store, hiring an expensive taxi, or finding someone to give them a ride which reduces their independence. As much as possible, some try to make do with more costly local convenience stores.

Without a safety net

Unfortunately, at a time when many did not know where to turn, the Bush administration and other conservative politicians continued to support efforts to deregulate industry, reduce programs for the needy, and privatize government services while they passed tax reductions for corporations and upper income taxpayers.

Collective action through our government has long been the principle way that we address social and economic concerns in our country. The Bush administration and its supporters appeared content to challenge this basic American principle and reduced the ability of the government to respond to the needs of middle and lower income citizens. In fact, some analysts suggested that the seemingly endless cycle of tax cuts and service reductions reflected nothing less than a goal of dismantling the government.

Even as many workers looked for assistance to help them with retraining, job searches, medical insurance, rent or mortgage payments, and grocery expenses, governments at all levels faced budget shortfalls due to massive tax cuts for the wealthy and corporations. As a result, federal, state, and local governments have reduced or eliminated many essential services. For most taxpayers, the so-called tax cuts of the first term of the Bush presidency were service cuts rather than tax reductions. High income taxpayers simply hire these services from private sources while middle and lower income taxpayers have little recourse except to bear the impact of the service cuts on their quality of life.

Taxpayers with children in the educational system paid increased fees for athletics and extracurricular activities and increased tuition costs at state colleges. Local school boards found it more difficult to replace or expand crowded or obsolete facilities. City and county governments found it more difficult to maintain, much less improve, important municipal services including fire and police protection as well as emergency medical services.

One of the primary targets of the antigovernment forces was the public school system. Conservatives often claimed that public schools were ineffective and expensive luxuries of government. However, their more likely targets were the teachers, instructors, and professors who opposed their efforts to dismantle government.

An educational chasm is developing across our country. During the coming years, those with a good education are more likely to prosper while those less educated are more likely to lose ground. Nonetheless, despite the advantages of higher education, projections suggest that the percentage of people graduating from college will show little growth over the next 20 years.

Many educators have become concerned over the growing role of "merit aid" that provides financial assistance to students regardless of need. In an era of flat budgets, this means that there is less need-based aid at most schools. As a result, colleges and universities are less diverse on a socioeconomic basis. Student bodies increasingly consist of a growing number of students from upper middle class families, a scattering of foreign and minority students, and a declining number of students from lower income families. The "winners" win again.

While conservatives worked on dismantling the government, including its safety nets for the needy, the privatized and deregulated world that they were creating was doing its part to dismantle the lives of the nation's workers. Although the economy began a modest recovery in 2003, the quality and quantity of jobs lost during the preceding years were not returning. Unemployment continued to impact huge numbers of workers, particularly in manufacturing. Government programs designed to assist in such difficult economic times were often no longer available or had reduced their services.

Unfortunately, as essential as education is to survive in our current society, it is no panacea. As mentioned earlier, in the global economy, even many middle income professionals in this country are finding it increasingly difficult to obtain employment that utilizes their education and provides adequate compensation and benefits.

One of the consequences of aggressive global capitalism has been the breakdown of the mostly informal, employment "contract" that existed between the employee and the employer. In the past, the employee made a commitment to the employer and in exchange received the assurance of a long term position. Today, all positions are essentially short term. There is little commitment on the part of the employer. As a result, there is little commitment on the part of the worker. For this reason, corporations must resort to ever stronger controls and procedures to direct the work of employees who no longer have a personal relationship to the business.

This breakdown of the employment contract may also be contributing to the breakdown of the social contract throughout our society. Just as the global economy has cost corporations the commitment of their employees, the breakdown of the social contract has led to citizens who are no longer connected to their neighbors and communities. We see the result in the growing alienation, anger, and despair among many of our citizens.

Decline and decay

Accompanying the breakdown of the employment contract and social contract for individuals is a breakdown in the institutional and physical infrastructure of our nation. As we continue to transfer wealth from the lower and middle income segments of our society to the wealthiest segment of our society, we are reducing our investments in our collective future. Our public facilities, from government office buildings to public schools, continue to decay. As we privatize our utilities, we see a continued decline in the reliability of our electric power grid and telephone networks due to aging infrastructure, even as user costs continue to rise.

We are failing to adequately invest in environmental protection and energy conservation. Many cities struggle with obsolete and failing water and sewer systems. In my home state, Milwaukee continues to regularly dump untreated sewage into Lake Michigan when heavy rains overload Milwaukee's improved, but still inadequate, combined sanitary and storm sewer system. Sewer and water line failures are common occurrences in New Orleans. Officials are considering privatization of the system, but many worry about the problems that could arise from such a massive change. They might want to look at Peoria and Pekin, Illinois: cities that privatized their water and sewage systems, but have since returned to public control due to problems and high costs.

As we continue to face problems with our physical infrastructure, we remain seemingly indifferent to the continued decline in our collective skills and capabilities. The global economy is deskilling our country's middle class. We have become a nation of consumers, rather than producers. We are becoming heavily dependent on others to not only build, but also to design and operate our modern infrastructure. As corporations outsource even engineering work to other countries, we are losing the technological base to perform product design and development.

In the midst of a troubled economy, terrorist threats abroad, and a growing quagmire in Iraq, President Bush presented an ambitious vision for extended exploration of the moon and Mars. As usual, not many details of how we would fund and accomplish such an ambitious and controversial program accompanied his vision. In reality, our nation's astronaut program consists of three aging space shuttles, obsolete designs from another era, with no replacement in sight. Moreover, as of June, 2005, the United States had not launched any astronauts into space since the Columbia disaster and the subsequent grounding of the remaining space shuttles.

Much of the infrastructure and knowledge required to design and build large aerospace hardware either no longer exists or is only available outside of this country. Heavy manufacturing is a vanishing industry in our country. There are very few companies capable of building large ships, power plants, and similar structures. Today, we would find it difficult to repeat the Apollo flight to the moon even if we wanted to, much less implement the ambitious vision that Bush presented for Mars. As one headline put it, NASA will have to "start from scratch."

Given the state of the space program, the tax cuts and staggering budget deficits incurred during the first term of the Bush administration, the immense resources wasted in Iraq, and the still greater resources necessary to provide real improvements in domestic security against terrorist attacks, Bush's statements concerning Mars were simply another example of empty rhetoric. As with so many of his initiatives, there was little energy or action behind his words.

Nonetheless, at least we were once able to fly astronauts to the moon. We can't say the same for supersonic passenger travel. The only operational supersonic airliner was the *Concorde,* a joint venture of the French and British, and it is no longer flying. Passengers can no longer fly supersonically across the ocean. Many may believe that this is not a great loss considering the costs, emissions, and noise associated with supersonic travel. However, it is one more example of how our technological capabilities have stagnated or even regressed in an era of globalization and privatization.

We can also see technological stagnation in computer software, an industry with few regulations dominated by a few giant corporations that pursue an especially aggressive form of capitalism. Computer software, despite or perhaps because of its growing complexity, becomes ever more prone to failures due to bugs, viruses, and other problems. Increasingly, there is little we can directly do about these problems since many of the engineers and programmers working on these problems are no longer in our country.

The Third World

As a result of the forces of globalization, deregulation, and privatization, many communities throughout the industrialized world are taking on some of the characteristics of Third World nations. Perfectly adequate manufacturing facilities lie idle, while highly skilled former workers compete for a dwindling number of jobs, often at much lower wages. Absentee corporate owners move production from one community to another, from one country to another, in their search for ever smaller cost reductions. In their wake, they leave devastated local communities attempting to pick up the pieces and provide education, health care, and other social services for their residents. Despite their efforts, too many people suffer from inadequate medical treatment, dental care, nutrition, and education. They live in communities that outside economic forces have exploited and abandoned like any other impoverished colony.

Parallels with developing countries are particularly evident in agriculture. Due to economic pressures, on many family farms in this country at least one family member pursues alternative employment on either a part time or full time basis to supplement the farm income. These workers often find jobs in manufacturing plants where the work is usually repetitive, unpleasant, and, in some cases, dangerous.

Even when the wages are modest by urban standards, the jobs are often attractive because of the benefits that they provide. For some farm families, outside employment is the only way they can afford or obtain health insurance. When absentee owners close a plant with substantial rural employment, many families have no alternative except to go without insurance.

In much the same way, displaced agricultural workers in developing countries often seek jobs at assembly plants in Free Trade Zones, sometimes known as "maquilas." In these plants, they work under highly controlled, difficult conditions for very low wages, assembling clothing or other products for sale in developed nations. In some cases, workers are able to obtain jobs in manufacturing plants that are outside of the Free Trade Zones, but still owned by large foreign corporations. These plants provide much needed jobs in economies that are often losing their agricultural base, but wages are modest and the profits flow to outside owners. As usual, the long term future of a given plant is uncertain at best.

As communities in the United States and other developed nations begin to experience some of the problems that have long faced Third World countries, we may find it easier to understand the concerns that these countries have with the global economy and to support the changes that they seek. In addition, we may find that we can learn from their personal experiences in dealing with the problems of global capitalism.

Too often in the past, we have delegated our economic decisions to nameless managers of anonymous corporations. These managers made their "business decisions" to maximize short term profits without regard for their long term impact on the workers and communities in which they operate. Meanwhile, our government too often abdicated its constitutional responsibility to "promote the general welfare" and "regulate commerce" as it gave corporations rights and powers that were not in the public's best interests. Under the Bush administration, it has continued to pass legislation, reduce taxes, eliminate regulations, and sign trade agreements for the benefit of a few corporate winners.

Where are these changes taking us? According to an essay by Niall Ferguson, the richest 20% of the world's population had a total income in the 1960s that was 30 times that of the poorest 20%. By 1998, this number had grown to 74 times as much. In 1965 the per capita GDP of the United States was about 15 times that of Chad, one of the poorest countries in Africa. By 1990, the U.S. per capita GDP had grown to about 50 times that of Chad. Over the past twenty-five years, the poor have generally gotten poorer and the poor in Africa have suffered as much or more than the poor anywhere else.

Nonetheless, if we want to catch a glimpse of one version of the future, we would do well to take a careful look at Africa. Africa's decline provides a sobering example of how once prosperous communities can collapse and no longer function as effective societies; how things can go wrong for a society on a massive scale.

Paul Theroux, in his book *Dark Star Safari,* reports how the combined impact of colonization, globalization, overpopulation, disease, corruption, and war have left an entire continent economically destitute, environmentally devastated, and socially fragmented. Theroux returned to Africa forty years after he taught at a school in Malawi. He found an Africa that had regressed in many ways from the place that he knew as a young man: a continent in which hunger, disease, corruption, and violence have grown worse, as the educational, political, and economic infrastructure of many communities has fallen into shambles.

Although the problems of the cities and countries in Africa dwarf those in the United States and other developed countries, we should be careful not to ignore the warning that they provide. Africa's breakdown revolves around such issues as disruption of local economies, global competition, population growth, environmental problems, resource depletion, inadequate medical care, excessive military spending, reliance on war, political divisions, and widespread corruption. There are disturbing parallels between many of these issues and the problems that we are facing in the United States and throughout the developed world. Despite our inherent strengths and immense wealth, a similar decline, perhaps different in detail and scope, could happen here.

In order to minimize this possibility, we need to redefine our priorities. We need to focus on building strong local economies, protecting the environment, conserving our resources, providing medical care, reducing our reliance on military solutions, healing political divisions, and eliminating fraud and corruption.

We need to recognize the economy for what it is -- a human invention designed to meet the needs of society rather than to enrich the few with unconscionable wealth while allowing others to slide down the economic ladder. We need to select leaders who will recommit themselves to our Constitution, rather than the demands of shortsighted corporations and conservative ideologues.

♫ ♫ ♫

The Preamble to the Constitution states that one of the reasons that the people "ordain(ed) and establish(ed)" a new government was to "promote the general welfare." This clearly calls for the government to serve all of the people of our nation, not just those of one class, race, or creed. It also calls for the improvement of their welfare. This is not a laissez-faire attitude. The founders clearly expected something from their new government. They believed that good government would improve their welfare and that of other Americans. The American people have always seen our government as playing a critical role in building a better society. It is important to keep this in mind during times when some consider government a dirty word and issue continuing calls for more privatization of government services. They are not only ignoring over 200 years of history, but they are also challenging the foundation underlying the American Constitution.

Interlude One

♫ ♫ ♫

Missing notes

♬ ♬ ♬

The importance of memory

...our forefathers brought forth

♬ ♬ ♬

The violin has a long and rich history. Three hundred years ago, Stradivari and other luthiers finally captured the basic structure and design of the modern violin in their now treasured instruments. Although their instruments remain benchmarks, many current violin makers continue to develop new design ideas, construction techniques, and materials. We benefit from the collective efforts, past and present, of the countless violinists, composers, and luthiers who developed the music, instruments, and performance techniques that we enjoy. Regardless of the field, our debt to those who have gone before us should generate appreciation and humility as well as inspire us to add to their work through our own lives.

Memories and personal identity

A number of years ago, my mother began suffering from the kind of memory loss often associated with Alzheimer's disease. She had increasing difficulty performing simple tasks or remembering recent events. As the memories and experiences that made up her life gradually disappeared from her mind, it became more difficult to relate to her in any meaningful way. It soon became clear, that my mother needed a new place to live with a more appropriate level of care. Over the next three years, my mother made three moves, each time to a higher level of care due to her increasing needs. She was entering the final stages of her long life journey.

There is no way to know for sure whether or not my mother has Alzheimer's. She certainly displays many of the classic symptoms of the disease, but do you need a name? Does it change anything? My mother has become a dim shadow, an empty shell of the person that I once knew. As described by the title of Eleanor Cooney's excellent book *Death in Slow Motion: My Mother's Descent into Alzheimer's,* it did feel as if my mother was literally dying in slow motion.

Although it was difficult to deal with the care of my mother, where she would live, and what to do with her house and belongings, they were tasks that we could work through and resolve. It was much more difficult to deal with her continuing loss of memory. Our own identities are the cumulative result of a lifetime of memories. Without our memories, who are we? We have no basis to form our reactions to the present. The present becomes a stream of experiences no better or worse than the past. They are all the same -- they just are.

When we meet people, one of the ways in which we establish a rapport is to discover shared memories. With strangers on an airplane, it might be no more than to discuss a recent football game or news story. With friends, it may be to retell a humorous experience or recall a special occasion. With close relatives, it might to talk of times long past with relatives now departed or when we were growing up. It is virtually impossible to have a conversation without reference to the past. It is difficult to make plans for the future without remembering who we are, how we got to where we are, and where we want to go.

A business colleague of mine once had brain surgery that left him without any short term memory. We could talk about trips that we taken together in years gone past, but the recent past was not accessible. This made everyday living frustrating and difficult. He could not remember where anything was, including the location of his own home. The simplest daily rituals were almost impossible. He ultimately moved back to the town where he had lived as a child hoping that his old memories would help guide him through his days.

Memory loss is an insidious process. In many ways, we are the sum of our memories. As these memories gradually fade away, we begin to disappear. At first, there are only occasional missing or discordant notes. Soon, entire pages of the music of our lives disappear. Finally, there is only a faint echo of what had once been a vibrant, engaged person. The music ends even as life limps along.

National amnesia

Memory loss is not just a problem for individuals. In many ways, amnesia is at the heart of our global economy. The flagship of consumptive capitalism, the shopping mall, exists almost purely in the present tense. There are no references to the past or future. Advertising encourages us to enjoy the moment. Every day in the mall is like every other day. Stores may come, stores may go, but nothing ever changes. The owners carefully control and manage every moment to be just as comfortable and predictable as every other. Elevator music guides shoppers through a strange world filled with humanity, but devoid of interaction, affection, or conflict.

Many of our corporations pursue policies aimed at systematically ignoring both the past and the future. Accountants use procedures that deeply discount future returns from long term investments. Corporate managers place little value on the past; it gets in the way of their desire to maximize short term profits.

For this reason, corporations often discount the memories of their most experienced employees. Older employees remember that there are other ways of doing business. To avoid confronting these historical realities and to pursue their own personal agenda, many corporate leaders encourage the departure of older employees through layoffs, firings, offers of early retirement, or by otherwise marginalizing older employees. Corporate policies mandate the destruction of business records to avoid legal problems. Corporations also often engage in creative rewriting of their business histories for their own benefit.

Corporate mergers destroy the business practices, memories, and traditions of acquired companies and are reducing the economic diversity in our economy at an astonishing rate. In its place, the surviving corporations are replacing management diversity with one size fits all management practices. As we standardize the world, we are losing a vast storehouse of knowledge and experience that will be difficult to recover.

In addition to this loss of business memories, the government suffers from memory losses due to employee reductions, political distortions, and outright suppression of information. As a result, we fail to remember the successes as well as the failures of the past. We do not learn from the mistakes of past leaders and we lose sight of the values that have guided us through previous difficult times.

The totalitarian society that George Orwell describes in his novel *1984* uses the systematic suppression of memory and the modification of documents to maintain its power and control. By continual editing of the historic record, it ensures the infallibility of its statements and eliminates any unfavorable comparisons of the present with the past. It meets or even exceeds its goals by simply changing earlier projections after the fact. Similar advantages accrue by simply destroying or restricting access to documents and records.

Throughout the first term of the presidency of George W. Bush, secrecy was a continuing obsession for the Bush administration. It classified countless documents, including documentation regarding contracts and purchasing decisions, in the name of national security. Its use of secrecy as a primary tool of government also extended to its treatment of presidential documents.

Soon after taking office in 2000, Bush announced a sweeping executive order restricting public access to presidential papers from previous administrations. Even if the previous president had no objection, the administration reserved the right to prevent disclosure. In making these sweeping new rules, the White House paid no attention to its obvious conflict of interest regarding the treatment of papers of administrations involving George W. Bush's father, George H. W. Bush, as both vice president and president.

These rules enabled the Bush administration to prevent documents from the Clinton administration from revealing information on the administrations of Ronald Reagan and the senior George Bush that it might find embarrassing or inconvenient. The White House also decided to withhold thousands of pages of documents related to the Clinton administration from the commission investigating the 9/11 attacks despite the surprise and concern of former aides in the Clinton administration.

With virtually no input from the political opposition or the American public, the administration developed major policies and new legislative proposals at meetings behind closed doors with attendees whose names and affiliations remained confidential. Most notably, the White House resisted efforts to identify those who attended meetings led by Vice President Dick Cheney to develop the administration's energy policy.

Efforts by reporters and activists to gain access to government records through the Freedom of Information Act in many other areas regularly encountered resistance and delays. The administration even restricted access to the president himself. Officials kept protesters far away from any presidential appearances where they were invisible to the president and could not intrude on the carefully staged presidential drama. The staged nature of the administration's press conferences became so blatant that *Doonesbury* parodied it in a series of comic strips. As a result of this secrecy and management of information, it became routine for news reporters to turn to foreign sources to learn about the actions of our own government.

Preserving the past

Libraries and the books that they contain are the depositories of our collective memories. They contain the memories and experiences of past generations upon which we base our core values and guiding fictions. However, public libraries throughout our nation face declining budgets, reduced hours, or outright closure. As a result, many libraries increasingly consist of an eclectic mix of older, often obsolete reference texts and popular bestsellers. They no longer provide a comprehensive collection of great literature or the latest information.

Some people attempt to justify library reductions by pointing to the Internet as an on-line replacement for the book collections of libraries. This argument fails to recognize that the Internet, as large as it may be, provides access to only a tiny fraction of the world's printed material. It also contains much of questionable value due to a lack of oversight and review. In addition, Internet content is highly ephemeral. Robert Lucky noted that the average life of a Web page is only six or seven weeks -- hardly the basis of a proper storehouse of our collective memory.

Traditional books also provide access to information independent of controls imposed by technology, corporations, and governments. They provide an archival collection of memories independent of rapidly changing digital hardware and software. Traditional books do not require emulation of obsolete hardware to access older material or the migration of current material to new formats and systems to preserve their accessibility.

It may be no coincidence that the budgets of our libraries are among the first that we reduce when money is tight. Libraries threaten the efforts of the ideological extremists to rewrite history and structure the world to their advantage. They slash library budgets and hours due to budget shortfalls that they have often created. They demand unprecedented access to our library records through the Patriot Act. They attempt to restrict and monitor access to the Internet further limiting our ability to learn about the past. They rewrite textbooks in an attempt to make history support their current priorities. They slash the budgets of our schools and universities to diminish access to knowledge of the past and how to critically challenge the present.

As a result of a closed door government, inadequate news reporting, and suppressed histories, we are becoming a society that is unable to carry on an informed conversation on the important issues of the day. Too many people base their opinions on stereotypes and ideology rather than history, facts, and data. The result is polarization and discord too often orchestrated by our own leaders.

Curiously, the surge of interest in books about the founders of our nation resembles the way in which Alzheimer's patients seem to retain their most distant memories the longest. The Alzheimer's patient cannot reflect on more recent events which have faded from their memory. Similarly, our nation seems to collectively have forgotten the difficult times that we faced as a nation during the first half of the 20th century. We are unable or unwilling to recall the way that our nation responded to these problems with the innovative programs of The New Deal, The New Frontier, and The Great Society. These included the creation of such important institutions as Social Security, the Federal Deposit Insurance Corporation, the Peace Corps, and Medicare, among many others.

Our collective memory of these relatively recent events fades as we focus on more distant stories. We seem to be suffering from a national loss of short term memory. As a consequence, we fail to remember that our nation has faced powerful opponents in the past founded on totalitarian schemes from both the Communist left as well as the Fascist right. We have forgotten that it was not so long ago when corporations were responsible to the people, when the role of government was to take an active role in alleviating national suffering, and when the needs of ordinary people were a national priority. In order to prosper in the 21st century, we need to recover our memory of the 20th century.

One of William Faulkner's characters, in his novel *Requiem for a Nun,* famously said that "the past is never dead, it's not even past." Nowhere is this more evident than in our nation's embrace of preemptive war along with nuclear weapons as we simultaneously condemn terrorists and their use of weapons of mass destruction. Through our collective amnesia, we fail to remember that we developed the first nuclear weapons of mass destruction. We were also the first to use these weapons on civilian populations in Hiroshima and Nagasaki. When we condemn weapons of mass destruction, we would do well to consider the role that we have played and continue to play in their development and dissemination. As we try to understand the motivations behind terrorist attacks, we need to reflect on our own history.

Unfortunately, we are proving to have short memories even concerning events as recent as the 9/11 attacks. Upon reviewing the initial design proposals for the 9/11 memorial at ground zero, Maureen Dowd wrote of their collective failure to reflect what actually happened. Unlike the memorial at the sunken battleship Arizona in Pearl Harbor with its slow leak of oil, the proposals did not evoke the event. Dowd also notes that the designs did not possess a narrative structure as does the Vietnam memorial with its long wall of names in chronological order recording the deaths from that war. Finally, unlike the Holocaust Memorial, the proposals did not instruct the visitor as to the causes behind the attacks. Dowd titled her thoughtful column, the "Unbearable lightness of memory." We need to give our memories the weight that they deserve.

In some ways, the general public is ahead of both the government and private corporation in acknowledging the importance of the past. Many Americans have a great interest in genealogy and preserving the memories of older relatives through audio and video records. They search archives to build family histories. Some return to the homes of their ancestors seeking to reconnect with their past.

Members of some American Indian tribes are also recognizing the value of preserving their collective memories and traditions. Among the most important are their native languages. Until the 1980s, the only speakers of the language of the Blackfoot Indians in northwestern Montana were over fifty years of age. Early white settlers had harshly suppressed the language and the culture that accompanied it. As a consequence, many Indians subsequently also prevented their own children from learning it. Now, the Blackfoot and other tribes throughout the nation are beginning to recognize the value of the cultural memories and traditions embedded in their native tongue. They are creating immersion schools where young people receive a complete and modern education taught in their native language.

Examples such as this demonstrate that some people are beginning to recognize the profound importance of recovering our past. They understand the important role that our memories play in creating a sense of personal identity and integrity. As a nation, we similarly need to recover and preserve our history of both the recent and distant past.

♬ ♬ ♬

The phrase "missing notes" in the title of this book as well as this section, a metaphor stemming from the missing notes on a violin with missing strings, has multiple meanings. On a personal level, this metaphor refers to my mother's lost memories and the holes left in lives by those who are no longer with us. On a more general level, it refers to the lost or suppressed memories of our nation including its communities and businesses.

"Missing notes" also represents the inability of an increasing number of people to participate in our economic prosperity, the loss of the voices of the independent media, the decline of diversity in our national debates, and the suppression of the voices of the political opposition. At the most fundamental level, "missing notes" represents the emptiness that we feel in our lives and our nation when we are not whole. Without these missing notes, we will fail to achieve our full potential as a nation.

After my father died, his violin remained silent. A number of years later, my mother passed the violin on to me, and I planned to simply display it as an interesting artifact. However, I had a long standing interest in the violin, and, with the encouragement of my wife, I decided that I would begin taking violin lessons. I thought that studying the violin might provide some relief from my frustrations over the direction of our nation following the controversial 2000 election. On a personal level, I may have also looked at the violin as a way to reconnect with my fading memories of my father.

Although I had the violin, I still needed to find a teacher. Fortunately, my daughter had a friend who was an accomplished violinist and also gave violin lessons. Although most of her students were much younger than me, she was willing to accept me as her only adult student. And so, one early autumn afternoon, I went to a local high school for my first violin lesson. It was Monday evening, September 10, 2001.

Part II

♬ ♬ ♬

America after September 11

...certain unalienable rights...

Chapter 5

A time of division and discord

...domestic tranquility...

♫ ♫ ♫

The morning after my first violin lesson, I attended the monthly meeting of a business consultants group of which I am a member. Following the meeting, I walked out to my car and turned on the radio. The first thing I heard was a report that a plane had crashed into the Pentagon followed quickly by reports on plane crashes into the World Trade Center in New York City. I could almost hear the tumblers of a lock opening the door to a new and unfamiliar world. In the wake of my first violin lesson, music was far from my mind as I listened and tried to anticipate what the future would bring. In the immediate aftermath of this horrific and unprecedented tragedy, no one knew how this event would affect our nation and the world.

September 11

After the decision by the Supreme Court that effectively determined the next president, the Bush administration claimed that it had a mandate to proceed unilaterally on both the domestic and international scene. It consistently chose the most divisive topics for its attention. Rather than bind up a nation that the flawed election had divided, the administration and its conservative friends in Congress pursued an economic agenda that favored the wealthy and a social agenda embraced by the religious right. The concentration of wealth that had been underway since the Reagan era accelerated.

Other than rewarding its friends and supporters, the Bush administration appeared to see little need for an active government. Throughout his first six months in office, many commentators noted the extensive time that President Bush spent away from Washington and his lack of attention to his job. As mentioned earlier, in the summer of 2001, the White House announced that the president would be spending the entire month of August at his ranch in Texas, despite having already spent nearly half his first six months in office away from Washington. Many other senior government officials also decided to go on vacation during the month of August, 2001. Democrats complained, but Republicans, never strong supporters of government despite their patriotic fervor, saw nothing wrong with the president taking some time off. After all, a little less governing was desirable from their perspective. Unfortunately, the vacations could not have come at a worse time.

Richard Clarke and others had previously prepared an extensive plan for taking action against Al Qaeda near the end of Clinton's second term. Not wishing to begin a major new initiative during a time of transition, the plan awaited review by the Bush administration as Clarke continued to work in the White House. After the installation of the Bush team, Clarke was unable to attract much interest in the plan and little progress occurred. After considerable delay, partially due to Bush's extended stay at his ranch in Texas and the vacations of other members of the administration during August of 2001, the Principals Committee finally met to review Clarke's proposal on September 4, 2001.

Just one week after this belated review of a proposal awaiting action for over seven months, on Tuesday morning, September 11, 2001, Islamic terrorists took control of four commercial airliners on the east coast of the United States. They managed to crash two of these planes into the twin towers of the World Trade Center in New York, another into the Pentagon in Washington, while the forth plane crashed into a field near Pittsburgh, Pennsylvania following a brief and violent struggle with the passengers for control of the aircraft.

These crashes killed hundreds of individuals in the planes as well as approximately three thousand additional people on the ground. The twin towers collapsed due to the combined effects of the crashes and the intense heat generated by fires fueled by thousands of gallons of jet fuel. The total cost in human life, direct and indirect economic expenses, and psychological damage to the millions who witnessed these events unfold was staggering.

Preemptive and endless war

Following the attacks of 9/11, a president who had gained office through a controversial decision of the Supreme Court saw his popularity ratings change in an instant from mediocre to spectacular. The country clearly had undergone a severe trauma and felt an instinctive need to get behind our national leadership.

On the international scene, there was a huge outpouring of sympathy and support for our nation. Leaders throughout the world condemned the actions of the terrorists and recognized the need of the United States to take strong action to prevent such tragedies in the future, both in our country as well as elsewhere. Indeed, the meeting that the Bush administration finally held in early September of 2001 on the Clarke proposal to combat terrorism had already covered some of these very issues.

However, an administration that had received strong support from the nation and the world chose to take a highly partisan, divisive, unilateral approach in its response. Through its immediate declaration that "either you are with us or you are with the terrorists," the administration spread a cloak of fear across our nation that stifled dissent and had a chilling effect on the political opposition. It transformed support of its policies into a litmus test for patriotism among Americans and loyalty among our allies.

Instead of seeing the aftermath of the 9/11 attacks as an opportunity to join forces with both its political opposition as well as the rest of the world in condemning violence and endorsing the need for a unified response, it chose to go it alone. Sadly, in the earliest hours and days after the attacks, the administration had already begun to politicize the attacks. The Bush administration decided to act as unilaterally and thoughtlessly in its response to 9/11 as it had on domestic issues following the 2000 election.

Without congressional approval, the Bush administration declared a virtually "endless" war against terrorism. Few thought to question the meaning much less the logic of an "endless" war. How do we win an endless war? Why is it endless? In addition, as noted by Senator Bob Kerrey during the hearings of the 9/11 commission, terrorism is a tactic, not an opponent. It is like saying you will wage war against bombing missions. You can only wage war against specific identified opponents. Our real enemies are the radical religious extremists who have chosen to wage war against us. The specific tactics that they choose to pursue may vary from place to place or time to time.

It is more than a matter of semantics. Religious extremists who wish to destroy our nation may use a variety of tactics in addition to terrorism. In fact, by focusing on terrorism, we may lose sight of other tactics such as economic sabotage or cyber warfare which can also be significant threats to our nation. Once again, language does matter; imprecise, careless, and misleading language, due to politics or simple ignorance, prevents us from making the proper decisions.

In addition to the "endless" war on terrorism, the Bush administration adopted a policy of first-strike, preemptive war. Fifty years ago, Thomas K. Finletter, former Secretary of the Air Force, wrote in *The Atlantic Monthly* about the emerging nuclear standoff between the United States and the former Soviet Union. While recognizing the arguments in favor of preemptive war against an opponent growing ever stronger, he still stated that he did not believe that the Eisenhower administration, "...or any administration that will succeed it, would or will make preventive war."

Finletter's comments were far from the first time an American had expressed such sentiments. According to Virginia Postrel's book review of *Liberty and Freedom* by David Hackett Fischer, a Pennsylvania Whig commented in 1775 that the rattlesnake, an emblem for our country on Revolutionary War banners, always warns her enemies and "never begins an attack." The Bush administration justified its invasion of Iraq with a long list of reasons, none of which withstood closer scrutiny after the war began. It soon became clear that we had invaded Iraq for invalid reasons. We had lost forever any pretense that the United States would never wage a preemptive war. Secretary Finletter's hopeful prediction was in tatters.

George W. Bush's personal appearance and language, much like Ronald Reagan's, often brought forth the image of a ranch cowboy -- and much like Reagan, Bush sprinkled religious rhetoric throughout many of his pronouncements. The problem is that in American western movies, the good guys never shoot first; they only fire their guns in self-defense. Similarly, the Bible says that those without sin should cast the first stone -- religious rhetoric that you're unlikely to hear from the Bush administration.

Freedom

Although the administration vowed that it would not let the terrorists win, some actions brought unprecedented changes to the national scene, supposedly justified by the need for homeland security, without any real sense that our country was indeed more secure. The Patriot Act, passed by the Senate with Senator Russ Feingold of Wisconsin casting the sole dissenting vote, contained numerous provisions that reduced fundamental American rights in the name of fighting terrorism. Frightening parallels continued to grow between the direction that our government was taking our country and the world George Orwell described in his novel *1984.* The reputation of the ill-advised Patriot Act grew so low that even the Bush administration soon rarely referred to it by its deceptive name. Efforts to pass follow-up legislation met considerable resistance from members of both parties.

At the same time that the administration supported this attack on our basic freedoms, it failed to pursue measures that might have been more expensive for the government and private industry, but would have provided more meaningful protections. These include scanning all incoming shipping containers at U.S. ports, improving patrols along our coastlines, increasing inspections at our borders with Canada and Mexico, and providing improved security for passenger and freight trains. Although expensive, the vast amounts that we ultimately poured into Iraq would häve gone a long ways towards funding these meaningful improvements to domestic security.

The Bush administration's policy changes not only undermined basic constitutional freedoms and rights, but they also encouraged a xenophobic fear of foreigners through harsh and punitive policies for foreign residents, students, travelers, and immigrants. Through a special visa requirement for foreign journalists, our government denied reporters and writers entry into this country. Elena Lappin, a reporter on assignment for the British paper *The Guardian,* wrote in *The New York Times Book Review* of her personal experiences when officials detained, imprisoned, and finally denied her entry into this country.

Most Americans are unaware of the extent to which the government maintains various watch lists containing the names of persons who the government believes pose some sort of threat to our country. Although we may need some sort of list to alert public officials and potential employers of dangerous individuals, many of these lists do not contain sufficient information to clearly identify the named individual. As a result, the questionable accuracy of multiple, conflicting databases threatens our democratic freedoms.

For example, an article by Anthony Romero, the executive director of the American Civil Liberties Union, noted that a list of "specially designated nationals and blocked persons" contain 10 individuals with his name. Although some entries include date of birth as an additional screening measure, not all entries provide this information and for employment purposes, prospective employers cannot ask for date of birth prior to employment -- a sort of "catch-22."

Officials have stopped Senator Edward M. Kennedy at least five times as he attempted to board a plane or buy a ticket because his name appeared on a no-fly list. Only through the intervention of supervisors who recognized him was he able to board the flight. Furthermore, even after contacting the Transportation Security Administration twice, he still found himself delayed at the airport. If a U.S. Senator encounters these problems, what can those of us who are not so readily recognizable do? -- and how did his name get on that list?

In addition to confusing watch lists, early in 2005, the House passed the REAL ID Act, legislation supposedly aimed at restricting the ability of terrorists to carry out attacks in the United States. If passed by the Senate and signed into law, this act would impose numerous requirements on state motor vehicle departments regarding the issuance of driver's licenses. Many officials oppose these new requirements both because of their complexity and because they would force many drivers into either unlicensed driving or black market licenses, making them more difficult to identify and track. In addition, the act also contains more restrictive immigration rules for refugees seeking asylum in our country and limits the ability of the courts to review immigration decisions. In total, this legislation would drive many current immigrants further into the shadows and make it more difficult for prospective immigrants to enter the "land of opportunity."

Following the 9/11 attacks, the Bush administration also turned its back on international agreements such as the Geneva Convention regarding its treatment of "enemy combatants." Through the Patriot Act as well as other powers that it claims to possess, it has imprisoned many people under inhumane conditions at our base in Guantanomo Bay, Cuba, without charges or access to the outside world including attorneys. Despite using their declaration of endless war to justify their actions in Congress and to the public, it simultaneously argued in judicial proceedings that our prisoners were not "prisoners of war," but enemy combatants with minimal, if any, legal protections.

The United States prosecution of foreign aliens in our country shows similar disregard of international treaties. The Vienna Convention of 1963 requires that any foreigners arrested in our country be told of their right to legal assistance from the consulates or embassies of their own nations. This agreement also provides the thousands of Americans arrested abroad each year with similar access to our embassies for assistance. In 2004, the World Court in The Hague, Netherlands, ruled against the United States in a case involving 51 Mexicans imprisoned on death row in the United States who did not receive notification of their rights to seek assistance from Mexican authorities. Although the World Court has no enforcement power, this decision has led the Supreme Court to hear an appeal from one of these prisoners.

As a result of its words and actions, the Bush administration has in a few short years threatened to destroy the international order that the United States has taken a leading role in creating since the end of World War II. In the process, the world's view of the United States as an international beacon of democracy and freedom has rapidly changed to identifying us as an "irresponsible nation" that no longer plays by the rules. Through our unilateral abandonment of treaties and decisions to wage war, we have damaged our relationships with countless allies throughout the world. We will be paying the price for our errors of omission and commission for many years to come.

Lies and deceptions

As it sought to gain support for its controversial proposals and actions, highly respected sources noted that the Bush administration engaged in a consistent pattern of deceptions, exaggerations, and lies. Mainstream newspapers published columns such as "Truth is not a Bush priority" by Walter Cronkite and "Bush's lying now routine" by

Gordon Livingston. A commentary by Steve Chapman in the *Chicago Tribune* noted that the deceptions, exaggerations, and falsehoods used by Bush to justify the war in Iraq had parallels with the deceptions behind the ill-fated decisions that led to the Vietnam War. In his collection of essays *An Intellectual in Public,* Alan Wolfe expressed his view that in the 2000 election Bush's advisors discovered that "...there are simply no limits to how much you can lie in American politics and get away with it." Al Franken wrote an entertaining though well-documented book about the Bush administration entitled *Lies and the Lying Liars Who Tell Them.*

When caught in their lies, Bush and officials from his administration often attempted to explain them away as simple errors, oversights, or misstatements. Explicit warnings about the presence of weapons of mass destruction in Iraq gradually morphed into a variety of vague and ever-changing statements about Iraqi desires for these weapons or the possibility that they might begin programs to develop them. The famous photo op of Bush landing on the carrier Abraham Lincoln in front of a huge banner declaring "Mission Accomplished" faded into a confounding discussion of who requested the banner and an endless litany about the meaning of combat, major combat, military operations, and so on.

Another example of the deceptive rhetoric of the Bush administration concerned the supposed relationship between Iraq and Al Qaeda terrorist groups. They initially claimed that there were direct links between Iraq and Al Qaeda. After a number of sources discredited their claim, they shifted their rhetoric from making direct claims to a form of innuendo that still implied the same thing. The rhetoric got so absurd that it began making regular appearances in various political cartoons.

In an all too common tactic, Bush would promote and praise various programs in his speeches and personal appearances only to later cut spending requests for these same programs in his budget proposals. Bush's 2005 budget proposal contained many examples of this whiplash approach to governing including cuts to the Global

Fund to Fight HIV/AIDS, Malaria, and Tuberculosis, the Hope IV Housing Program, and the program to rehabilitate contaminated industrial sites -- all areas that he had endorsed at previous personal appearances.

Sometimes, the deceptions took the form of the suppression of information. A few months after Bush signed the bill authorizing sweeping changes to Medicare that may endanger the long term future of this critical social program, a Medicare actuary revealed the results of his analysis showing that the bill could cost the country more than $500 billion, $100 billion more than the amount considered by Congress. He believed the head of the agency failed to pass the information to Congress because the results exceeded the $400 billion limit set by a number of House Republicans.

Following the statements by the actuary, the Medicare discussion evolved into a debate over the rights of supervisors over their employees, whether the cost estimates were fully relevant, and the legal relationship between Congress and the Executive Branch, rather than focusing on the financial facts. Meanwhile, by February of 2005, the projected cost of the program over ten years was not $400 or $500 billion, but $724 billion.

Following the collapse of Enron, Bush and his staff were also less than forthright concerning the relationship of the Bush family, Enron, and Kenneth Lay. Whatever the exact form of these relationships, it is clear that they were numerous and extended back for many years. The corporation topping the list in *The Atlantic Monthly* magazine of the top ten employers by cumulative lifetime employee contributions to George W. Bush's political career was none other than Enron. And yet, from Bush's public comments, you might think that he had barely heard of Enron or Kenneth Lay.

Whenever someone attempted to call the administration on these lies, deceptions, and omissions, the administration responded with a vengeance not usually seen in American government. The effort by former ambassador Joseph C. Wilson, IV, to expose the deceptions involved in the president's 2003 State of the Union Address statements about Iraq and its supposed efforts to purchase uranium in Africa is one well-known example. A national columnist soon exposed the identity of Wilson's wife, a CIA agent, that he reportedly received from a White House source. Despite continuing efforts, the source of the leak of this confidential information remains unknown.

In Ron Suskind's book *The Price of Loyalty,* former treasury secretary Paul O'Neill provided critical descriptions of Bush's management style in the White House and described the president as unengaged at cabinet meetings. Following these public statements, the Justice Department began a probe of O'Neill for allegedly leaking secret documents to support his criticism. Ultimately, they cleared him of any wrongdoing insofar as administration officials provided the documents to him after their review and clearance as he requested.

The pattern continued with the publication of Richard Clarke's book *Against All Enemies.* In this book, Clarke again faulted the Bush administration for its obsessive focus on Iraq before and after the 9/11 attacks and the way in which the Iraq War detracted from our nation's efforts in combating terrorism. In this case, the criticism hit the administration especially hard since Clarke had worked closely with the Reagan, the first Bush, the Clinton, and the second Bush administrations on counter-terrorism activities.

In their heated responses, members of the Bush administration made multiple, often contradictory, accusations against Clarke trying to diminish the impact of his views. One would report that he "was out of the loop" while another stated that he "was in every meeting." One would declare that he didn't know what he was talking about while another suggested that it was his responsibility to have solved the problem. As a last resort, they fell back on the old chestnut that Clarke was simply trying to sell books. There were few attempts to respond to the actual content of his observations.

Form often triumphed over content. The Bush administration consistently endorsed programs and legislation featuring highly deceptive labels. The "Patriot" Act actually undermines the human rights that many of the founding patriots of our nation considered of central importance. As noted in a speech by Al Gore, this act exploited public fears for political gain and tended to weaken rather than strengthen the nation. It also distracted the country from more appropriate actions that would have contributed more to our national security.

The little known "Support Anti-Terrorism by Fostering Effective Technologies Act of 2002" (the so-called SAFETY Act) is part of the Homeland Security Act. Contrary to its reassuring and self-serving name, this act actually provides a safety shield for corporations rather than the public. It protects sellers of a wide range of products ranging from aircraft to computer software whose products receive the designation of "Qualified Anti-Terrorism Technology" (or QATT). QATT certification prevents victims from recovering damages from sellers of approved products following a terrorist attack -- hardly enhancing "safety" or "homeland security" for the nation.

The "No Child Left Behind" legislation encountered opposition from educators across the nation who complained about receiving too many mandates with too little funding and excessive emphasis on standardized testing programs. This legislation drained resources from other areas while producing children trained to pass a specific test without necessarily being able to function as responsible citizens and critically analyze today's issues. Of course, cynics might suggest that was exactly the goal of the legislation.

Similarly, the administration's "Clear Skies" initiative actually allowed corporations to avoid installing the latest pollution control equipment on their power plants. Changes to Medicare, that allegedly focused on improved drug benefits for seniors, included little publicized provisions that moved us closer to the privatization of the entire Medicare system for the benefit of health care corporations. Many opponents described another Bush proposal concerning the legalization of immigrant workers in this country as actually a temporary worker program controlled by and for corporate employers. A note in *Time* magazine described the American Jobs

Creation Act as the "No Lobbyist Left Behind Act" and a classic of pork-barrel politics. In the Bush administration and the Republican Congress, the rhetoric rarely agreed with the reality.

In one of the Bush administration's most surreal actions, it proposed removing the distinction between farm raised salmon and wild salmon. By declaring farm-raised salmon as equivalent to wild salmon, the overall number of salmon increases, reducing the need for protections under the Endangered Species Act. The proposal conveniently ignores the likely decline in actual wild salmon without these protections. The same report on this proposal in *Time* magazine noted that the administration had previously proposed to reclassify workers to increase manufacturing employment as well as to reclassify radioactive waste from "high level" to "low level" in order to reduce disposal costs.

And so we have "wild" salmon that aren't, "low level" nuclear waste that isn't, and "clear skies" that are getting more polluted. The motto of the Bush administration seemed to be that when substantive action is expensive or politically unattractive, resort to rhetoric.

The policies and actions of the Bush administration have squandered much of the goodwill enjoyed by the United States throughout much of the world. Instead, we are fast becoming the nation that almost everyone dislikes. Ironically, we have managed to retain the enmity of our foes while infuriating our friends. At home, rather than promoting the general welfare, the Bush administration has created division and discord. In its ongoing imperial edicts and rhetoric, the Bush administration has catered to the wealthy and powerful, restricted our freedoms, and divided our nation.

George Soros has drawn a parallel between the beliefs and actions of the Bush administration and a financial bubble. Financial bubbles take a kernel of reality in a nonsustainable direction. Soros suggests that the administration's quest for American supremacy is a bubble with great dangers for our nation. The kernel of reality driving the bubble is that the United States does occupy a position of great power in the world today. However, distorting this reality into the view that our country can and should use its power to impose its desires throughout the world is not sustainable, a bubble that sooner or later must burst. In the language of this book, this bubble has grown from deceptive guiding fictions regarding our wisdom and power that are more fiction than truth and that divide rather than inspire us as a people.

Rather than continuing to believe that we have all the answers and that our power is virtually unlimited, it is time for us to reconnect with our core values of democracy, freedom, and equality. We need to restore harmony to our nation and the world before it is too late. Otherwise, our future may parallel that of many other nations and empires who arrogantly abused their wealth and power.

♫ ♫ ♫

The Preamble to the Constitution calls for the government to "insure domestic tranquility." During presidential campaigns, candidates not infrequently proclaim that, if elected, they will unite the nation. George W. Bush was no exception. When new administrations take office, one of their first acts is often to make an appeal for unity and the support of all Americans. In fact, these calls usually usher in a "presidential honeymoon" when the opposition speaks more softly and the new president seeks conciliation as the new term begins. As seen in this chapter, despite the controversy of the 2000 election and the attacks of 9/11, the Bush administration almost immediately sought confrontation and created division, rather than unity much less "domestic tranquility." However, it continued to maintain its close relationships with corporate America. The following chapter will discuss some of the consequences of these relationships and the aggressive capitalism that the Bush administration supports.

Chapter 6

Scandals, frauds, and deceptions

...a fair deal...

♫ ♫ ♫

Achieving even a moderate level of skill on a violin requires years of weekly lessons and daily practice for most students. A young student can sit down at a piano and immediately play simple tunes. Playing a single note on a violin with the correct pitch, not flat or sharp, is a difficult task. Playing a series of notes requires extreme dexterity from the violinist's left hand and complex motions of the bow with the right hand and arm. It sometimes takes days or even weeks for a new student to properly play a simple tune. The use of vibrato with the left hand to create a wavering tone adds to the difficulties. Even master violinists with years of concert experience continue to work on some aspect of their vibrato or fingering. The demanding nature of the instrument generates a sense of integrity. There simply are no short cuts or tricks with the violin.

Stock market scandals

There is a long history of market distortions and manipulations through speculation and fraudulent activity. Abuses in the 1920s contributed to the Great Depression and led to new financial regulations for the stock market and other investments. Nonetheless, creative individuals regularly try to find new ways to beat the markets, much like a compulsive gambler tries to find new ways to beat the house.

In the 1990s, hedge funds became very popular on Wall Street. These funds, virtually unregulated, invested in a wide variety of so-called derivative investments whose value depended on a complex array of other investments. Exploiting small differences in returns between these related investments, so-called arbitrage investors attempted to lock-in a relatively small, but seemingly certain return. Although these strategies initially generated handsome profits, their highly leveraged nature possessed an equally powerful ability to lose money when the small gain became a loss.

In the 1990s, one of the most spectacular stories of going from boom to bust involved Long Term Capital Management. After several years of amazing returns, the accumulated losses in this firm's derivative investments were so large that they threatened the stability of the entire financial system. Eventually, the Federal Reserve system stepped in and oversaw efforts by various private Wall Street bankers to maintain the viability of the system. Through the actions of these private bankers, the financial markets continued to function, the Wall Street power brokers maintained their collective wealth and power, and those managing the fund lost hundreds of millions in paper profits. Many wealthy investors in the fund lost virtually their entire investment in this ill-advised and unregulated scheme.

On the heels of the hedge fund collapse in 1998, the stock market experienced a rapid run-up driven in large part by speculation in technology and Internet stocks. Entrepreneurs formed new Internet businesses almost every day chased by a seemingly inexhaustible supply of investment interest. Companies with minimal sales revenues and no profits reached market valuations that placed them among the most valuable businesses in the world.

Brokers encouraged stock purchases in a bloated and unrealistic market. Analysts pumped the stock of companies even when they were well aware that the prospects for the underlying businesses were dim. Investors sought ever larger returns on stocks that had already produced huge gains. Needless to say, this irrational behavior could not last and the Internet bubble collapsed in 2000.

Following the collapse, authorities penalized a number of brokers, accountants, and analysts for their part in creating an unsustainable bubble. Of course, this did little to help the individual investor who lost money in the fiasco, often without any direct involvement, but simply through mutual funds that included Internet firms in their portfolios. As with the hedge funds, the need for oversight and regulation was clearly apparent.

The mutual fund industry has also come under attack for the way in which large investors have received more favorable treatment compared to average investors. Some funds allowed selected large investors to take advantage of anticipated changes in the valuation of the mutual fund before average investors. Once again, the playing field in the financial markets was far from level. Without adequate regulation and oversight, certain individuals took advantage of their privileged positions to gain an unfair advantage.

There has been considerable political pressure, particularly since the election of Ronald Reagan in 1980, to increase the use of market forces to make our decisions and set our priorities. Under the best circumstances, the ability of the market to make decisions that will bring long term benefit to our society has always been debatable. However, when individuals and firms in positions of power are able to apply undue influence, ceding our decision-making to the market becomes ludicrous.

The collapse of Enron

Through deregulation and privatization, there are now ample opportunities for individuals and companies in other industries to manipulate the system for their own massive gain through varying degrees of subterfuge, deception, and illegality.

One of the most prominent examples has been the deregulation of the electric power industry. The growth of Enron, a giant corporation led by an executive with close ties to the Bush administration, was a direct result of privatizing the production and distribution of electric power. Its manipulative practices perhaps created and certainly exacerbated the California power crisis and ultimately led to the firm's bankruptcy. As a consequence, thousands of investors, employees, and taxpayers suffered through a combination of lost jobs, lost savings, higher taxes, and higher rates.

Since it occurred in the immediate aftermath of the 9/11 attacks, the Enron bankruptcy received relatively little scrutiny by the public and mass media. In different times, this story would have been the story of the year. At the time, it was the biggest corporate bankruptcy in history; Enron had grown to be the fifth largest corporation in the United States. Enron employees had contributed more than those from any other corporation to Bush's political career according to the previously mentioned list in *The Atlantic Monthly*.

Unfortunately, by 2004, not only were Enron's links to the Bush administration receiving minimal attention, but it remained unclear what degree of success prosecutors would have in prosecuting those at the highest levels of the company. Despite their high compensation and apparent power, senior executives are often able to avoid prosecution by claiming ignorance of activities at lower levels of their company. Ironically, the claims of authority and responsibility that executives often use to justify their often outrageous compensation packages, virtually disappear whenever investigators examine corporate misdeeds.

The human costs and financial losses associated with the collapse of Enron were due to inadequate oversight of its business decisions and individuals taking advantage of a recently deregulated industry. Even conservative investors lost a huge amount of money simply because their mutual funds or pension accounts included Enron in their portfolios, often as a traditionally safe, utility stock.

The problems created by deregulation, privatization, and permissive capitalism are not limited to corporate giants such as Enron. Early in 2003, the CBS television news show *60 Minutes* carried a report on the sad story of Montana Power. For many years, Montana Power had provided its customers with electrical power at low rates while maintaining happy employees and satisfied investors. However, a new state law allowed Montana Power to leave the power industry and become a telecommunications company in its search for improved financial returns. It sold its power generating dams, coals mines, and transmission lines, and used the proceeds to build 26,000 miles of fiber optic cable across northern plains states.

Almost immediately, it became evident that there was vast over-capacity in the telecommunications industry and the value of Montana Power stock plummeted. Employees lost their jobs, investors and retirees suffered financial losses, and electricity rates skyrocketed. These high rates resulted in the closure of mines and additional job losses. The consequences devastated Butte as well as the entire state of Montana. Sad stories like Enron and Montana Power demonstrate the importance of often criticized government regulations to control speculative, deceptive, and illegal activities.

Privatization is not the panacea that some believe. There are many goods and services that do not lend themselves to delivery by the private sector. Many believe that the costs outweigh the benefits of privatization and deregulation in such important industries as telecommunications, broadcasting, electric power, air travel, and health care. Deregulation in these industries has resulted in confusion, increased costs, decreased reliability, and reduced access to important products and services.

A good example occurred in the fall of 2004 with the fiasco related to the production of the flu vaccine. Severe shortages developed when one of only two producers was unable to deliver its half of the national supply due to problems with contamination. In this case, the dangers in relying on only two suppliers with production facilities outside our country became clearly apparent. Depending on a small number of private corporations, driven by demands for low costs and high profitability, for such a critical product, simply does not make sense.

Another example of an area where privatization has led to a variety of problems is the operation of prisons. The various abuses by the profit seeking corporations providing this difficult service suggest that it should return to the exclusive and direct control of the government. Providing responsible care for the prison population requires a long term perspective with strong moral overtones that does not work well in a profit oriented, market based system. The market takes a short term perspective without adequate regard for long term risk, moral considerations, or effects on other parties.

Deregulation and privatization may be appropriate for some economic activities and decisions, but they do not provide the protections that our society needs and demands for many services and products. Rather than depending on the vagaries of the market and lowest cost bidding, closely regulated businesses or the government itself should be the preferred providers for critical products and services.

Public sector scandals

Scandals and abuses are by no means limited to the private sector. They also occur in the government. Throughout history, acceptance of bribes, illegal payments, and misuse of public funds have been continuing problems. Today, our problems are sometimes more subtle. Conflicts of interest, both real and apparent, have assumed greater importance as the financial and political consequences of decisions increase and the circles of power grow ever tighter.

For example, Congress halted a deal between the Air Force and Boeing regarding the leasing of tanker aircraft due to inappropriate behavior by a government official involved in the negotiations. It appears likely that Boeing will have to contend with stiff competition from Airbus in Europe when contract negotiations reopen.

In another example, some see a conflict of interest in the close relationship between the vice president and Supreme Court Justice Antonin Scalia at a time when many disputes involving the Bush administration are going to the Supreme Court. Unfortunately, those involved in controversial decisions often appear satisfied to insist that they have no conflict of interest while failing to recognize that it is the appearance of a conflict that is the problem.

The immense amount of money required to run for public office also creates problems. Those receiving large campaign contributions often must choose between the interests of their constituency and those who provide the cash. Barbara Freese, in her book *Coal: A human history,* describes the role played by coal and global warming in the 2000 presidential election. Although most analyses focused on the debate over the close results in Florida, Freese notes that Al Gore helped negotiate the Kyoto Protocol that the coal industry opposed. The coal industry also worried about how a Gore administration concerned about the environment might limit mining practices that remove entire mountain tops in the West Virginia coal fields.

According to Freese, the coal industry tripled its campaign contributions and generously supported the Bush campaign. Subsequently, West Virginia, usually a strong Democratic state, supported Bush with a 52% majority. If West Virginia had voted for Al Gore, its 5 electoral votes would have made him the next president. Soon after taking office, Bush weakened environmental restrictions and their enforcement for coal plants and refused to support the Kyoto Protocol. A coal industry representative duly noted the "payback" for their efforts in making Bush president. Money once again asserted its power and few people are even aware of the role that it played in West Virginia and the election.

By 2004, the United States had not only rejected the Kyoto Protocol, but it also blocked efforts to begin substantive discussions at a United Nations conference on global warming in Argentina. Attendees wanted to include the United States under an earlier 1992 agreement on climate change that our country had signed. However, the United States position at the conference was it wanted no written or oral reports from any seminars on climate change held under that protocol. As a result, the conference could only schedule a single meeting next year to "exchange information."

The flow of individuals between corporations and the government compounds the problem. Government officials often take high paying corporate jobs after leaving their public positions. Conversely, corporate executives often receive appointments to high level government positions or have the inside track to elected office due to their wealth and connections. Vice President Dick Cheney was previously the chief executive officer of Halliburton, a large government defense contractor. In the summer of 2004, the Securities and Exchange Commission fined Halliburton $7.5 million for providing investors inaccurate reports of its profits while Cheney was CEO. Although Cheney, through his attorney, denied any involvement in the accounting changes that led to the fine, Halliburton remained under investigation by the government for a number of other alleged violations.

Shortly before the 2004 election, the FBI broadened its probe of Halliburton related to a $7 billion contract for restoring Iraqi oil fields. According to a *Time* magazine article, the objections to the lack of competitive bidding for the five year contract by a senior Army contracting specialist involved in the negotiations may have threatened her career. These various examples illustrate the problems that can develop from the cozy relationship between government officials and major contractors or supporters.

Exploiting our guiding fictions

In some ways, the misuse and distortion of our guiding fictions may be the greatest public sector scandal of them all. It undermines our ability to make decisions consistent with the core values of our nation. In the name of equity, we insure that the wealthy get a larger tax cut because they pay the most, rather than helping the needy. In the name of establishing justice, we enact and enforce harsh penalties for common street crimes while imposing minimal sanctions, if any, for white collar crime that steals billions in the markets. In the name of religion, we support moral legalism without accepting responsibility to help the poor, the sick, and the needy. While praising democracy, we create gerrymandered districts, restrict access to the polls, and tolerate inaccurate counting of votes.

From its earliest days, this has been a nation of diverse peoples seeking new opportunities free from tyranny. They found a land that valued individual freedoms, democratic elections, political opposition, and justice under the law. A lengthy Revolutionary War and bloody Civil War helped ensure and define these freedoms for future generations. Despite the mistakes of the past, our collective dedication to basic human rights and democratic ideals have formed a solid foundation upon which to build our nation.

Today, the actions of some threaten these collective values. Corporate executives, capitalizing on conservative initiatives in deregulation and privatization, exploit and manipulate the economy through a variety of complex, often unethical, and sometimes illegal, maneuvers. They report profits that aren't there. They produce products that don't perform. They avoid taxes they don't want to pay. They outsource every job except their own.

Meanwhile, wealth from these executives and their corporations finances friendly candidates, supports corporate lobbyists, and even seeks direct redress of their grievances through petitions that they promote through massive advertising campaigns. The Democratic governor of California lost his job, eleven months after winning his second term, to a celebrity with no previous experience in government in a recall process initiated by a wealthy individual. George W. Bush became president with high level connections and wealthy supporters, a discredited election process in the state where his brother is governor, and legal maneuvers in a Supreme Court dominated by justices appointed by Republican presidents.

Conservative political leaders accuse anyone who challenges these handouts to the rich and powerful as engaging in "class warfare," while labeling conservative efforts to weaken environmental protections, a "Clear Skies" initiative. Our country invaded Iraq based on claims of an imminent threat from weapons of mass destruction that weren't there. Our leaders told us we were bringing peace and democracy to a nation that wanted us to leave and that saw little but continuing bloodshed and destruction. Reminiscent of the party slogans in George Orwell's novel, *1984,* fairness meant inequality, peace meant war, democracy meant domination.

Among the many guiding fictions of our nation are such aphorisms as honesty is the best policy, everyone deserves a fair deal, and equal opportunity for all. These principles have never been literally true, but most people tried to observe them as best as they were able. Today, we have lost any pretense of adhering to them in a world filled with spin doctoring, taking what you can, and favoring the wealthy. What is going on here? Is anyone paying attention?

♫ ♫ ♫

Americans expect "a fair deal." This expectation undergirds the social and legal contracts of our market based society. Republican President Teddy Roosevelt called it "a square deal" and said that no one deserved more or should receive less. Democratic President Franklin Roosevelt offered "a new deal" when the old one wasn't working. Among the most important guiding fictions of our country is that everyone deserves fair treatment. The effects of the scandals, frauds, and deceptions within the private sector and the government on the middle class since 2000 suggest that we are again at a time that calls for a new deal, a fair deal for all Americans.

Chapter 7

A state of endless war

...the common defense...

♫ ♫ ♫

For the beginning violinist, simply playing the correct notes is a challenge. Later, while playing more difficult pieces, the student must learn to anticipate the upcoming notes. At times, a single bow stroke produces multiple notes sometimes requiring a quick crossing to a different string. Changes in the key signature as well as accidental sharps or flats occur without warning. One finger must sometimes cover two strings at the same time, and double stops require the bow to simultaneously excite two strings. The left hand may have to shift position to reach the higher notes. The violinist must think ahead to prepare for what is to come. In much the same way, our nation must look ahead and anticipate the consequences of its decisions.

The axis of evil

The attacks of 9/11 generated a huge outpouring of support for New York City, a desire for national unity in the face of great loss, and a genuine international expression of grief and sympathy. The audacity and immensity of these tragic attacks was difficult to comprehend. In the coming weeks, we all mourned the loss of human life, suffered from the emotional and physical toll that they took, and pondered what they meant for the future of the world, our nation, and our own lives. There was a widespread expectation both at home and abroad that the United States would take whatever action that was possible against those who supported and directed the attacks.

Following its declaration of an endless war on terrorism, the administration focused its attention on Afghanistan, home of Taliban extremists as well as Al Qaeda training camps supported by Osama Bin Laden. The White House, with broad bipartisan support and little international opposition, initiated military action aimed at overthrowing the oppressive Taliban regime and destroying the training camps. Fortunately, a strong rebel military force, the Northern Alliance, already controlled the northeast corner of the country. This alliance, as well as former Soviet republics to the north, provided assistance as well as an initial base of operations for our ground troops. Without their active assistance, our invasion of Afghanistan would have been much more difficult.

In a relatively short time, U.S. led troops entered the capital, Kabel, and forced the Taliban forces to disperse into the mountains or neighboring countries. The U.S. then began the difficult task of establishing a new government, consolidating control of the more remote areas of the country, and tracking down Taliban forces in the mountainous border regions between Afghanistan and Pakistan. These were all challenging tasks, particularly since the Bush administration already had its eyes on another target, Iraq.

Even though the long term future of Afghanistan and its surrounding areas was still quite uncertain, Bush gave a speech in which he chose to broaden his vision and identified Iraq, Iran, and North Korea as an "axis of evil." In so doing, he attempted to garner political support by aligning his policies and actions with those pursued by our nation against the axis nations of Germany, Italy, and Japan in World War II. The unnecessary and arbitrary linkage of Iraq, Iran, and North Korea in a political sound bite ignored threats from other nations also run by autocratic and repressive regimes. It also contributed to a sense of desperation in Iran and North Korea that would further aggravate our problems with these nations.

Despite the questionable accuracy and wisdom of this declaration, it soon became clear that the real focus of the administration was Iraq. The extent to which this was due to Iraq's strategically critical location in the Middle East or its possession of the world's second largest petroleum reserves remains unclear. Aside from these considerations, the administration used an assortment of other reasons to justify a possible invasion of Iraq.

One of the arguments that it used was the removal of Iraq's weapons of mass destruction. Although extensive inspections by officials from the United Nations had failed to uncover any such weapons, the administration insisted that it had clear evidence that Saddam Hussein possessed or was pursuing chemical, biological, or nuclear weapons. Senior officials in the White House summarily dismissed the failure of United Nations' inspectors to locate any of these weapons. Ultimately, they forced the premature removal of the U.N. inspectors over the objections of many that we should give the inspectors additional time to continue their work since Iraq did not pose an imminent threat to anyone.

Throughout the summer and fall of 2002, administration policies seemed to reflect an obsession with power and control more driven by ideological dogma than facts and logic. The administration was talking openly about the need for preemptive war as a regular policy for the first time in our nation's history. Mainly monologue and not much dialogue filled the mass media. There was little tolerance of dissent or respect for the opposition; minority views appeared to be irrelevant. In addition, the ongoing debate over Iraq distracted the nation from discussing other important issues including rebuilding Afghanistan, fighting terrorism at home, restoring the economy, preserving human rights, and protecting the environment.

While the rhetoric from the Bush administration reached a fever pitch, the leaders of the Democratic opposition remained strangely silent. With a few notable exceptions, including Senator Feingold from Wisconsin, most congressional Democrats seemed unable to articulate a strong critique of the policies and actions of the administration following 9/11 and its plan to attack Iraq. In August of 2002, my wife and I joined a group of citizens from throughout Wisconsin at Senator Herb Kohl's Madison office to express concern over the proposed war in Iraq. Many also expressed frustration with the weak opposition to the proposed war by the Democrats.

Following the meeting at Senator Kohl's office, we joined many others in a nationwide effort opposing the anticipated war in Iraq. Through Move-On and other political groups, we expressed our deep concern over the statements of the administration, contacted Congress as well as the White House, signed petitions to the United Nations, installed yard signs, and posted bumper stickers. In early 2003, on the eve of the war, we joined a large group in a peace vigil at the state capitol building in Madison.

Richard John Neuhaus, in his pro-war article "Just War and This War," written before the Gulf War in 1991, lists seven criteria for a just war. These include that the war be undertaken only as a *last resort*, that it right a *grievous wrong*, that it is by *legitimate authority*, that it defend against *great injury*, that it have a *high probability of success*, that the goals be *commensurate with the cost*, and that the *immunity of noncombatants* be respected.

The administration's proposed war against Iraq failed virtually all of these tests. Our country acted before the completion of international inspections. What grievous wrong did it right? Iraq had not attacked or threatened this country. We did not have broad international approval. Who did the war defend against what great injury? It was always unlikely, as what we euphemistically called "collateral damage" would subsequently confirm, that the war would respect the immunity of noncombatants. The war's vague, ever shifting goals and uncertain outcome still do not appear commensurate with its increasing costs, both direct and indirect.

In his opposition to the Iraq War, former President Jimmy Carter wrote a succinct summary in *The New York Times* using similar criteria for a just war. In his analysis, he wrote of a number of viable options to war, the military's concern about so-called collateral damage to civilians, the lack of a convincing link between Iraq and the 9/11 attacks, the international disagreement over authorizing the war, and the uncertainty whether the war would improve the current situation. In addition to objections raised by current and former national leaders, a member of the U.S. Foreign Service Corps resigned in protest over the administration's pursuit of war with Iraq. Several former CIA officers also expressed their belief that Bush had slanted intelligence information to support his case for war.

Opposition by observers in other countries was also strong. John le Carré wrote an opinion piece for *The Times of London* that described our country's reaction to the 9/11 attacks as one of the United States' "periods of historical madness." His article criticized the erosion of our freedoms following the attacks as well as our military stance against Iraq, a country with substantial oil, but no clear connection with bin Laden or the terrorist attacks. Perhaps just as important as his criticism of the proposed Iraq War, le Carré observed that without the attacks and the imminent war, our country might have given more attention to the administration's involvement with the Enron debacle, its regressive policies on taxation, its unilateral withdrawal from numerous international agreements, and its abysmal record on the environment. Distraction and misdirection are keys to success when you are playing a political shell game.

During the Revolutionary War, France, Poland, and other European countries provided invaluable aid to our fledging nation. Without their active support, the history of this continent might well be very different and the United States might not exist. Similarly, during both World Wars, the United States fought as part of broad alliances. Unfortunately, the Bush administration saw less need for the endorsement of others and relied on our military power to enforce its will. During the debate over Iraq, it ignored the opposition to war from many of our closest allies. Its stance resembled that of many past leaders with delusions of grandeur who believed that their power was so great that they could do whatever they wished. More often than not, their arrogance had sad consequences.

Ironically, even many of Iraq's own neighbors opposed the war on Iraq. Turkey, one of our closest allies in the region and a member of NATO, refused to allow the United States military passage through its territory to attack Iraq on its northern border or to provide troops during our occupation following the invasion. In Afghanistan, unrest continued with vast areas not under government control. And in our own country, we were about to waste resources that we needed to combat terrorism within our own borders.

War in Iraq

As feared, in the spring of 2003, the administration dismissed diplomatic efforts, told weapons inspectors to leave Iraq, and invaded Iraq without the approval of the United Nations or the support of most members. It formed a patchwork "coalition of the willing," consisting of Britain, several Eastern European nations, and a number of mostly smaller nations, that provided modest military contributions and an illusion, if not the reality, of broad international support. Against the hopes and wishes of many, the son who was president followed in the footsteps of his presidential father, even though death and destruction were the logical consequence, and there was little or no plan for what was to come. As with most wars, the costs would be much higher than expected, and it would prove much easier to start than to end.

Soon after the war in Iraq began, our local church held a brief ceremony one Sunday evening in which members placed about eight hundred wooden crosses on a small mound near the church. The mound was part of a restored prairie area that the church had burned to remove undesirable weeds and unwanted growth. The blackened earth served as the perfect backdrop for the display in which each cross memorialized the death of a soldier or civilian who had died in the war. At that time, an estimated 130 American soldiers had lost their lives along with 32 British soldiers, thousands of Iraqi soldiers, and an estimated 2000 Iraqi civilians.

In addition, there were seven larger crosses. Four of these larger crosses represented four thousand lives lost in the war in Afghanistan, while the other three crosses represented the three thousand lives lost in the 9/11 attacks. Members also placed stones laid on the ground to symbolize the Islamic deaths in both Iraq and Afghanistan. A brief service concluded the ceremony, and we all returned quietly to our homes. The crosses remained for several days as traffic streamed past. They provided a powerful statement on the human cost of the political and diplomatic failures that led to war.

Following our initial military successes, Bush, after a grandiose landing on an aircraft carrier just off the coast of California, stood in front of a banner that proclaimed "mission accomplished." Depending on your source, the White House either proclaimed "the end of combat" or "the end of 'major' combat." As time passed, the White House spin on this incident evolved into a claim that the banner merely reflected the successful completion of the mission of one specific aircraft carrier. Of course, the president has never, before or since, landed in his flight suit on a carrier at the end of its tour of duty. Whatever the White House said or meant to say, combat continued. Soldiers and civilians from the United States, Iraq, and other countries continued to die at a steady pace.

Today, the number of crosses representing the soldiers and civilian lives lost in Iraq and Afghanistan would be much larger. Dawn Turner Trice wrote a column for the *Chicago Tribune* following her visit to a local resident who had filled his yard with small American flags representing just the American soldiers lost in Iraq. In her column, she interspersed 1,027 small crosses representing the deaths of those American soldiers. Although many readers supported her column, others complained and repeated now discredited arguments in support of the war.

By the spring of 2005, over 1,600 U.S. and coalition soldiers, many more Iraqi soldiers, and tens of thousands (by some estimates, perhaps as many as 100,000) Iraqi civilians had died during the U.S. invasion and occupation. In addition, well over 10,000 American soldiers suffered injuries, many of which were very severe. Excellent medical care had significantly reduced the number of battle deaths, but many of the wounded had much more serious injuries. The overall casualties were substantially greater than in any other U.S. military action since the Vietnam War, including the first Gulf War.

Weapons of mass destruction

As conflict continued in Iraq and the administration insisted that we "stay the course," its assertions regarding Iraq came under intense scrutiny. President Bush's claim, in his State of the Union address in 2003, of an attempt by Iraq to buy uranium "in Africa" carried great weight among many people as the administration tried to build public support for war. However, as mentioned earlier, a senior government official soon reported that sources within the government had known for some time that this claim was erroneous.

When a noted columnist subsequently revealed, in a scandalous breach of security, that this official's wife was also a CIA agent, the columnist claimed that he had received this information from sources in the White House. Nonetheless, the White House refused to establish an independent investigation or commission to look into in this breach. The administration claimed that an investigation by the Justice Department was sufficient.

Belatedly, Attorney General John Ashcroft announced that he was "recusing" himself from the investigation on December 30, 2003. The announcement received relatively little public attention since it was the heart of the holiday season and the day before New Year's Eve. It also coincided with the administration's "announcement" of a ban on ephedrine and related products despite the fact that the effective date of the ban was still unclear. Once again, secrecy and misdirection served the administration's desire to distract the attention of the public from the real issues.

Furthermore, what real meaning did "recuse" have in this case? The investigators were still in the Justice Department and ultimately reported to Ashcroft. Normally judges who sit in judgment recuse themselves when there is a conflict of interest. Did Ashcroft plan to make the final decision? Was he recusing himself from doing the investigation (which he wouldn't do anyway) or was he recusing himself from controlling the direction of the investigation (not creditable since he had already made his imprint and his presence would continue to influence the investigation whether explicitly or implicitly). Instead, the entire process gave the distinct appearance of being simply a charade.

By the fall of 2004, United States forces had yet to find any evidence of weapons of mass destruction or related development programs. In December of 2004, the search for WMDs in Iraq ended. According to an article by Dafna Linzer of *The Washington Post,* the leader of the search filed a report in September of 2004 that failed to confirm virtually any of the assertions that the Bush administration made regarding WMDs in Iraq.

Along with claims of weapons of mass destruction, the administration made a variety of other accusations to justify their actions in Iraq. As mentioned earlier, one of the most troubling was the recurring suggestion, sometimes made directly and sometimes through innuendo, that in attacking Iraq and removing Hussein, we had removed an ally of Al Qaeda and those terrorists responsible for the 9/11 attacks. Although we found minimal connections between Iraq and the 9/11 attacks or between Iraq and Al Qaeda, members of the Bush administration continued to report or imply such connections with such great regularity that it became another frequent topic of political cartoons.

As various officials and journalists continued to discredit its claims, the administration began to argue that the goal of its military invasion of Iraq was to establish democracy in that country and build a democratic model for the Middle East. Unfortunately, their unwillingness to relinquish any power or authority in Iraq to international agencies such as the U.N., much less the Iraqis themselves, did not convince others that they were serious. Again acting unilaterally, we installed national leaders that met our own criteria and desires. Ceremonies supposedly turning over control of their country to Iraqis were as usual more about form than content.

Some religious clerics and their followers resisted efforts to create a new constitution along western lines. Whenever they or other Iraqis resorted to violence, the administration and news media in our country invariably referred to them as insurgents, terrorists, or foreign fighters. Although some carried out terrorist attacks against the Iraqi people in probable efforts to destabilize the country, many others fought as a resistance movement against what they saw as an unwelcome foreign invasion force.

As our efforts to create a stable society and model democracy encountered substantial opposition from the Iraqi people, the administration argued that at least we were safer without Saddam Hussein in power in Iraq. The only problem with this simple claim is that it too was probably false. The war destabilized Iraq, attracted many new recruits to extremist terrorist groups, resulted in a dissemination of Iraqi weapons throughout the region and probably beyond, and created a climate of hostility towards the United States much greater than before.

Ironically, and there is considerable irony in the entire sad story, as administration rhetoric emphasized democracy and basic human rights, a scandal erupted concerning the humiliation, abuse, and torture of Iraqi prisoners by American soldiers and interrogators. Initially, complaints in this area had focused around our detention of prisoners at Guantanamo Bay in Cuba. However, in May of 2004, a sordid story of prisoner humiliation, abuse, and torture also emerged from our prison facilities in Iraq.

As people in this country as well as throughout the world exploded in outrage over these abuses, preliminary investigations revealed that the Red Cross had complained about the abuse of prisoners in Iraq for many months before the May revelations. Furthermore, investigators attempting to trace the origin of these abusive practices learned that Secretary of Defense Donald Rumsfeld had authorized harsh interrogation practices at Guantanamo in late 2002. Early in 2003, Rumsfeld approved a new code of conduct that although less harsh than before still endorsed practices that many people would consider highly abusive and, in fact, forms of torture.

Since 9/11, the Bush administration had created a climate in this country as well as Afghanistan, Iraq, and our prison at Guantanamo Bay that encouraged callous disregard of basic human and legal rights. The horrendous disclosures from Iraq are just one example of how this attitude manifests itself as it passes down the chain of command. Doug Cassel noted that respect for human rights is not simply a nuisance, but a strategic asset and national value of our country. It is another of the guiding principles that has made our country strong. The scandals in Iraq and at Guantanamo regarding our mistreatment of prisoners brought immeasurable damage to the reputation of our nation that will take many years to mend.

Consequences

Where had lashing out in various directions at our friends and foes gotten us? What had we accomplished with our embrace of unilateral war? Although the initial military victory was rather swift, uncertainty continued to hang over Afghanistan. Establishing a stable government that received broad recognition throughout Afghanistan proved to be a long and difficult job. Our military forces, at the end of a long and difficult supply line, maintained a tenuous control over limited areas. Regional warlords still exercised considerable control over large sections of the huge country. Terrorist elements and remnants of Taliban forces appeared to remain, either in remote mountainous regions and other neighboring nations such as Pakistan.

Our country was also facing growing problems in Iraq. Ironically, an administration, known for its obsession with control and political planning, had failed to adequately plan for the period beyond the initial invasion of the country. It failed to anticipate the widespread looting and devastation that spread across Iraq with the fall of the Iraqi government, it underestimated the number of troops required, and it failed to provide the proper military equipment for our forces, including armored vehicles and personal armor.

In the spring of 2004, the Pentagon delayed troop rotations home in order to increase available forces in a continuing effort to maintain order in a deteriorating situation. The Pentagon also called additional members of the reserves to active duty for extended tours of duty in Iraq and Afghanistan. As fighting escalated in cities throughout Iraq, it decided to send in additional armored equipment including Abrams tanks and Bradley armored fighting vehicles that the Pentagon initially thought were unnecessary. The Bush administration's aggressive demands on our military forces stretched even its immense resources to the breaking point and significantly reduced the ability of our military to respond to future crises.

In *Battle Ready,* a book by Tom Clancy in cooperation with retired Marine General Anthony Zinni, General Zinni expressed his belief that the concept and planning behind the Iraq War were wrong. According to an article by Vincent Schodolski, General Zinni describes the preparation and execution of the war as reflecting at least "negligence and irresponsibility" and at worse "lying, incompetence and corruption." Similarly, several senior officers involved with the war expressed concern that we might be winning some battles, but losing the war strategically. In fact, our invasion of Iraq has given our opponents fertile ground for recruiting and training a new generation of terrorists.

Although we removed corrupt regimes in Afghanistan and Iraq, we also destabilized regions of critical importance. These instabilities have provided our opponents in Iran an opportunity to increase their influence in Iraq. We have pushed adversaries such as Iran and North Korea into a corner and made their future actions less predictable and possibly more dangerous. Their nuclear activities along with the Bush administration's plans to develop new nuclear weapons technology have threatened the future of the Nuclear Nonproliferation Treaty that since 1970 has helped reduce the spread of nuclear weapons.

Our preemptive military actions have encouraged Israel to act unilaterally against the Palestinians. Its actions have placed new and difficult barriers, both figurative and literal, to peace in the Middle East. We have set a dangerous example in our treatment of prisoners of war, so-called enemy combatants, and citizens of this country as well as those of our allies who fail to pass our often arbitrary and imprecise screening measures. Once again, we have demonstrated that violence begets violence. It is easier to destroy than to create.

Rather than bringing us together, the Bush administration has engaged in an endless series of needlessly divisive actions. It has pursued policies that have weakened the world order and isolated our country from other nations. As a result of our misplaced priorities and ill-advised militarism, our country suffers from loss of respect throughout the world, decreased support from our friends, and increased political polarization at home.

Unjustified military action also distracted us from taking needed steps in the fight against terrorist activities in this country. Richard Clarke in his testimony to the 9/11 commission noted that his strident criticism of the president stems from Clarke's belief that the war in Iraq had undermined the war on terrorism. Due to the expensive, ongoing conflict in Iraq, we were short of time, resources, and money to implement other important steps against domestic terrorism.

In April of 2004, Senator Robert Byrd gave a speech in the Senate comparing the situation in Iraq to the story behind the poem *The Charge of the Light Brigade* by Lord Tennyson. As in the poem, heroic soldiers are serving in an ill-conceived blunder of a war in Iraq. More than a year after the opening of conflict, we still had no effective plan to deal with the aftermath of the war nor any exit strategy from the morass they had created. Analysts estimated that the costs associated with occupying and rebuilding Iraq, much of which we destroyed with our own bombs would exceed $200 billion by the fiscal year beginning in October, 2004. Meanwhile, threats remained from unsecured nuclear weapons and dangerous material throughout the world, inadequate inspection of shipping containers entering our harbors and airports, and weapons entering our country through its lightly patrolled borders.

As a nation, we have always tended to pride themselves on "American ingenuity," one of our many guiding fictions. When our country needed to make the best use of limited naval resources in the early years of our republic, it created the *U.S.S. Constitution,* "Old Ironsides" -- an innovative frigate that combined maximum firepower in a relatively small, fast ship to gain significant tactical advantages. When we were struggling at the start of World War II, we responded with what some Japanese historians called "characteristic Yankee boldness and ingenuity" to launch the Doolittle Raid and bomb Japan using heavy bombers flown from an aircraft carrier.

Instead of ingenuity or creativity, the Bush administration simply resorted to traditional military actions and claimed, as the situation deteriorated, to be "committed" and "determined." While these can be admirable characteristics, at some point, they segue into "stubborn" and "boneheaded." Faced with a deteriorating situation in Iraq, the Bush administration dug in its heels and refused to consider any changes to its approach.

Jim Hoagland in his commentary in the *Chicago Tribune* noted that President Bush's speech to the nation on May 24, 2004, failed to adequately address a number of harsh realities surrounding war in Iraq and lacked the honesty that he owed the nation as it faced the problems created by this tragic war. Nonetheless, denial was the name of the game for the president as he sought reelection -- and the polls suggested that for many voters, it seemed to be working.

♫ ♫ ♫

The Preamble to the Constitution calls for the government to "provide for the common defense." Section 8 of the Constitution gives to Congress the power to declare war, to make rules concerning captures on land and water, and to raise, support, provide, and maintain our military forces. At a time when we face threats from a diverse range of conventional and unconventional weapons, delivered in a wide variety of ways, against a broad array of targets, the Bush administration used virtually all of our military resources to wage conventional wars against regimes in Afghanistan and Iraq. However, after a successful invasion of Afghanistan with the help of the Northern Alliance, the administration soon lost interest as it focused its attention and resources on Iraq. The Iraq War, now seen by most as at least premature, if not unjustified, consumed vast amounts of human and material resources to destabilize an entire region. The ultimate outcome in Iraq and Afghanistan remains highly uncertain. Meanwhile, the Bush administration, having already waged preemptive war, often used the banner of its self-declared "endless" war on terrorism to justify many of its other actions.

♬ ♬ ♬

Chapter 8

Our immune system under attack

...checks and balances...

♫ ♫ ♫

The role of the teacher or coach is essential in learning many complex skills. Even highly successful professional athletes have coaches to help them refine their technique or direct their conditioning program. Professional golfers have swing instructors to review their swings, eliminate bad habits, and improve their fundamentals. In much the same way, violinists work with teachers to hone their skills, master new pieces, and otherwise improve their abilities. A teacher is able to see problems that even an advanced violinist may not recognize on their own. A coach can detect and correct bad habits as well as refocus the violinist on the fundamentals. Similarly, the United States depends on a complex system of checks and balances to catch our mistakes and keep us moving in the proper direction.

The societal immune system

In our technological society, we take many steps to reduce the incidence of injury and illness. Our children learn how to safely navigate a world full of potential hazards. Engineers design products and buildings to reduce the risk of injury to their users or occupants. Instruction manuals, protective guards, and warning devices contribute to the safe use of products. Immunizations protect us against diseases that we once accepted as an unavoidable part of life.

When we do suffer injury or illness, our bodies have powerful immune systems and recovery processes to help us survive. They have the power to heal wounds, mend broken bones, and even in some cases, regenerate damaged parts. Antibodies enable our bodies to survive the many toxic antigens present in our environment. Medical procedures are available to assist our bodies in their recovery through the use of antibiotics and other drugs as well as surgical procedures to repair damaged parts or replace entire organs.

Much like our bodies, our government, organizations, and businesses may malfunction and need repair. They may suffer the consequences of poor decisions, illegal behavior, or simple bad luck. And much like our bodies, they also need an effective immune system to protect against disease and ensure their rapid recovery.

Our societal immune system includes the various institutions that help identify and correct threats to our individual freedoms and attempts to misuse power. These include actions that are not consistent with our core values and threaten our long term health and survival. The first line of defense in our society is the division of power between our major institutions. These include such groups as the political opposition, independent news media, educational institutions, religious groups, professional societies, labor unions, trade associations, regulatory agencies, and judicial courts. The differing views and priorities of these institutions reflect the diverse values and desires of the members of our society.

Each institution and organization also has its own internal immune system. These immune systems may take many different forms. In the business world, the employees, management, officers, directors, and stockholders of a corporation all possess a certain amount of power and influence over the direction of the business. In government, we have executive, legislative, and judicial branches to provide checks and balances on the exercise of unlimited power by any one branch. In addition to this separation of power, the Bill of Rights in our Constitution helps protect basic human rights throughout our nation.

Since the founding of our nation, these various systems of checks and balances, within our government as well as other national and international institutions, have identified and corrected abuses and mistakes. Our nation is at risk if we disregard or disempower these important systems.

The media

A 2003 article by Samantha Power in *The Atlantic Monthly* on the virtual collapse of the economy in Zimbabwe, "How to kill a country," suggested that a healthy democratic society requires an outspoken media, a healthy opposition, an independent judiciary, and periodic, presumably fair and open, elections.

We live in a nation in which these critical factors are in danger of no longer performing their vital functions. Researchers have found that stress can weaken our body's immune system. Similarly, the attacks of 9/11 weakened the checks and balances that serve as our nation's immune system.

The ability of our news media to provide a strong and independent voice is declining. Through corporate mergers and consolidations, a handful of giant corporations control most of the major media. Concentrated ownership, demands for profits, reductions in news staff, secrecy restrictions, self-serving rhetoric, and weakened regulations have all contributed to the decline of the media as an effective part of our societal immune system.

Most major cities have only a single daily newspaper. The surviving newspapers often use a format, pioneered with great success by *USA Today,* that features an entertainment focus, attractive graphics, and brief stories. Even smaller communities are finding that large companies increasingly own and control their daily or weekly local newspapers. For example, following a 2004 purchase by The Gannett Co., 11 daily newspapers and numerous other publications serving communities in central and northeastern Wisconsin are now under the centralized control of a single owner.

An article in *Isthmus,* a weekly newspaper in Madison, described the impact of centralized control at the *Wisconsin State Journal* in Madison. It reported that a new editor had reassigned a popular, long time columnist and discontinued his column. The article quoted the editor as stating that other reassignments would also occur in order "to help the newsroom speak with one mind." The desire for centralized control of content apparently superseded the desire for balanced reporting from a variety of perspectives.

Despite efforts to boost circulation, many people do not subscribe to any newspaper and those who do are often too busy with their work and families to take the time to read much of it. Both groups receive what little news they get through "sound bites" broadcast on commercial television and radio stations.

Unfortunately, a few corporations also control the major television networks as well as many cable channels. In addition, deregulation has enabled large corporations to put together chains of newspapers, television stations, and radio stations that control news coverage over large regions and even the entire nation. One large corporation now owns well over 1000 radio stations.

With the decline in both the availability and consumption of serious news in all forms of mass media, our democracy suffers as the lack of informed citizens makes meaningful debate difficult. Some counter these concerns with observations that people now receive their news and information from a much wider diversity of media sources including countless Internet sites, a great variety of news magazines, cable and satellite television, and satellite radio. William Powers, in his article in *The Atlantic Monthly* "The Massless Media," claims that for most of our history the mass media segmented its audience by various demographic and political factors. For example, in the 19th century, there were many newspapers corresponding to a great diversity of political factions and parties.

However, in today's world, two major parties dominate the political scene. Rather than a diversity of views, the political debate divides along bipolar lines. As a consequence, it is more difficult for the public to hear a variety of views on critical issues facing our nation. Commercial demands drive coverage towards those stories that will receive the highest ratings rather than stories that are the most important for the public to hear.

The role of big money is more important than ever before in attaining political office, influencing public opinion, and lobbying public officials. Ed Garvey, a former candidate for governor in Wisconsin, has noted that in the past statewide candidates could simply visit radio stations in communities across the state. They were usually quite willing to do an on-air interview during which the candidate could communicate directly to the electorate.

Distant corporations now own most of these stations, and many radio stations no longer have a local news staff. Computers, prerecorded material, and distant announcers fill the airtime, and local interviews are often no longer possible. A similar situation exists with the local newspapers. Rather than meeting with editors at individual papers to obtain endorsements, a single corporation representing a single political perspective selects one candidate for all of its newspapers to endorse. In addition to these challenges, candidates must now purchase most of their media access.

The problem is compounded as the mass media continue to reduce their serious news coverage and public affairs broadcasting. John Nichols quipped at a Madison, Wisconsin, conference on the media that it is cheaper to cover celebrity news, weather reports, and macramé lessons than send correspondents around the world to cover hard news. Instead, there is a proliferation of reality television shows -- which have little connection to reality; news magazine shows -- reflecting our obsessions with celebrity news, consumerism, and militarism; and game shows -- offering easy riches in our winner-takes-all, lottery-driven society.

In the publishing business, large corporations have acquired many formerly independent publishers. The remaining publishers focus on best sellers and best selling authors. Intense competition is also creating financial pressures on the remaining small publishers.

They publish fewer titles each year. As a consequence, there is great pressure for every new title to be successful. There is less room for error than in the past and less ability to take a chance on a book with uncertain commercial prospects. A more competitive market and tight budgets even limit the ability of university presses, often an outlet for books with limited audiences, to take commercial risks.

China, with its amalgam of a repressive totalitarian government and a full throttle capitalistic economy, presents an unnerving glimpse of where these trends may be taking us. According to a report on National Public Radio, China views bookstores as entertainment for the masses -- purely focused on the personal sphere. Shoppers can find books on business, career development, hobbies, and even pornography. However, they will not find books intended to change society, despite living in a culture that grew out of revolutionary literature. Today, many people in China do not see politics as relevant to their lives. They are uninformed and apolitical -- a phenomenon becoming all too familiar in the United States.

Another disturbing trend is the blurring of the line between professional journalism and political entertainment. Many people obtain their news from talk radio hosts who focus on entertainment and controversy, making little pretense of being objective. The 2004 Republican Convention featured interviews on the convention floor that organizers presented to the convention delegates as well as across the nation on C-SPAN. Although the interviewers looked and sounded like reporters, they were in fact members of the public relations staff of the Republican Party. Their reports resembled news broadcasts while they were actually political presentations.

Even in their news programming, the media is beginning to believe that what sells is coverage slanted towards a particular partisan perspective. The Fox News Channel, seen by many as right leaning, beat the major networks in ratings during the Republican National Convention despite being a cable outlet with more limited reach than the broadcast networks. Similarly, much of the success of

Michael Moore's documentary film, *Fahrenheit 9/11,* depended on its appeal to those left of center.

Some suggest that it is becoming necessary for media outlets to align themselves with a particular political point of view in order to be successful. This trend, at the very least, illustrates how far we have moved away from the ideals of our founders. Guiding fictions such as freedom of speech and freedom of the press bound us together as a nation and enabled us to respect differing views on important questions. The mass media, grounded in these founding principles, covered a diversity of views and attempted to find common ground rather than to exploit partisan divisions.

Sadly, many people do not recognize the central importance of freedom of speech and the press in a democracy. The results of a 2004 study of high school students found that more than one in three high school students thought that the First Amendment goes "too far" in guaranteeing these rights and only half of the students in the study supported newspapers' right to publish articles without prior permission by the government. As we lose sight of these unifying ideals that we can all endorse, we are splintering into factions without the shared inspiration that enables us move forward together.

Speaking out

In addition to the mass media, organizations, such as labor unions, churches, and schools, are also important elements of our societal immune system. They provide a diversity of voices in the never-ending national dialogue over where we have been, where we are, and where we are going. Unfortunately, many of these organizations have suffered from declining participation and flat or declining budgets. These problems have diminished their ability to contribute to the national debate.

For many years, the membership and influence of organized labor has declined. The decline began with the movement of manufacturing jobs from labor friendly northern states to southern states generally more hostile to labor unions. The movement of jobs offshore and the resulting reduction in bargaining power of domestic workers has accelerated the loss of labor power.

In addition, encouraged by President Reagan's firing and replacement of air traffic controllers in 1981, corporate managers have adopted more aggressive and public stances against unions. For example, corporate managements are making increased use of the lockout. Under a lockout, companies lock their doors to union employees on strike without a contract while remaining free to hire nonunionized replacement workers. To compound the problem for the union and workers, the companies can also declare contract negotiations to be at an impasse and make the temporary employees permanent replacement workers. These techniques are a strong disincentive against strikes, formerly one of the labor movement's most powerful weapons.

Rather than seeking improved wages or benefits, union workers find themselves trapped in a world of hostile employers, decreasing compensation packages, and vanishing jobs. In December of 2004, a workers' union rejected contract concessions proposed by a Wisconsin manufacturer. Three days later, the company announced its plans to close die-casting and machining plants employing 603 workers involved in the dispute. It is hard for unions struggling to simply survive to be strong participants in the national dialogue.

Along with the declining impact of the labor movement on our national scene, mainstream church bodies are finding it increasingly difficult to speak with a strong voice on the important moral, social, or political issues of our day. Roman Catholic leaders, speaking from a more traditional perspective, often have a difficult time gaining the ear of their progressive American members, much less the nation.

Mainstream Protestant denominations also have problems resolving differences between their leadership and individual members, but they face additional challenges as well. Membership in mainstream Protestant churches continues to decline. From 1993 to 2002, the percentage of Americans who considered themselves

Protestants declined from 62% to 53%, while those not following any organized religion increased from 9% to 14%.

In addition to declining membership, the roots of many mainstream Protestant denominations are in smaller ethnic churches whose differences in language and culture became less relevant as the older members passed away. For many, there seemed little reason not to combine these smaller organizations into larger church bodies. Some felt that mergers would lead to efficiencies of scale, much like the arguments that executives use to tout the benefits of proposed corporate mergers. Others subscribed to a vision of a unified Christian Church preaching God's message throughout the world.

As a result, many smaller denominations combined into larger, national churches built around beliefs, policies, and social statements that were sufficiently generic and apolitical to be acceptable to a large, often diverse membership. Comprised of congregations from throughout the country, they found themselves unified around the idea of unity rather than around any sense of commitment to a common set of values and beliefs. Ironically, this severely limited their ability to speak with a unified voice on important issues.

Lutheranism, the religious tradition of my own family, has its own unique difficulty in speaking out on current issues. Lutherans developed their theology around the doctrine of the "two kingdoms." From this perspective, we live our lives simultaneously in both the Kingdom of God and the Kingdom of the World. As H. Richard Niebuhr put it, in his book *Christ and Culture,* we live in Christ and in the world at the same time. While this tradition places a neat dualistic spin on the problem of resolving the relationship between the harsh realities of the world and our spiritual beliefs, it is a disempowering perspective. It too often results in Lutherans becoming passive observers of life, refusing to take an active role in building a better world. When faced with a moral dilemma, Lutherans can quietly slip across the line into the Kingdom of God and abstain from any personal involvement or responsibility.

And so for a variety of reasons, mainstream Protestant churches have ceded the political stage to fundamentalist Christian groups. These fundamentalist groups are quite willing to fight for the legalistic view of Christianity and morality that they endorse. The media too often accepts their narrow and exclusivist religious beliefs as the defining measure of Christianity. They ignore the millions of Americans who belong to mainstream churches that consider themselves Christian, and often evangelical, but do not support the extreme views of these fundamentalist groups.

With the unions in retreat and mainstream churches silent, it is not surprising that the conservative right has relentlessly attacked the public educational system, one of the last remaining strong and independent elements of our societal immune system. Public schools must now teach to narrow performance standards, deflecting their attention from preparing their diverse student body for life in a complex society. While attempting to meet conflicting requirements with ever dwindling resources, educators face opponents more interested in ideology than education. Through private schools and home schooling, children avoid the benefits of diversity in favor of a homogeneous setting comprised of others just like themselves -- not the recipe for a strong society unified behind common ideals.

Opponents of public education reveal their real goals in their comments on funding and test scores. If test scores remain low or decline, they criticize the public schools and demand that they forfeit their funding to private schools. If test scores remain high or increase, they claim that this shows that public school budgets are higher than needed. Whether scores are high or low, they conclude that we should reduce the funding of public schools -- a classic example of "heads I win, tails you lose."

At the college and university level, public financial support has also declined. Conservative politicians often justify these funding reductions by telling us that the public revenue is just not there. It's not there because too often they have returned it to the wealthiest segment of society in the form of tax cuts, corporate welfare, and the war in Iraq. As a result, corporate financial support is becoming increasingly essential to schools at all levels. Unfortunately, along with their funding of scholarships, research grants, equipment, facilities, and special programs come implicit constraints on what the educational system can do or say.

Despite our central role in creating and hosting the United Nations, one of the most important elements of our global immune system, the Bush administration and its conservative supporters persist in undermining this unique international organization. For over fifty years, the United Nations has serve as an antibody to conflict, hunger, and disease throughout the world. Although far from perfect, it has often brought healing to the world through its forums, negotiations, and actions. Nonetheless, the administration has withdrawn its support from many important U.N. activities, such as the Population Fund, the U.N. agency that runs family planning programs throughout the world.

The Bush administration's attitude was perhaps best illustrated when, despite failing to obtain U.N. endorsement of the war in Iraq, it simply proceeded with its unilateral decision to wage war only to return to the international community for help as things went bad. The ill-advised actions of one U.S. administration have threatened the future of this important institution.

The political opposition

The second requirement for a strong democracy, a healthy political opposition, has also struggled. Following the 2000 election, the Bush administration and its supporters in a conservative Congress systematically marginalized and ignored the political opposition, including the majority that voted for Al Gore. Then, in the aftermath of the national disaster on 9/11 and with the public rallying around our flawed national leadership, the political opposition, with only a few exceptions, became reluctant to speak out against the policies and actions of the administration.

To a significant extent, this was due to the Bush administration's use of the trauma of the 9/11 attacks to silence any opposition. It created an "either-or" climate in which you were either for its positions or you were against our country. You either supported the administration or you supported the terrorists. In addition, other factors contributing to the silencing of the opposition included its continuing depression and frustration over the 2000 election, shock and confusion following the attacks of 9/11, skyrocketing public support for the president, intimidation by the news media, and perhaps a simple lack of imagination.

In some ways, the Bush administration may have simply worn down the opposition through its sheer number of outrageous actions and policies. Maureen Dowd wrote a column in the spring of 2004 entitled, "Bush's world of fantasy." She listed about two dozen examples of the contradictions, hypocrisy, and denial that permeate the Bush administration. A few months later, *The Onion,* a satirical newspaper originally published in Madison, Wisconsin, ran a supposedly humorous story with the headline, "Nation's liberals suffering from outrage fatigue." The satire in the article actually painted a rather accurate picture of how many Americans felt.

It is difficult to mount a serious opposition when every day reveals new military actions or threats, new tax cuts for the wealthy, additional environmental breaks for corporations, more restraints on civil rights, additional spending cuts for social programs, more sweetheart deals for defense contractors, new challenges to our democratic processes, more blurring of the line between church and state, and so on.

Whatever the reasons, with the mass media controlled by a small number of giant corporations generally sympathetic to conservative policies and more interested in ratings than political discourse, it was difficult to hear alternative views or opinions. Ironically, the foreign press presented the strongest and most outspoken opposition to the administration. Unfortunately, in the new world of concentrated media, these reports rarely received adequate coverage by the news media in this country.

The polarization and extremism evident in our politics has weakened the ability of our system of checks and balances to moderate the power of any single branch or political faction. One party has achieved almost complete control of all three branches of the federal government. Although similar concentrations of power have occurred in the past, a more diverse array of powerful, independent institutions served as a check on the power of the government. Without these checks, the majority is free to virtually ignore the minority. Unfortunately, at a time of a sharply and evenly divided electorate, those in control act as if they have received a mandate from the people and exploit every possible maneuver to concentrate their power and increase their control.

The Republican controlled Congress often meets with little or no input from the Democratic minority. During the closed-door conference committee sessions of House and Senate negotiators to develop the changes to Medicare, the majority Republicans allowed no House Democrats and only two Democratic Senators, neither of which was the Senate Democratic minority leader, to participate. The marginalization of the substantial Democratic minority in both houses was virtually without precedent. The majority leaders routinely presented thousands of pages of new legislation for the first time just hours before voting.

The use of harsh and insulting measures to strengthen the control of the Republican leadership over the legislative process even extended to members of their own party. The conservative House leadership regularly extended fifteen minute roll call votes, sometimes as much as three hours, as it applied unconscionable pressure on Republican members to support the party position.

The opposition provides a counter balance to the inherent strength of the elected majority. It provides societal antibodies to fight against the diseases of extremism. Totalitarian states tend to self-destruct because they do not receive the benefits of a strong political opposition. In a democracy, the majority needs the minority to curb its arrogance and power. One of the strengths of our society has been its ability to recognize that while the majority may rule, it must never trample on the rights of the minority. The opposition is able to critique actions of the majority in ways that often provide insights essential for the maintenance of a strong society.

The scientific community has traditionally been an important part of our nation's checks and balances. However, the Bush administration and its supporters often ignored or suppressed widely accepted scientific information when it disagreed with their views, justifying their actions using deceptive scientific evidence.

There was a time when our nation ridiculed the former Soviet Union for the sometimes ludicrous ways in which it used science and the arts to serve the needs of its totalitarian state. One of the most egregious examples was the ideologically inspired theory of genetics known as Lysenkoism. An editorial in the *Scientific American* expressed concern over the ways in which the Bush administration was misusing science for its own political purposes and noted that it brought to mind Soviet-era distorted science like Lysenkoism.

The extensive web of scientific advisory committees is a key link between members of the scientific community and the government. Here again, the Bush administration skewed the membership of advisory committees towards those scientists who supported the views of industry and the administration even when those views conflicted with generally accepted scientific information.

A 2005 article in *Scientific American* magazine by David Michaels, former assistant secretary for environment, safety and health for the Department of Energy described how industry groups fight regulations by imposing an impossible standard of absolute certainty before agreeing to the need for regulatory action. Michaels presents examples in which companies hired researchers whose work obscured rather than clarified the scientific evidence. They sought to create ambiguous results and uncertainty in order to argue that new regulations are unwarranted. The Bush administration has embraced this philosophy through the use of researchers that tend to favor industry positions and through institutionalizing guidelines that emphasize uncertainty rather than protection.

The Secretary of Health and Human Services disbanded scientific groups working on solutions to problems in genetic testing and research, presumably in response to a fundamentalist religious constituency that opposes work in these areas. President Bush replaced several members of his handpicked Council of Bioethics who supported research on human embryo cells with members opposing such research as well as abortion. The administration also reorganized a number of committees on environment health so that industry scientists dominated the membership and reviewed health standards for their own companies.

Sometimes administrators ignored the results of research funded by their own agencies. For example, in March of 2005, the Environmental Protection Agency (EPA) announced new rules limiting mercury emissions from power plants that were substantially weaker than those advocated by environmentalists. Although EPA officials claimed that the costs of tougher standards were much greater than the projected public health benefits, a study funded by the EPA at Harvard University estimated health savings from restrictions similar to those announced by the EPA of nearly $5 billion per year. This is about *100 times* greater than the $50 million a year savings cited by the EPA and suggests that tougher restrictions would be justifiable from a public health standpoint. An EPA official attempted to marginalize the report by claiming the study was late and that crucial elements of the study were flawed. In fact, the report had met its January 3, 2005, deadline and the EPA had received a briefing on its methodology earlier in August of 2004.

Another good example of how the administration ignored scientific reality was its policy on tactical nuclear weapons. As it criticized and attacked other nations that possessed or might be seeking weapons of mass destruction including nuclear bombs, the administration aggressively pursued additions to our already excessive armory of these weapons and developed more aggressive policies for their use. In particular, overturning decades of work at limiting nuclear weapons, the administration declared that it supported the development of tactical, bunker-busting nuclear bombs, allegedly to destroy terrorist strongholds with their weapons.

However, an article in *Physics Today* reported that the most robust weapons can only penetrate about 50 feet into the earth and still remain functional. The destruction of bunkers at depths greater than 50 feet requires nuclear weapons substantially larger than those dropped on Japan at the end of World War II. Exploding at a depth of only a few dozen feet, the quantity of earth would be insufficient to contain such large blasts. As a result, huge amounts of highly radioactive and dangerous fallout would result. Depending on the density of the surrounding population, civilian casualties could be very high, possibly reaching hundreds of thousands in urban areas. As in so many other areas, the Bush administration simply ignored, suppressed, or was ignorant of the facts.

The judiciary

The third leg of a strong democracy, an independent judiciary, was increasingly the subject of political machinations. Conservatives continually complained about liberal, activist judges despite Republican presidents having nominated much of the federal judiciary including 7 of the 9 Supreme Court justices. The president described the political opposition to several of his judicial nominees as "shameless" despite the successful confirmation of over 95%. His demand for absolute rubber stamp approval of all judicial nominees without any meaningful questioning or review threatened the political independence of our justice system and the health of our democracy.

The Republican leadership in the Senate also objected to the Democratic use of the filibuster to block some of Bush's judicial nominees despite the fact that Democrats used this tactic for only 10 individuals out of more than 210 nominees from 2001 through April of 2005. Senate Majority Leader Bill Frist described this use of filibusters as "a formula for tyranny by the minority." With the Democrats having approved more than 95% of the president's nominees, their actions certainly didn't constitute "obstructionism" or "tyranny by the minority." However, Frist's demand for 100.00% acceptance of all nominees would force the Democratic minority to sit back and quietly submit to "tyranny by the majority."

To suppress the Democratic opposition, Frist hinted that he might support use of what some describe as the "nuclear option." Under this tactic, the presiding officer of the Senate, Vice President Dick Cheney, would rule that filibusters against judicial nominees are unconstitutional, a simple majority of 51 senators would approve his ruling, and the same simple majority would then approve the nominees. This would be much easier than obtaining the 60 votes to break a filibuster or the 67 votes to change the rules of the Senate.

One would think that Democrats could challenge the legitimacy of such a high-handed process in the Supreme Court -- but conservative strength on the court makes victory there highly uncertain. Not surprisingly, conservative wordsmiths called the nuclear option the "constitutional option" despite their demands that Senators simply give their rubber-stamp approval to all judicial nominees. Without a careful review that leads to occasional rejections of some nominees, the constitutional duty of the Senate to provide "advice and consent" becomes meaningless.

In another example of an apparent conflict of interest between the judiciary and the executive branch, there was considerable controversy concerning the relationship between Vice President Cheney and Supreme Court Justice Antonin Scalia. At a time when the Supreme Court addressed whether or not Cheney must release information related to the administration's energy policy, Cheney and Scalia went on a hunting trip together. Scalia opposed efforts to have him recuse himself from the case by claiming that despite the trip with Cheney his impartiality still could not be reasonably questioned.

Whether or not this is true, there is little doubt that the trip, at the very least, created the appearance of a conflict of interest.

Ironically, at the same time that Scalia found himself embroiled with issues related to secrecy in the executive branch, he gave a speech on the Constitution during which he directed officials to stop the audio recording of his comments. The officials soon destroyed the tapes, an act for which Scalia subsequently apologized even though it was too late to reverse the damage. In 2005, despite continuing concerns by some over his willingness to defend basic constitutional rights, Scalia apparently began a campaign to improve his image when it appeared that he might become the next Chief Justice.

Ironically, that role may become less important in light of legislative efforts to include "court stripping" provisions in legislation that preclude any judicial review. Although the legislative and executive branches of our government have made many attempts to limit judicial power throughout the history of our country, none of these were successful until the spring of 1996. At that time, Congress passed legislation, including The Prison Reform Litigation Act and The Antiterrorism and Effective Death Penalty Act, that limited the power of the federal courts with regard to these bills. In the summer of 2004, opponents of same-sex unions included court stripping provisions in the Marriage Protection Act passed by the House.

The constitutionality of these provisions is uncertain, but it is clear that some conservative legislators care less for our system of checks and balances than for imposing their own beliefs on others. In fact, ever since the controversial intervention of the Supreme Court in the 2000 presidential election, abuses of the separation of powers, constitutional requirements, and other long standing traditions continue to move our country towards a true constitutional crisis.

A new dark age?

Meanwhile, while the nation endured endless confrontations on domestic issues, critical questions regarding the 9/11 terrorist attacks remained unanswered. We may never have a full and complete accounting of the events up to and following the attacks of 9/11. These events caught the nation almost totally unprepared. There were failures in the airline security systems, failures in the military to anticipate and respond to an attack on domestic targets. There were failures by the government to respond to strong hints that something was going to happen, possibly involving aircraft. Failures by engineers and architects to recognize the inherent vulnerability of towering steel structures to fire.

When a commission finally began its investigation of the 9/11 attacks, the Bush administration resisted requests for documentation, access to appropriate personnel, and even the time to perform the complete investigation that the country deserves and needs. In addition, in order to quickly complete a report that could receive broad bipartisan support, the commission chose to avoid controversial topics that might reflect poorly on either party or threaten the global corporations that exert such powerful influence over Congress.

Nonetheless, many believed that the final report of the 9/11 commission was a well-written attempt to address at least some of the issues raised by the 9/11 attacks. As noted in an article published by the *Chicago Tribune* in December of 2004, following the conclusion of its 12 part series on Islam, the report called for working more closely with moderate Muslims to implement reforms and create opportunity within the Muslim world. The article describes a story in which the late King Hussein of Jordan reportedly warned of the similarities, both good and bad, between Islamic extremists and people like himself. Moderate Muslims understand quite well how the grievances created by American foreign policy can result a violent response. We need to better understand their views.

As the administration pursued its endless war on terrorism, few of our leaders called for a study on the origins of terror. Other than superficial condemnations of religious extremists and violence, there has been little discussion of American economic, diplomatic, and military actions that may have motivated the individuals behind these attacks. These include, among many others, American hegemony of the global economy, our dominance of such global institutions as the World Bank and the International Monetary Fund (IMF), our support of autocratic rulers, our withdrawals from international agreements, and our continuing reliance on military force.

Exactly who or what are we fighting in our so-called war on terror? What are the roots of the hatred, especially in the Islamic world, towards the United States? What can we do build bridges between nations rather than continuing to engage in ongoing militarism? Many believe that even to pose such questions is unpatriotic and disloyal to our country -- a strange and troubling reaction in a nation that prides itself on its plainspoken honesty.

Strangely, as our representatives in government generally failed to provide adequate leadership in getting to the root of the problems behind terror, others stepped into the breach. For example, Michael Schuler, senior pastor at First Unitarian Society in Madison, wrote shortly after the 9/11 attacks about the origins of terror in *The Capital Times.* John Talbott, a former investment banker, in his book *Where America Went Wrong,* entitled a chapter "Why do they hate us? -- What world opinion could tell America." Gilles Kepel, in his book *The War for Muslim Minds: Islam and the West,* critiqued the Bush administration's response following the 9/11 attacks. Despite their diverse backgrounds, these writers as well as others are willing to ask the hard questions and to move beyond simple condemnation of the terrorists towards a better understanding of the sources of their hatred and actions. Such analyses help us to better understand ourselves and respond more effectively to the challenges that we face.

Some also worried that the political machinations exploiting the fear generated by the terrorist attacks were causing us to lose sight of the ideals of our own revolution of 1776. Barbara Ehrenreich, in her July 4th, 2004, commentary in *The New York Times* "Their George and ours," notes more than a few similarities between the abuses of King George III found in the Declaration of Independence and the objections of the political opposition to George Bush's administration in our own time. These include the curtailment of the legal rights of U.S. citizens, the misuse of our military forces, a lack of accountability and a resistance to judicial review, and the assertion of royal or executive privilege.

Cullen Murphy, in his article in *The Atlantic Monthly,* identifies similarities between the society we are becoming and the Middle Ages. He notes that we have a growing tendency to harass or persecute those who challenge the ruling class. Verbal communication through cell phones is replacing writing as our preferred choice of communications much like medieval society. Private corporations, controlled by a few executives, are becoming centers of power and wealth much like the medieval church or royal courts. These corporations control or influence the goods and services that we buy, where and how we work, and whether or not we have health insurance and retirement benefits. Rather than serving public interests, they are taking on the characteristics of private fiefdoms responsible to no one but themselves.

In a similar vein, Art Winslow, in his review of Jane Jacobs' book *Dark Age Ahead,* described her concern that we may be entering a new dark age. Throughout our nation, she sees signs of what she describes as a "spiral of decline" and "an abyss of mass amnesia" in which we are losing the cultural underpinnings of our society. Our fiscal and social policies are destroying our sense of community much as they have already destroyed family farms and much of the local farm economy in many small towns.

While some might consider the title of Jacobs' book "over the top," Jacobs notes that such economic institutions as the International Monetary Fund, The World Trade Organization, and the World Bank have already brought about a new dark age to millions of people in Africa and Asia. These tools of the so-called Washington Consensus of fiscal austerity, privatization, and deregulation operate behind closed doors beyond the reach of individual citizens, their elected representatives, or domestic courts. They are the underpinnings of a globalization movement that has enriched and empowered private corporations while bringing misery and suffering to people in many nations, including our own.

Perhaps most importantly, Jacobs notes that the "stabilizing forces" that have served our nation in the past are becoming "ruined and irrelevant." Instead, small groups of the elite are making decisions in secret that can have far reaching effects throughout our country and the world. We may never know who made these decisions or why they made them, but we will suffer their consequences. It is essential that we take action now to restore our national immune system so that it can provide checks and balances against that forces that threaten to divide and destroy our society.

♫ ♫ ♫

Our system of "checks and balances," as well as the closely related "separation of powers," are among the oldest guiding principles of our nation. The concept of separating the powers of government between different institutions goes back to Montesquieu and is in the Virginia Declaration of Rights written by George Mason shortly before Thomas Jefferson drafted our Declaration of Independence. John Adams also wrote in 1776 of the importance of a judiciary independent from the legislative and executive branches so that each could serve as a check on the other. In 1788, these ideas formed the basis for our government under the Constitution. Over the years, political leaders have made numerous efforts to undermine the separation of powers established in the Constitution. The actions of the Bush administration represent just the latest efforts to circumvent these constitutional safeguards as well as other elements of our national system of checks and balances. However, the system of checks and balances is resilient and has the ability to bounce back from efforts to undermine it. Whether in politics or sports, Americans prefer to see a balance of power.

Chapter 9

From democracy to oligarchy

...all are created equal...

♫ ♫ ♫

The strings in an orchestra usually perform in a semicircle around the conductor with the first violins on the far left, followed by the second violins, violas, and cellos, with the double basses typically behind the cellos on the far right. The stringed instruments are relatively quiet compared to the brass, woodwind, and percussion instruments. It takes a great number of strings to balance the strength of the sound from these inherently louder instruments. An orchestra of one hundred musicians may have a total of about sixty stringed instruments. Despite their relative weakness as individual instruments, the strings provide a musical flexibility and range not available in most other instruments. As a result, they often take the lead in a symphonic orchestra and dominate its sound. They are a musical metaphor for the power of the people in a democracy.

Fair and open elections

According to Samantha Power's article "How to kill a country" in *The Atlantic Monthly,* the holding of periodic, presumably fair and open, elections is another important characteristic of a healthy democracy. Unfortunately, our democracy is far from healthy. We preach to other nations about their need to adopt more open and democratic processes, but many worry about the fairness and integrity of our elections. Others see our links with our elected representatives growing ever weaker.

In the 2000 election, the need to resort to extensive legal battles finally resolved by an appointed judiciary rather than our elected representatives further weakened our democracy. In addition, this election revealed numerous flaws in our voting procedures and equipment. Although the Help America Vote Act allocated $3.8 billion dollars in 2002 to improving voting, many problems remain.

In fact, some solutions to the problems created by hanging chads on punch card ballots may actually have made things worse. Many jurisdictions have gone to electronic voting systems using touch screen technology that do not leave a paper trail with which to audit the results or to perform a recount. Optical scanning technology is a more attractive approach that requires each voter to complete a paper ballot that officials can review and recount if there are any concerns. However, at this time, relatively few jurisdictions use this or any similar system that can both quickly and accurately count votes as well as provide a paper trail for the purpose of recounts.

The use of provisional ballots whenever there is a question concerning the registration or eligibility of a voter has added another layer of confusion and uncertainty. Unfortunately, the legislation creating the provisional ballot failed to state clearly where the voter should cast such a ballot. This omission has already resulted in serious problems. In an Illinois election in March of 2004, Chicago officials accepted only about 7% of the provisional ballots that voters cast in that city. In addition to voters incorrectly completing the form, officials rejected provisional ballots due to voters going to the precinct where they lived rather than the one in which they had registered -- a violation of Illinois voting rules.

Reports after the 2004 election in the key state of Ohio included numerous complaints on voting irregularities. Problems at polling places led to the disqualification of thousands of provisional ballots, electronic voting machines apparently transferred votes to the wrong candidate, and inadequate numbers of voting machines, particularly in poorer districts, resulted in voters waiting in long lines for hours. In frustration, many voters walked away without voting. In a Third World country, we would condemn such problems with disgust and frustration. In our country, many citizens and leaders seem to accept them with barely a passing thought.

Another serious threat to our democracy is the creation of gerrymandered districts that create safe districts for as many of one party's candidates as possible while minimizing the number of districts where candidates from opposition parties might win. There are two basic approaches to gerrymandering. One is to place as many opposition voters as possible into a single district. This "packing" process ensures that the opposition will win that district, but reduces their chances in the surrounding districts. The other approach, "cracking," is to divide opposition voters into multiple districts such that opposition candidates are unlikely to reach a majority in any district. Gerrymandering makes a mockery of our representative democracy by reducing the likelihood that the distribution by party of the elected representatives will reflect the overall distribution by party of the voters.

In the past, the process of redistricting a state was so burdensome that it was unusual to consider more than a few geographic configurations. The process of forming districts was a tedious process that restricted the ability of either party to create a significant advantage. As a result, legislatures went through the process infrequently, usually once every 10 years after the census. Today, computers enable the rapid consideration of an almost unlimited number of different geographical arrangements and encourage frequent redistricting.

As a consequence, some current congressional districts include noncontiguous areas, while others have outrageously contorted shapes. One article in the *Chicago Tribune Magazine* described a twisted North Carolina congressional district as resembling a "writhing snake." According to another report in *The Atlantic Monthly,* a Florida congressional district includes a "Democratic" district consisting of two disjoint pieces separated by Tampa Bay and surrounded by "safe" Republican districts. The report suggests that packing and cracking in Florida has led to an eleven-seat majority for the Republicans in Florida's congressional delegation despite an even split between the parties in the voting population.

Similar examples of efforts to thwart democracy exist in other states as well. In 2002, a hotly contested and highly controversial state election in Texas led to the first Republican majority in the state House in 130 years. The new Republican-controlled legislature subsequently developed a gerrymandered plan to redraw the Texas congressional districts in a manner highly favorable to Republican candidates. Democratic legislators made headlines when they briefly left the state in opposition to the new proposals from the new Republican majority. Some reports estimated that the final redistricting plan enhanced Republican political demographics in perhaps as many as seven congressional districts in Texas.

In the aftermath of the redistricting uproar in Texas, criminal investigators looked into campaign financing in the 2002 election campaign prior to the redistricting. In September, 2004, a Texas grand jury indicted fundraisers with links to U.S. House Majority Leader Tom DeLay on charges related to illegal donations to Republican candidates for the Texas legislature -- donations that helped create the new Republican majority that redrew the congressional map in Texas to favor future Republican candidates. A few days before the 2004 election, the Supreme Court deferred final judgment on a Democratic challenge to the constitutionality of the redistricting plan pending further review by a lower court.

Soon after the announcement of the indictments, a House ethics committee report criticized Delay's arm-twisting tactics in obtaining passage of bills. Six days later, the same committee rebuked DeLay for requesting federal aviation officials to locate the missing Democratic legislators during the Texas political feud surrounding redistricting and also for actions that suggested a link between political contributions and legislative action. This was the third time that the committee had criticized DeLay. The actions of DeLay and his associates have caused damage to our democratic processes that may be difficult to repair.

Protests

Following the 9/11 attacks, the Bush administration and its supporters also discouraged the opposition through systematic attacks on free speech rights. Statements and political ads from the White House continually claimed that there was no middle ground in the war on terrorism. Criticism of Bush or the war in Iraq meant you were disloyal, unpatriotic, soft on terrorism. Recording artists making critical statements suffered widespread criticism and destruction of their records. Conservative web sites listed those celebrities and entertainers considered unpatriotic because of their opposition to Bush and his policies.

The administration also restricted the ability of average citizens to express their displeasure with its actions and policies. It managed public events featuring President Bush to ensure that he would see no protesters. Protesters as well as simple bystanders sometimes found themselves arrested and held in jail without justification. After hours or even days of uncomfortable detention, they sometimes received an apology from the authorities, but these unjustified arrests discouraged them and others from the future exercise of their constitutional rights. Conservative forces also attempted to suppress the political activities of nonprofit organizations as well as so-called 527 organizations that provided one of the few remaining outlets for the political opposition.

In one particularly strange, but nonetheless disturbing example, the federal government prosecuted Greenpeace after its protesters boarded a ship as it approached Miami Beach with a cargo of mahogany. The protesters wanted to draw attention to what they believed was an example of illegal logging activity by unfurling a banner on the ship. After their arrest, they faced misdemeanor charges for their protest. In addition, fifteen months later, the government charged their organization, Greenpeace, under a 19th century law designed to prevent brothel operators from boarding ships as they were about to dock. This obscure law, dormant since the 19th century, exposed Greenpeace to significant financial penalties, a lengthy probation, and potential loss of its tax-exempt status: another example of legal overkill in pursuit of ideological purity.

One of the most insidious actions against the free exchange of ideas and information grew out of the indignation of some over an incident involving partial nudity during the half-time show at the 2004 Super Bowl. In response to this "wardrobe malfunction" as well as other incidents involving coarse or vulgar language on the airwaves, the Federal Communications Commission subsequently put forth a "zero tolerance" policy for on-air obscenities that some believe endanger the future of live news telecasts. Whereas, it is possible to control the content of scripted entertainment, broadcasters have little control over live news reports, images, and interviews. The potential penalties for violations of the new policy are so severe that it may even limit the public's ability to view live news events.

It is not just the broadcast media that are operating under new restrictions with onerous penalties. The computer software industry has promoted passage at the state level of the Uniform Computer Information Transactions Act (UCITA) to govern software purchases. This legislation, already passed in Virginia and Maryland, is aimed at restricting the ability of consumers to sell, lend, or even give away software that they have purchased. Rather than treating it like a copyrighted book that consumers cannot duplicate, but can otherwise pass along after they no longer need it, software would receive unique and highly restrictive protection. This corporate-friendly legislative approach would place a particular burden on nonprofit and human rights organizations who often depend on "hand me down" computers and software due to their limited budgets.

Yet another attack on the open exchange of information occurred in the fall of 2004 with new regulations regarding the publishing of works by authors from certain designated countries.

Fortunately, a group of professional and scholarly publishers filed a lawsuit against the Treasury Department's Office of Foreign Assets Control challenging the constitutionality of the new restrictions.

These various attempts by the Bush administration and its supporters to suppress protesters and control the free exchange of information threaten the very heart of our democracy. Without the continuous challenging and questioning of their actions, we are in danger of moving ever closer to a totalitarian state.

Amazingly, during Bush's 2005 tour of Europe, in anticipation of his meeting with President Vladimir Putin of Russia, Bush emphasized that "our alliance stands for a free press, a vital opposition, the sharing of power, and the rule of law" -- important democratic values expressed through our guiding fictions that the Bush administration and its conservative supporters have so often undermined or ignored. It's not surprising that Putin later demonstrated some irritation over Bush's objections to the actions that Putin had taken within Russia to consolidate his power.

The California recall election

Another discouraging attack on our democratic system occurred in the fall of 2003 with the successful recall of California Democratic Governor Gray Davis. In some ways, conservative efforts to remove President Clinton from office through impeachment in the final years of his presidency foreshadowed this recall. Efforts to remove the president did not focus on any particular malfeasance in his performance as president, but rather emphasized his personal behavior regarding a matter that had little connection with how he did his job. It was hardly an adequate reason to impeach a two term president, and fortunately, the effort to oust Clinton failed.

In the case of California, a wealthy individual began and funded an effort to recall the state's governor with $1.7 million of his own money. Although there were very few precedents for such an action, it was most unsettling because the movement called for the recall of a governor who, only 11 months earlier, had won his second term in a general election. Gray Davis was not an unknown quantity. He was not inexperienced. He had not demonstrated any fundamental incompetence for the job. He was not guilty of any crime or scandal. In many ways, he was a victim of circumstances far beyond his control. The state suffered from economic problems associated with a national recession aggravated by corporate manipulation of the deregulated electric power industry in California.

As discussed previously, one of the central players in market trading of energy contracts and manipulation of the California power industry was Enron. Following its rapid climb to the fifth largest corporation on the Fortune 500 list, Enron collapsed into bankruptcy late in 2001, leaving financial chaos and ruin for many of its employees, customers, suppliers, and investors. Virtually lost in the aftermath of the 9/11 attacks was not only the close relationship between Enron executives and the Bush family going back at least as far as the administration of Bush's father, but also the way in which the entire episode discredited the deregulation mantra endlessly repeated by conservative politicians and commentators. In fact, many months later, recorded comments of some Enron employees clearly revealed their arrogance and greed in manipulating the cost of electrical power in California.

Ironically, instead of expressing their anger and frustration at Bush or the many Republican politicians beginning with Reagan who have embraced deregulation and privatization as the answer to almost any problem facing our country, the public voted to recall a second term governor who inherited a deregulated California power industry from his predecessors. In fact, Davis was a Democrat, a party whose members have generally questioned and resisted pressures for deregulated capitalism and a privatized economy even as deregulation and privatization measures consistently failed to fulfill the promises made by their Republican supporters.

Although the individual who started the California recall process ultimately dropped out of the chaotic campaign, over one hundred candidates remained to compete for a simple plurality of votes on the recall ballot in order to become the new governor. Not surprisingly, the winner, Arnold Schwarzenegger, was a movie star whose name recognition and financial resources were almost overwhelming advantages in a short campaign. It was difficult for any other candidate to gain much traction with so many candidates and no primary to narrow the field to a more reasonable size.

The California recall election for governor provides further evidence of the poor health of our election processes. However one might feel about the details, the reality is that a small minority was able to use extraordinary measures, rather than a regular election, to fill a major political position in our country. Echoing the end of the 2000 presidential race, the results filled another important executive position through an atypical process that emphasized the use of big money, a famous name, and connections to high places. A small number of wealthy individuals and celebrities were able to overturn the reelection just a few months earlier of an incumbent governor to a second term and install a celebrity candidate with minimal qualifications or experience related to the position.

In another hotly contested election in the state of Washington, a wealthy Republican candidate attempted to reverse the results of a close race for governor. In December of 2004 following a meticulous hand recount of all ballots, the Republican Secretary of State declared the Democratic candidate the new governor by a razor thin margin of 129 votes out of 2.9 million votes cast. However, the wealthy Republican candidate refused to follow the lead of both Al Gore and John Kerry in their own narrow defeats for president and concede the election. Instead, he responded with a letter to the Democratic winner asking that they jointly request that the legislature order a new election, despite the lack of any evidence of fraud or misconduct.

By April of 2005, the controversy had evolved into an expensive lawsuit involving both parties. Finally, in June of 2005, a judge in the state of Washington upheld the election of the Democratic candidate.

According to an Associated Press report, the Republican candidate said that, due to this decision and the political composition of the Washington Supreme Court, "... I am ending the election contest."

Oligarchies

In many ways, our government is becoming an oligarchy, government by the elite few: more specifically, a plutocracy, government by the extremely wealthy. Wealth and celebrity are distorting our basic democratic processes. Elections are becoming irrelevant as the rich and famous dominate campaigns, reverse results that they do not like, and increasingly put themselves on the ballot.

The two major parties nominated candidates for president and vice president in 2004 who were millionaires many times over. In the case of George W. Bush and Dick Cheney, their policies blatantly expressed the views of the plutocratic elite as they endorsed round after round of tax cuts for wealthy taxpayers as well as global corporations. Although the positions of John Kerry and John Edwards were more sympathetic to the needs of the middle class, both had long since entered the ranks of the independently wealthy.

Political power continues to grow ever more concentrated in a relatively small number of wealthy individuals, corporate executives, and famous celebrities. This select group controls immense financial resources to support their own political and personal agendas. Powerful ideologues in Congress control access to desired committee assignments, control the legislative agenda, and even assert considerable influence over future elections. These forces have compromised the ability of the legislative branch to provide independent oversight of the other branches of government.

Through sophisticated use of the mass media and computer analysis, persons of wealth and power are able to encourage and exploit the highly polarized views of the electorate. They assert an influence over our country far greater than their numbers or knowledge. A disproportionate number of our successful candidates for high elective office come from the ranks of the wealthy and famous. In the past, the winning political candidate was often the one who was best able to propose solutions to problems that bridged the gap between diverging views. Today, the winning candidate is more likely to be a wealthy individual willing to exploit cultural divisions for political advantage.

There are great dangers when we concentrate political power and economic wealth in the hands of a relatively small elite oligarchy of plutocrats. The Bush administration has its own set of guiding fictions that depart significantly from the founding principles of our nation. Rather than recognizing that every vote counts, they believe that the few know best. Rather than supporting freedom for all, they support controls on the many for the benefit of the few. Rather than creating a society with a broad and prosperous middle class, they support policies that create a bimodal society in which there are a few winners and many losers. Jack Beatty, in an article in *The Atlantic Monthly,* described Bush as seeking a society "in which to those to whom much is given, more is given."

As we lose control of our nation to this oligarchy, economic pressures discourage participation by the average citizen in the various institutions of our societal immune system. Even with two incomes, most middle class families have a difficult time maintaining their current lifestyle. With the middle class running short of time and money, local governments, church groups, civic organizations, and professional groups are all experiencing difficulty in recruiting leaders and new participants.

Democracy depends upon an informed and engaged population. Along with a shortage of time and money among middle and lower income Americans, there has been a general deterioration in the quality of public discourse in our nation. The print and broadcast media have encouraged lowest common denominator entertainment and news. As long as our culture emphasizes wealth, celebrities, and sound bites over knowledge and substance, democracy will continue to take a back seat to oligarchy and plutocracy.

In his article in *The Progressive,* Bill Moyers emphasized that our country cannot survive being "half oligarchy" anymore than it could survive being "half slave." In his call to action, he urged us to stand up and fight for democracy. He noted that the forces supporting social inequalities are strong, but so are those who call for justice, fairness, and equality.

♫ ♫ ♫

"All men are created equal" is probably the central guiding fiction of our nation. As discussed earlier, it is certainly not literally true from virtually any perspective. However, it expresses many of our most cherished ideals. These include our belief that everyone deserves fair treatment and a chance to live their life in peace, that everyone's rights are deserving of protection by the state, and that everyone should have a voice in making our collective decisions. Unfortunately, rather than strengthening our democratic processes, recent actions by the Bush administration and its supporters in Congress are moving our nation towards an oligarchy in which decisions are made by and for the elite few.

Interlude Two

♬ ♬ ♬

Broken strings

The growth of malignancies

...weeds in the garden...

♫ ♫ ♫

One day, when I opened the case of my violin, I saw a rat's nest of strings lying on top of the violin. The tail gut that secures the tail piece holding the strings had broken, releasing the strings, and allowing the bridge to fall over. Another time, I heard the peg for the D string crack when I tried to turn it. High humidity had caused it to become swollen in its hole. Later, the technician in our local music shop also pointed out a severe warp in the bridge. He recommended making a new bridge as well as replacing the broken maple peg with a harder, ebony peg. A few months after these repairs, I heard a buzz and felt an unusual vibration in my violin. A tiny crack between the top plate and a side rib needed regluing. The repair and maintenance of a violin is an endless process. Strings break, bridges fail, seams open, heel guts break, necks crack, and so on. If necessary, technicians can take apart and reassemble the entire violin. Except in extreme cases, the instrument is almost always repairable.

Bad news

Tuesday, November 5, 2002, was election day. The country was in the midst of an active debate over a possible war in Iraq and political feelings were running high. In a tragic accident, Senator Paul Wellstone had just lost his life along with several others in a plane crash during the final days of the campaign. Former Vice President Walter Mondale stepped in to run for the seat that Senator Wellstone had previously held. The outcome of this hotly contested race in Minnesota might determine control of the Senate.

Unfortunately, the results of these mid-term elections were discouraging to those concerned with the direction that our country was moving. The Republicans regained narrow control of the Senate by winning a number of close races. Vice President Mondale was unable to retain the seat formerly held by the late Senator Wellstone for the Democrats. According to a post-election commentary by Bill Moyers on his public television show, *NOW,* the Republicans outraised the Democrats by $184 million. The Republicans now controlled both houses of Congress, the White House, and enjoyed a conservative leaning majority in the Supreme Court.

A few weeks after the election, bad news also arrived on a personal level when I learned that I had a malignant colon tumor that required immediate surgery. Despite some recent health concerns, I had not anticipated the need for surgery to remove a cancerous section of my colon. Much like the time when I first opened my violin case, the doctors had looked inside me and found the human equivalent of broken strings.

Death, rather than an abstract idea for the distant future, suddenly became an imminent possibility. A few years before, I had read *Arrows of Longing*, a collection of letters between the writer Anaïs Nin and her friend Felix Pollak, edited by Gregory Mason. In this book, Mason suggests that their final letters, written as Nin was dying of cancer, reflected a longing for what was as much or more than what might be. These were exactly my feelings as I wrestled with my health problems. I longed for what was, more than what might be. I wanted to return to a time when my body was young and strong. In some ways, my desires paralleled the feelings of many Americans following the attacks of September 11 -- depressed by the horror, they longed for what was.

Fortunately, following surgical removal of the tumor, I was able to resume my usual lifestyle with virtually no changes. I found it hard to think about the whirlwind that I had just been through. Was I a cancer survivor? Was I a cancer victim? A column by Julie Deardorff in the *Chicago Tribune* on the "Live Strong" yellow wristband campaign supported by Lance Armstrong noted that cancer patients have a wide range of views of the term "survivor." For some, it brings forth images of the holocaust, for others it suggests that the cancer has left when they know that it can often reappear. For me, my experience with colon cancer had gone so well, I found it hard to accept that, at least for the present, I was indeed a "survivor."

Malignancies and society

There is a fine line between the orderly growth of healthy cells in your body and the chaotic, uncontrolled growth of cancerous cells. It is ironic that in some ways cancerous cells demonstrate, in overabundance, the very characteristics that we need to live. Healthy, living organisms need to continuously produce new cells to replace old cells that die. Malignant growths take this process to the extreme and can destroy the ability of the body to function normally.

Malignant growths serve as a metaphor for the ways in which a society can become dysfunctional. Just as our bodies need to find the right balance between healthy and uncontrolled growth, our nation needs to find the right balance between stability and growth, between order and chaos, between stagnation and anarchy. In a world of perfect order, there is no change, no growth. In a world of complete chaos, there is no structure, no direction.

In the aftermath of the 9/11 tragedies, fear caused some in our country to embrace a dangerous mixture of nationalism, militarism, and privatization. Nationalism ignores the critical partnerships that we need to succeed in a shrinking, interconnected world. Militarism replaces diplomacy with an endless cycle of death and violence. Privatization neglects the role of collective action by the community.

Ironically, at the very time when we need to seek out new and creative responses to our problems, we gravitated towards simplistic solutions. Internationally, we placed too much emphasis on the use of force. The result was to drive away our friends and to damage our standing in the international community. We repeated in our actions in Iraq as well as our rhetoric concerning the "axis of evil" some of the same mistakes that we made a generation ago in Vietnam.

Domestically, we accelerated our embrace of privatization, allegedly to strengthen the economy, but in reality aimed at benefiting the wealthy and the corporate benefactors of those in power. Robert Kennedy, Jr. wrote of the dangers of unfettered capitalism and the corporate control of government. In particular, he quoted Franklin Roosevelt's warning that "the liberty of a democracy is not safe if the people tolerate the growth of private power to a point where it becomes stronger than their democratic state itself. That, in its essence, is fascism -- ownership of government by an individual, by a group or by any controlling power."

Peter Drucker observed in his book *The End of Economic Man: The Origins of Totalitarianism,* published at the onset of World War II, that totalitarian, fascist governments are essentially neither socialist nor capitalist. Rather their repressive dictatorships simply want to maintain the operation of a regimented industrial system in support of an aggressive nationalistic agenda. Leadership in such a society stems from cultural and religious attributes rather than economic distinctions. Non-economic military forms such as recognition, status, and function serve to camouflage the economic inequities that fascism tolerates.

The linkages between government and the corporate world that the Bush administration and its friends in Congress were so keen to suppress and keep hidden from public scrutiny were leading us in the direction that Roosevelt and Drucker had described. We were seeing the emergence of an oligarchy of plutocrats that pursued nationalism, militarism, and privatization couched in religious language to garner support even from those their policies harmed.

Ironically, the principles, strategies, and tactics that our nation pursued following the 9/11 attacks bore more than a passing resemblance to those of the extremist forces that threatened our nation. In fact, George W. Bush described the terrorists as "the heirs to fascism" even as his administration embraced his own versions of nationalism, militarism, and privatization, The policies of the Bush administration and the views of those who threaten our nation have their roots in parallel needs to control, intimidate, and suppress others. Much like the uncontrolled growth of a malignant tumor in our bodies, ideological dogmatism does not tolerate competition.

The metaphor of malignant growth frequently suggests itself whenever ideologies adopt extremist views that tolerate no opposition and claim to possess exclusive rights to the truth. Franklin Foer, in his review of John Dean's book *Worse than Watergate,* notes that Dean has amassed evidence of "a cancer growing on the presidency." At the same time, Michael Ignatieff, in his article "Lesser Evils" suggests that Islamic terrorism may have metastasized into "a cancer of independent terrorist cells."

Unfortunately, there are other parallels in the history books to our current problems. According to an article in *Physics Today* by Ella Ryndina, authorities of the former Soviet Union arrested Lev Landau, their future Nobel prize winning physicist, in 1938 along with two of his colleagues for distributing a leaflet opposing the policies of the government. The leaflet stated that "innocent people were being thrown into prisons and no-one can tell when his own turn will come," that, in a betrayal of the October Revolution, a "clique has carried out a Fascist coup...for the sake of [their] own power," and that the secret police under this clique are "slaughtering defenseless prisoners," "catching unsuspecting innocents," "plundering national property," and "concocting absurd court trials."

Though clearly more extreme, this description of Soviet rule in this 1938 leaflet contains chilling parallels to some of the actions of our own country after 9/11. These include the growing intimidation, suppression, arrest, and jailing of protesters, the indefinite imprisonment of suspects who are often innocent of any wrong doing, and the torture and abuse of prisoners in Iraq and Guantanamo.

Through overuse, comparisons with Hitler and Nazi Germany have for some become virtual clichés, but this is no reason to ignore the real lessons from that horrific period of history. According to Richard Rhodes, in his Pulitzer Prize winning book *The Making of the Atomic Bomb,* Nazi domestic strategies in Germany prior to the Second World War included leading the masses away from politics, strict censorship and control of the press, and attacks on liberalism along with its ideals concerning individual liberties.

Many of the tactics of the Bush administration reflect similar themes. For example, the Bush administration often trivializes political discourse with sound bite aphorisms. It encourages ridicule of thoughtful, extended responses to its proposals as illustrated in its treatment of comments by John Kerry during the 2004 election campaign. Although explicit censorship may be relatively rare at this time, the Bush administration and its supporters restrict public debate through intimidation of the media, the cooperation of friendly media owners, the use of "embedded" or "friendly" reporters, virtual control of all three branches of government, suppression of protesters, and administrative constraints on publishers. Liberalism in all of its many dimensions as well as its supporters are regularly scorned.

One astounding example of the impact of media intimidation was in the refusal of all three major networks at the end of 2004 to broadcast a *paid* advertisement produced by the national United Church of Christ (UCC). The ad featured a bouncer refusing entrance to church to two gay men, a young black girl, a Hispanic man, and a person in a wheelchair. The punch line was that UCC churches do not turn people away.

While the networks cited vague policies against "issue" or advocacy advertising and controversial religious ads -- apparently they believe that you should only advocate for a non-religious product or service and that churches should not express their views even when they are inclusive rather than exclusive. CBS noted in a written explanation to the UCC that it also found the ad unacceptable because of the Bush administration's proposal of a constitutional amendment regarding the definition of marriage. However, in our society, proposals by the president or anyone else are just that, proposals -- open to public debate and criticism by anyone who wishes to comment.

In May of 2005, Frank Rich wrote an essay in *The New York Times* in which he reviewed how the Bush administration has criticized and intimidated the mainstream media in order to avoid public scrutiny of the administration's lies and failures. Rich wrote his essay in the aftermath of an over-the-top reaction by the Bush White House to a report, soon retracted, in *Newsweek* magazine concerning desecration of the Koran by American interrogators. Despite White House posturing, Rich noted that there remain many fully substantiated examples of American interrogators exploiting the Muslim beliefs of our prisoners in their interrogations. The details of the *Newsweek* article might be incorrect, but the message at its core, that interrogators have abused the religious beliefs of our prisoners, is still accurate. In addition, a subsequent report by the Pentagon confirmed five incidents in which our personnel did mishandle the Koran, either by accident or intentionally.

Rich notes that the administration's exaggerated concern for truth and accuracy regarding the *Newsweek* article contrasts sharply with its own actions. These include the lies and deceptions used by administration officials in justifying the war in Iraq, in responding to questions regarding the need for more armored Humvees in Iraq, and in defending their failure to secure munitions depots in Iraq after our invasion. In addition to its extreme criticism of the media, the desire of the Bush administration to operate behind closed doors and restrict access to public documents further undermines the ability of the news media to function as an alternative voice in our society.

A similar example occurred the following month in June of 2005. According to an article by Jill Zuckman in the *Chicago Tribune,* Senator Dick Durbin from Illinois, and the second ranking Democrat in the Senate, gave a speech on the Senate floor criticizing the Bush administration and its mistreatment of prisoners at

Guantanamo Bay. After reading a report from an FBI agent complaining about the mistreatment, Durbin went on to add that if he hadn't identified the mistreatment as involving prisoners held by Americans "you would most certainly believe this must have been done by Nazis..." Rather than responding to the substantive content of his speech concerning the abuse of these prisoners, the White House and the conservative opposition chose to focus on those few words in Durbin's speech. Clarence Page observed in the *Chicago Tribune* that the agent's report did indeed sound like "the horrors of a mad regime," but that it took some imagination to see Durbin's words as smearing all of our troops as Nazis. Nonetheless, the controversy intimidated Senator Durbin into apologizing for his comments, and once again the content got lost in the rhetoric.

Hannah Arendt, in her book *The Origins of Totalitarianism* quoted by Richard Rhodes in *The Making of the Atomic Bomb,* states that totalitarianism "destroys all space between people." Throughout history, there have been many examples of physical oppression by literally forcing people to live in confined spaces. During World War II, the Nazis forced the Jews to live in walled ghettoes and later concentration camps. In the 1880s, our nation placed American Indians on reservations comprised of land, often less desirable, that provided a small fraction of the freedom that they once enjoyed. In some cases, these allocations also exacerbated conflicts between opposing tribes fighting over the same space -- a "divide and conquer" side benefit of restricting their land.

However, there is more to freedom than simply physical space; our democratic institutions also need space. Expanding on Hannah Arendt's observation that totalitarian regimes destroy the space between people, Azar Nafisi in her book *Reading Lolita in Tehran,* emphasizes the need for space in democratic societies. We need space for dialogue, opposing views, and minority voices. The concentration of media ownership, the importance of big money in political campaigns, the emphasis on celebrity, and the political dominance of ideological extremists have all contributed to a loss of public space in our society. There is less room for what Nafisi calls the "cacophony of voices" that is essential for a democracy.

The Madison author, Parker Palmer, has spoken of the importance of "public places" for democratic society. In the past, there were places like city streets, parks, schools, clubs, and so on where we could meet strangers, encounter divergent views, and engage in dialogue. Unfortunately, in a world of private shopping malls, gated communities, private schools, theme parks, and electronic media, there are ever fewer public places that provide these opportunities for democratic processes to function. As a consequence, we are less able to alleviate our fears, negotiate conflict, and empower ourselves to confront abuses of power.

In a world of dwindling public space, the government finds it easier to suppress individuality and force society to conform to its ideological views. The Bush administration is moving us towards a society in which there simply is no room for divergent thinking. It suppresses opposing points of view and claims that you either support them or you are helping the terrorists. Its religious zeal in gathering support for its views and its rejection of any alternative opinions are bringing us ever closer to the point where our individual freedoms vanish in the crush of conformity; freedom of speech means little if there is no place to use it.

In *The Making of the Atomic Bomb,* Richard Rhodes reports that the Nazis named their first anti-Semitic law, "The Law for the Restoration of the Professional Civil Service." This law led to one-third of the academics at major German universities losing their positions because of their Jewish heritage. Contrary to its title, this discrimination was not professional, and focused on expulsion, rather than restoration. Ironically, as it tore apart the lives of those expelled under the act, it also cost Germany many of its finest scientists.

Similar discrimination on racial or ethnic grounds in our own country remains an ominous possibility. In December of 2004, researchers at Cornell University released the results of a nationwide poll that showed that 44 percent of those surveyed favored restricting the civil liberties of Muslim Americans in some fashion. These included 27 percent who supported national registration of Muslim Americans, 22 percent who supported racial profiling aimed at Muslims, and 29 percent who supported the use of undercover agents in Muslim organizations. Views such as these, and the extremist rhetoric that encourages them, are another example of the malignant attitude that threatens the future of our democracy.

We often object to religious extremism in other countries that discriminates against other faiths, preaches hatred, promotes violence, and restricts the rights of women. However, religious fundamentalism increasingly dominates our own nation and presents a similarly exclusivist view of the world. Its adherents too often see themselves as God's chosen people, driven by their ideology to military, economic, diplomatic, and cultural domination of the world. Religious extremism of any flavor is destructive to peace and stability. The health of an individual or society depends on the contributions of a diverse array of systems and components. It is essential to nourish and encourage the orderly, balanced growth of all parts of our bodies and society.

We need to be ever vigilant to the emergence of malignant growth, whether literally in our own bodies or metaphorically in our nation. This is particularly true during times of stress. As mentioned above, research has shown that stress can weaken the resistance of individuals to illness. The nervous system appears to communicate with the immune system and chooses short term survival over long term health. An analogous effect occurs within our larger society. After the trauma of the 9/11 attacks, many people, consumed by stress and fear, appear willing to accept without question virtually any action by our government.

Why are so many Americans silent as our leaders foment division and blindly drive us towards the edge of a cliff? It is not unlike many other countries and empires that have suffered under despotic rulers and ill-advised policies. How many Germans protested as Hitler led Germany down the path to its destruction, how many South African white citizens objected during more than 40 years of apartheid, and how many Argentineans objected to policies that divided and weakened their country? Some are too tired to care due to working two jobs, caring for the kids, and trying to keep their family running. Others simply don't want to be bothered. They want to enjoy life, and let someone else do the heavy lifting. Some are so committed to their own ideology that the thought of abandoning their preconceptions and assumptions is too frightening to consider.

The life of empires

For many of us, the period of life from about fifty to sixty-five is a time of changes. Parents die, children go off to school and get married, grandchildren arrive, employment changes, and health concerns grow. In the United States, there is no common name for this transitional time -- some call it "the third age." The hymn *I Was There to Hear Your Borning Cry* by John Ylvisaker may capture the essence of this period when it speaks of an age when you are "not too old, no longer young."

Nations also pass through similar stages of life that vary greatly in length depending on their circumstances. In the aftermath of World War I, a number of smaller states, following very brief appearances as independent nations, disappeared into the rather short-lived empire that was the Soviet Union. A number of these states have since been reborn as new nations.

Following World War II, former long time world powers, such as the United Kingdom and France, entered what may become for them a long period of senior citizen status on the world political scene. At the same time, other nations, including Japan, China, and India have developed renewed positions of economic, diplomatic, and in some cases, military power. The newly enhanced roles of these ancient societies continue to evolve as they become major players in the modern economic and political world.

On the other hand, as we enter the 21st century, our nation may have entered the transitional period between middle age and senior citizen status. Some have described the world cruise of our Great White Fleet at the beginning of the 20th century as a sort of coming out occasion for the United States. By the end of World War II, our country had reached the peak of its power and had a wide range of economic, military, and diplomatic resources. Since then, our ability to dominate the world has slowly faded even as some of our leaders pretend otherwise. We are no longer at the peak of our powers, nor are we in complete control of our destiny. Many people throughout the world are beginning to see the United States as more a part of the problem rather than the solution.

Today, the age of empires is nearly over. The United States is perhaps the only remaining example. Although the U.S. is primarily a "virtual" empire with relatively little territory and only a few remaining overseas possessions, it remains the only country able to project its power and influence throughout the world. It does this through military, economic, cultural, and diplomatic strengths unmatched by any other nation. The actions of the Bush administration following the attacks of 9/11 have certainly squandered a substantial portion of our power in all four areas, but we retain, for now, our ability to exercise considerable influence wherever and whenever we desire. How long we will be able to maintain this position is an open question.

Milan Kundera, in his novel *The Unbearable Lightness of Being,* suggests that when the founding idea of an empire crumbles, the empire fades away. The Soviet Union collapsed when it no longer could maintain its guiding fictions of economic equality and prosperity built around the Communist ideas of Marx and Engels. The United States observed the collapse with unjustified self-satisfaction. Rather than rejoicing in our success, we should be asking ourselves how such a large and powerful nation could disintegrate so quickly and completely.

Our powerful military forces have tended to mask our decline. Despite the continuing rhetoric regarding our need for an antimissile, "Star Wars" defense against a long-range missile attack, it is now apparent that we face serious threats from seemingly more mundane weapons. Although we have developed an awesome array of military forces for conventional warfare, they have limited usefulness against modern terrorist tactics and their weapons.

It may take a number of years before we fully understand the meaning of the attacks of 9/11, but they have already challenged our long standing presumption that the oceans protect us against direct attacks. However, we can also see them as the latest insult in a string of events that began with the debacle of the Vietnam War and continued through oil embargoes, the Iran hostage crisis, and terrorist attacks against our interests throughout the 1980s and 1990s. Much like our personal experiences with growing older, it is not easy for a nation to adjust to the inevitable weaknesses that emerge over time.

We need to be more intentional about where we are going. We need to engage in long range thinking and planning. Too often, we have moved ahead on a proposal, such as the war in Iraq, without adequate thought as to why we are doing this, where will it lead, and what will we do then. Such thinking might have avoided some of the tragedies, costs, and frustrations that we experienced in Iraq following the declaration of "the end of combat."

As we grow older, injuries and illnesses that a younger person might be able to easily overcome can overwhelm our bodies. A broken bone or simple cold can lead to complications that can threaten our very survival. In much the same way, older nations can fall victim to incidents that might not threaten younger, more vigorous nations. Earlier in our history, we were able to use our vast land and resources, both natural and human, to overcome almost any obstacle that we encountered. Today, it is dangerous to believe that we are immune to the same fate that has befallen former world powers including the Soviet Union, the United Kingdom, and France.

Rather than resorting to militarism, we need to develop new strategies for meeting the economic, political, and military threats that we face. Militarism encourages leaders to overreach and often leads to disaster. Pursuing diplomatic and economic steps to reduce the desire and ability of future terrorists to attack our country is not condoning the attacks of 9/11.

We need to realize that the long term health of our nation depends on taking a balanced and thoughtful approach to our problems. As a nation and as individuals, we do not achieve health and happiness when each day is a new crisis. Good health requires that we slow down and reflect on where we are going. As a first step, we need to reject those individuals and political leaders who poison the atmosphere with cries of militarism and "endless war."

As we develop a more mature grasp of our role in the world, we may even discover new ways to reinvent ourselves as a nation. Much like middle-aged people often take on second or third careers, the United States may find ways to renew itself and return again to the vigor, enthusiasm, and ingenuity of its youth.

♬ ♬ ♬

The phrase "broken strings" in the title of this book as well as this section has multiple meanings. At the most basic level, "broken strings" refers to the frustration that we feel when we experience brokenness in our lives, everything from broken violin strings to broken health. It also refers to the broken nature of many of our societal institutions and systems. Most importantly, it refers to the malignant efforts of some to restrict our individual freedoms and rights, to impose one particular set of religious values on our nation, and to move us closer to a fascist form of government controlled by the rich and powerful. However, just as technicians can repair broken violins and physicians can mend broken bodies, our people and their institutions can restore wholeness to a divided nation.

Part III

♫ ♫ ♫

Seeking new alternatives

...a new birth of freedom...

♫ ♫ ♫

Chapter 10

Renewing the economy

...American ingenuity...

♫ ♫ ♫

Many students begin their study of the violin when they are quite young, perhaps in preschool or elementary school. Some suggest that the difficulty of the instrument demands an early start in order to become an accomplished player. This is probably true for those who aspire to reach the highest levels of ability. Nonetheless, there is no reason why a student of any age can't learn to play the violin. They may never become as good as they would have had they started at an earlier age, but the older adult student can learn to play well enough for their personal satisfaction and to perform with others. Although it requires a commitment to study and practice, the biggest hurdle, as with so many things, is deciding to begin.

From reacting to acting

A question that continues to engage many scientists and philosophers is whether we invent or discover mathematics. It is often striking how well mathematics can help us understand how the world works. Is this because the world is inherently mathematical? Or is it because we only ask those questions that lend themselves to mathematical analysis? Is God a mathematician? Or is it just a coincidence that we happened to have invented a way of the looking at the world through mathematics that is so useful? Have we and the universe of which we are a part evolved through what we now see as mathematical relationships? Or are these relationships the metaphorical street light that illuminates only a small part of the world in which we live?

In a similar way, some people believe that we are in control of our lives, while others believe in a God that has predetermined our future, and still others emphasize the role of blind chance. It certainly seems that we influence our lives through the hundreds or even thousands of decisions, both big and small, that we make every day. However, it also seems clear that there are many factors that we cannot control. Do we direct our lives? Or are they the result of external actions beyond our control? Has God or some cosmic computer program predetermined the way things are and will be? Do our decisions make a significant difference or are we prisoners of fate? Are our lives more like an invention or a discovery? Are we reacting or acting? Is life an active or passive process?

At this moment in our nation's history, many people seem to have adopted a passive attitude about their lives and the future. They often express fatalistic views about their inability to influence the companies where they work, the communities where they live, or the governments that regulate and control their lives. For some, this fatalism stems from their religious belief in a God that is pulling all the strings. For others, it stems from a feeling of impotence in an increasingly chaotic world. For whatever reason, too many people have decided to nestle into their homes, withdraw to their television sets, and simply watch the world go by.

A large number of Americans have decided that there is no need for them to vote since they believe that the results will not make any difference in their lives. They do not participate in community organizations, volunteer to work on special projects, or even stay informed on critical issues. They regard their work as merely a way to earn their living. Life has become simply something that happens to them rather than an experience they can direct.

However, a small, but growing number of people are rediscovering that they can influence the direction of their lives as well as the world in which we live. They are taking a more active role in making the changes that they feel are necessary in their neighborhoods and communities.

Many people are also seeking to regain control of their economic lives. They are returning to school to pursue new career directions. When their work does not provide the opportunities or work environment that they desire, they are starting their own businesses. They are joining with others to respond to threats to the economic health of their communities and local businesses.

For example, the uncontrolled growth of big box stores has become a blight on the national landscape. It has restructured the commercial and social life of entire communities. Due to its concern for the historic character of Vermont, the National Trust for Historic Preservation has designated the entire state as one of the 11 most endangered places in the country due to the continued spread of big box stores. In response to these concerns, many communities are considering or have passed regulations restricting the development of these mega-stores.

In 2004, a highly contentious debate took place in Chicago over plans to construct two new Wal-Mart stores. Council members became particularly upset over Wal-Mart's tactic of using of pollsters to identify residents who supported construction of the new stores and then to connect those residents to council members' phones, in some cases without the residents even understanding what was happening. At a subsequent council meeting, members voted to approve one store, the first in Chicago, but denied the other due to concerns over its impact on local businesses.

Mike Ivey, in his 2005 article in *The Capital Times,* discussed local efforts throughout the country to restrict the proliferation of huge "big box" stores. He noted the many empty Wal-Mart stores as well as numerous vacant big box stores from other chains lying idle across the nation. These buildings are often too large for most local businesses and too small for other national chains that continue to desire ever larger buildings. As a result, they stand as dark, ugly monuments to forgotten impulses of corporate retailing.

Efforts to restrict the size of mega-stores stores often face stiff opposition from their corporate owners. In May of 2005, *The New York Times* carried a report on a tough fight over the size of big box stores in Flagstaff, Arizona. Voters repealed a local ordinance restricting the size of new big box stores by a margin of 365 votes out of 17,000 votes cast. According to local newspapers, Wal-Mart, with a nearly $300,000 campaign supporting the repeal, outspent those opposing the repeal by a margin of nearly 10 to 1. After running one controversial ad that compared the existing law to Nazi book-burning and censorship, Wal-Mart apologized, apparently without noting its control over the books and magazines carried in its stores. As a consequence of the repeal, new big box stores will grow ever larger, continue to dominate the commercial activity of the region, and create difficult problems when they decide to close their doors.

Efforts have also begun to curb abuses of corporate power. Senior management controls the nomination and election processes for the board members of most corporations. As a consequence, corporate directors too often support the company's management rather than serve as independent representatives of the shareholders. The result is a circular process in which the shareholders play no significant role. Corporate shareholders, both individual and institutional, are trying to correct these weaknesses in the corporate system. In the wake of fraud and scandals following the collapse of the Internet bubble, they have increased their use of shareholder lawsuits to obtain changes in corporate governance. The demands of these lawsuits include more independent directors, restrictions on executive compensation, and tighter audit requirements.

Large investors, such as mutual fund companies, are turning to specialized research firms to provide assistance in analyzing complex financial statements and deciding how to cast their proxy votes at corporate meetings. This advice helps large investors to better understand the risk factors and to encourage proper corporate behavior at the companies in which they invest.

Accounting firms that perform corporate audits are taking stronger positions against executives who fail to disclose information during the audit process. In late 2004, a conflict between Deloitte & Touche, a corporate auditor, and its client, Molex, Inc., resulted in an almost unprecedented request from the auditors that the Molex board remove both the chief executive officer and chief financial officer from their executive positions. When the board refused this request, the subsequent resignation of Deloitte & Touche threatened the company's stock market listing since independent auditors had not reviewed its latest quarterly results.

State officials have also begun to take a more aggressive role in investigating the aftermath of the market bubble and bankruptcies of the late 1990s. These investigations, led by the efforts of New York's state attorney general, Eliot Spitzer, have exposed many abuses in financial markets. Numerous brokerage firms, other financial institutions, and high level executives have paid substantial penalties for actions and inactions that included inadequate staff oversight, special trading arrangement for large customers or insiders, and excessive compensation for favored individuals.

Federal agencies have also begun prosecuting some of the executives responsible for the most egregious behavior. Although the pace has been slow, at least partially due to the weak laws in these areas, and some of those most responsible have not yet faced responsibility for their deceptions and fraud, progress is occurring. Hopefully stiff penalties, including substantial fines and prison sentences, will, at least in some cases, inspire changes in behavior within financial markets and corporate offices. Alex Beam reviewed a number of books about the leading characters in these various abuses of corporate power in *The Atlantic Monthly.*

Changes are also occurring at the international level. In late 2003, negotiations at a meeting of the World Trade Organization in Cancun, Mexico, broke down when a bloc of developing nations refused to go along with the plans of the developed world, including the United States. Similar objections by the poorer nations at a

Western Hemisphere economic meeting considering a so-called "Free Trade Area of the Americas" resulted in a much weaker agreement that gives individual nations greater freedom to manage their own economies.

The success of the developing nations has further encouraged local leaders in those nations. These leaders recognize that the current global economic system is unfair and ineffective in its management of economic resources. For this reason, they often develop tactics that explore the boundaries of current laws and regulations.

Cooperatives and other alternatives

Argentina is one of the countries at the forefront of efforts to find more effective and equitable solutions to its economic problems. A country with a history that includes years of social unrest and countless military coups, Argentineans endured repressive domestic measures during the internal "dirty war" of the 1970s as well as an ill-advised war in the Falkland Islands with the United Kingdom in early 1980s.

In the 1990s, Argentine leadership embraced the twin mantras of privatization and deregulation to rebuild the nation's economy. Rather than solving its problems, these strategies led to foreign ownership of land and manufacturing facilities, plant closures by absentee owners, and vast unemployment. The collapse of both the agricultural and manufacturing sectors brought hardships to its people and virtually bankrupted central and provincial governments. Only 350 foreign owners, mainly American, now own nearly one-sixth of Patagonia, the vast southern region of Argentina.

After this chaos, Argentina has resisted further efforts of outsiders, including the International Monetary Fund, to manage and control its economy. Workers have confronted absentee owners who closed many of their factories because they failed to meet desired profit expectations. However, the workers were still willing to work, and many of these dormant plants remained useful at least for domestic production.

As a consequence, worker cooperatives have emerged to reopen idle factories. Using a law of expropriation, some cooperatives have obtained legal ownership of the plants under the condition that they pay for the building and equipment within a specified time period. Other efforts by worker groups to reopen facilities have led to legal conflicts as well as illegal occupation of vacant plants. By 2003, there were about 100 workers' cooperatives operating failed businesses instead of their original owners. The 2005 Madison Film Festival included a powerful documentary movie, *The Take,* that tells the story behind several of these Argentine cooperatives.

In December of 2004, reports from Argentina indicated that the economy was once again growing, unemployment was falling, the currency was stable, and exports were growing. The government remains focused on the creation of jobs and internal consumption. It continues to move away from the IMF and insists that returns to foreign creditors are dependent on its continued economic recovery.

Interestingly, even as European and other investors from wealthier countries remain leery of the Argentine economy, businesses from other Latin American countries, who understand less stable economies, are increasing their investments in Argentina. The Argentine approach seems to be leading to prosperous relationships within the Latin American regional economy.

In a similar manner, Paul Theroux in *Dark Star Safari* describes a furniture supplier in Malawi who found success distributing African-made furniture that is more affordable than that imported from outside Africa. Economic trade is not simply a question of local versus global; regional and sub-regional trade relationships offer many opportunities for local businesses, often with fewer problems than global relationships.

In the United States, we face similar problems as Argentina when companies abandon still useful facilities and labor forces to seek lower cost locations in other countries. Increasingly, the location of choice for manufacturing and design is China. An article by Ted Fishman reported that China's economy, growing about 6% per year, is already the sixth largest in the world and is third in trading behind the U.S. and Germany. It currently graduates five times as many engineers as the United States. Although the U.S. still spends five times as much as China for research and development, our higher wages mean that this much larger budget can support less than 2 times as many researchers as in China.

Although China claims that its urban per capita income is about $1000, many urban couples are able to earn $5000 per year through a combination of two wage earners working at multiple jobs. Since their purchasing power in China is about five times that of a worker in the United States, the buying power of this Chinese couple is equivalent to $25,000 in the United States, which approaches that of many middle class American couples. The rapid economic growth of China coupled with the indebtedness of the United States means we are no longer dealing from a position of unchallenged strength in the global economy. We need to adjust our economic and political thinking to fit these new realities just as Argentina and other Latin American countries are beginning to do.

As in Argentina, cooperatives are playing an active role in the United States, particularly in the agricultural sector. Some of these cooperatives, like the Maple Leaf Coop in Wisconsin, are small and focused on providing distinctive, high quality products for specialized markets. Others, like Pipestone Family Farms in Minnesota, are large farmer owned businesses. Pipestone supplies piglets to its farmer owners who bring them to market weight. It is the only top 10 national pork producer owned by family farmers.

Large corporations dominate the supply of farm inputs such as seeds, fertilizers, equipment, and animals as well as the distribution and processing of farm products. Family farmers have a difficult time surviving when they are squeezed between these powerful economic forces. Pipestone Family Farms gives its member owners greater control over their piglet supply, an input variable. On the output side,

Community Supported Agriculture (CSA) is an innovative approach to the distribution side of agriculture. Through CSAs, farmers are able to distribute their produce directly to the consumer on a weekly basis for a fixed fee. In addition to better returns, they are able to educate their customers about their farms and obtain advance payments that help finance their businesses.

Cooperatives are also finding a role for those seeking to improve access to health care insurance for farmers, other self-employed individuals, and employees of small businesses that do not provide medical coverage. The Wisconsin legislature passed a bill that will provide a structure for such a cooperative approach that resembles a program already in operation in Minnesota.

Unfortunately, as with so much in our growth and profit oriented society, cooperatives are not necessarily a panacea. There are now reports of cooperatives that have grown so large and powerful that they may threaten rather then enhance the success of small farmers. Dairy Farmers of America (DFA), the nation's largest dairy cooperative, attempts to influence the price of dairy products for the benefit of its members. However, the legality of its trading strategies is unclear, and some dairy economists have expressed concern over practices that undermine the integrity of market pricing.

In addition, both federal and state authorities are investigating DFA for possibly monopolistic practices. Dairy farmers in Louisiana are attempting to halt the sale of a small milk processing plant to DFA. They object to the way in which DFA has purchased smaller cooperatives, signed supply agreements with bottling plants, and vertically expanded into trucking and other aspects of the industry. This growth has given DFA the ability to control much of the dairy industry throughout this county. Its opponents argue that its actions, including supply agreements with foreign suppliers, often fail to benefit local dairy farmers.

In Minnesota, farmers are suing the former executives at an ethanol production cooperative that they had recently sold. The lawsuit alleges misconduct in the sale which occurred just as the price of ethanol increased and which led to golden parachute payments to the chief executive and other officers of the cooperative. Not surprisingly, giant cooperatives can generate some of the same problems as giant corporations.

Although cooperatives have a long history in agriculture, the cooperative form of organization is enjoying a renewal of interest in other fields as well. For example, some small towns are resorting to cooperatives to revitalize their decaying shopping districts. After their general clothing store closed, the residents of Powell, Wyoming, had to travel 23 miles to Cody or 100 miles to Billings, Montana, to meet their clothing needs. Inspired by a small town in Montana with a similar problem, a local group got together and sold shares to 429 shareholders at $500 a share to raise the funds necessary to open a new community-owned general clothing store. *The Merc* exceeded sales expectations during its first two years of operation and soon opened an annex to provide children's clothes. In addition, the store has stimulated sales at neighboring businesses.

In another example, as large chains and big box stores were driving many pharmacies out of business, a number of new independent pharmacies opened in the Madison, Wisconsin, area. Some have benefited from the purchasing power of the Independent Pharmacy Cooperative in Sun Prairie, Wisconsin, just outside of Madison, the largest purchasing cooperative of its kind in the United States. In addition to providing excellent customer service, these independent pharmacies sometimes offer specialty products and services not available at their larger competitors. Nonetheless, they still face many difficulties surviving in a world dominated by large corporations and health maintenance organizations. These companies sometimes require consumers to obtain their medicine from distant pharmacies through the mail, completely bypassing the local market.

Not surprisingly, the corporate world is rarely supportive of new and innovative alternatives to traditional business models. For example, smaller Wisconsin communities often find it difficult to obtain adequate attention from private Internet or cable TV providers.

This can range from lack of access to high prices and poor service. For these reasons, some communities have started their own municipal cable TV or Internet systems. Private cable TV or Internet providers are not happy about these alternatives to their services. Industry-sponsored legislative proposals have attempted to either ban municipal utilities from providing these services or to place new restrictions on their operation.

Technology and survival

The use of appropriate technology and the ability to control the direction of a business are sometimes the keys to survival. Many people are beginning to recognize that smaller businesses are often more efficient than large corporations and able to do things that might not be possible in a larger concern. For example, family farm owner John Bobbe wrote in the *Door County Advocate* that Gary Frank of the University of Wisconsin found in his research that the most efficient dairy herd size is from 50-100 cows. Larger herds may generate more revenue, but they are not the most efficient in terms of income per cow.

Smaller dairy herds also allow farmers to graze their cows in pastures rather than keep their cows confined. The animals are healthier with less need for antibiotics, the workers do not have to maintain and operate centralized manure processing systems, and the consumers receive a better product. The benefits are significant enough that confinement livestock operations are illegal in Sweden, according to an article by John Peck on small scale family farms.

The primary beneficiaries of the creation of super-sized farms are often the corporations that provide the equipment and the banks that provide the financing. Local communities gain relatively few jobs from highly automated "dairy factories" that often bypass local suppliers of goods and services. In addition, local residents face air and water pollution issues as well as increased traffic. Smaller farms can be more efficient and provide a better quality of life for farm families as well as more support for local businesses.

Just as there are arguments concerning the growth of large corporate super-farms, there are raging debates over the use of genetically modified crops. Zambia, in southern Africa, has resisted the importation of genetically engineered corn due to concerns over its potentially harmful effects on people and the environment. In this case, their specific concern revolved around the inclusion of a gene selected from a bacterium for its ability to help the corn resist certain insects. Although it is widely used in the United States, officials in Zambia, along with many in the European Union, believe that there are still too many uncertainties concerning its long range impact.

Ironically, other reports indicate that some farmers in Brazil are illegally using genetically modified soybean seeds because of the much higher yields that they provide. The conflict between environmental impacts and increased profits drives arguments concerning the use of genetically engineered crops. Another thread running through these arguments is resentment towards the power and hegemony of the United States and its global corporations.

Even before the emergence of new varieties through the use of the latest genetic engineering, seed companies strongly encouraged the widespread use of their hybrid seeds. These hybrid seeds have generated mixed feelings among third world farmers and political leaders. Although they may have some advantages over local varieties, they are either sterile or their offspring do not perform as well. Farmers must return to the seed companies each year to purchase new seeds. On the other hand, native varieties may perform better under local conditions in the long run than hybrids. They also allow farmers to obtain next year's seeds from this year's crop.

Similar stories exist for other businesses that must compete in highly competitive markets dominated by larger corporations. For many years, Apple Computer, a leader in computer technology since its introduction of the *Apple II* personal computer, has created a long line of innovative new products and technology. Following the introduction of its highly successful *iPod* music player, it took the leadership role in creating a usable, cost effective approach to legal downloading of popular music through its *iTunes* business.

Even though its market share of the personal computer market has dwindled to the low single digits due to the dominance of Microsoft software, Apple continues to thrive. Meanwhile, Microsoft has endured product patches, computer viruses, tough sanctions in Europe against its bundling practices, new competition from free software such as Linux and Firefox, and continued delays in the introduction of its new operating system. Smaller can often mean quicker, more innovative, and sometimes, more sustainable.

Authors and musical performers are also reacting to the growing dominance of global corporations in the publishing and recording industries. Writers are attempting to regain control of their creative output by self-publishing their books, either traditionally or through e-books, and by marketing their books through the Internet or other nontraditional distribution channels.

Recording artists are searching for ways to gain improved financial rewards and increased control over their music. *ArtistShare* is a new Internet business that sells CDs over the Internet for musicians who want a more direct route to their customers and a larger share of the revenue stream. An article on this new approach to distribution described a highly successful composer who, despite substantial commercial success with her first three albums through traditional channels, failed to make money on any of them. Using *ArtistShare* to direct market to her customers, she hopes to finally gain some reward for her efforts.

Renewing the local economy

One key to revitalizing local economies devastated by job losses when companies move their operations in search of lower cost labor in this country or overseas is to involve local investors in the formation of new businesses.

The cookware industry in Wisconsin, formerly a major employer in many smaller communities, has suffered through a series of plant closures. Following the closure of a huge plant in Manitowoc, Wisconsin, local investors with assistance from the state and federal government were able to put together a package that enabled them to purchase the facility. They plan to produce coil aluminum stock and add contract manufacturing in the near future. Similar opportunities to recycle abandoned facilities exist throughout our country. They require creative approaches in finance and engineering to encourage new uses for existing facilities.

In addition to repairing the damage to our communities when businesses leave or declare bankruptcy, it is also important to search for novel approaches to retaining existing businesses. One of the problems facing many communities across the United States is loss of grocery stores to serve local neighborhoods. Elderly, lower income, disabled, youth, and many others without access to transportation are finding it much less convenient to meet their grocery needs. Unfortunately, the grocery business continues to consolidate into a smaller number of corporations that try to serve their customers from a dwindling number of ever larger stores.

This corporate consolidation can create unexpected problems at the local level. For example, the new owners of a neighborhood grocery store in Madison chose to close the store and consolidate its operations with another store some distance away. However, they retained control of the old building and prevented any other competitive grocer from filling the void in the neighborhood left by the closure.

Fortunately, a local agency provided limited transportation services to the surviving grocery store for those in need using funds from the United Way and government grants. In addition, about two years after the closure of the neighborhood store, the new owners agreed to subsidize operation of an expanded, regularly scheduled shuttle service to their remaining grocery store. They also agreed to waive a lease prohibition against a competitive grocer occupying the site of their former store.

In a sharply different example, Schoep's, a Madison ice cream maker, leases space to the Jenifer Street Market, a small neighborhood grocery store, at below market rates. The store provides groceries and deli services to local residents and Schoep's employees. It also helps create goodwill for Schoep's products and improves relationships with its neighbors surrounding its quiet residential location. This type of symbiotic relationship, that combines elements of private, public, and cooperative ownership, is a good example of the creativity that helps build stronger communities.

A role for government

Many state and local governments are beginning to recognize the importance of taking a more active role in economic development. Some state governments are taking a direct role in the formation of new businesses through the use of state resources to invest in aspiring entrepreneurs. Others are passing legislation that encourages or maintains local business ownership. In Illinois, banking regulations that restrict bank expansion have led to a highly fragmented banking industry. Despite many bank mergers and the purchase of several major banks by out-of-state businesses, new bank formation continues at high rate. Although these banking regulations may have discouraged the development of large banks in Illinois, they have encouraged the formation of many strong locally owned banks.

Local governments are also passing ordinances that provide tighter controls over land use through zoning, sale of development rights, and public land purchases. They are regulating the demolition of older houses purchased as "teardowns" and restricting the size of new houses to preserve the scale of existing neighborhoods. Private developers are creating new neighborhoods, often based on ideas from the New Urbanism, that use smaller lots clustered around neighborhood parks. The use of public spaces linked by sidewalks to homes featuring front porches creates environments more suitable for interactions between neighbors. Working together, individuals, businesses, and government can create a better society.

In order to build a stronger economy, we need more than continuing appeals for more deregulation, privatization, and market-based decisions. Appropriate regulations help to support our core values. They protect the environment from those driven only by profits. They protect our workers from employers who see them as just another resource to exploit. They protect our financial markets from unfair and fraudulent behavior.

At the federal level, the new Sarbanes-Oxley legislation mandates a number of reforms in the management and reporting of corporate financial information to help protect investors. It attempts to increase the authority and independence of corporate auditors. Complex transactions of the sort engaged in by Enron that do not appear on the corporate balance sheet now require enhanced disclosure. It requires corporate management to certify their financial reports and provides penalties for violations of these requirements.

However, new regulations are not enough. Privatization of important public services has too often led to scandals and market chaos rather than the efficiencies and savings that some predicted. For many goods and services, the government, rather than private businesses, is often the most logical, efficient, and reliable provider. We need public ownership of parks, wildlife refuges, and similar lands to provide long term protection. Enron and the California power crisis demonstrated that we need public ownership of many utility functions as well as public oversight of private providers.

In the fall of 2004, a British supplier of the flu vaccine was unable to supply its share of the vaccine to the United States and shortages quickly developed. Vaccine production tends to be a low profit, commodity business with substantial liability risks. For these reasons, many manufacturers have no interest in it. It is another good example of an area that may require a more direct role for the government -- perhaps, in this case, actually operating the vaccine production facilities.

Making better decisions

Even at its best, the market, despite its acknowledged strengths, gives little attention to ethics or morality. It emphasizes short term supply and demand; it rarely projects very far into the future. It fails to consider a wide range of qualitative impacts, both good and bad. It ignores economic activity outside of the money economy.

However, today we have many markets that are far from ideal. Rather than large numbers of sellers and buyers trading with similar power and information, we often find a small number of giant companies selling to a large number of buyers who have much less power and information than large corporations. The relationship is inherently unequal. It is difficult for the consumer to make an informed decision, to consider alternatives, or to hold the seller accountable.

How can we restore strength and vitality to our nation's economy? A flawed market cannot make all of our decisions for us. We must renew government's role as the collective voice and power of the people. We need to develop new approaches to decision-making that look beyond the immediate future and consider the full range of costs and benefits in any particular action. We need to take active steps to make real our claim that the United States remains a land of opportunity for all Americans.

We must ensure that the responsibilities and obligations of corporations reflect the privileges that they receive. We need to broaden our rules of fiduciary responsibility to enable corporate officers and directors to take a broader view of their responsibilities. We need to encourage economic diversity and local ownership of businesses. We need to find new ways to focus our economic priorities on quality over quantity, lifetime costs over initial cost, conservation over production.

As we consider these questions, we should be careful not to allow false information to mislead us. Jonathan Koomey, in his article in *Spectrum* magazine, makes a number of suggestions on how to avoid misinformation or deceptive data. These include: talk to the experts in the field -- experts care and are more often accurate; however, don't believe everything you read -- even experts are sometimes wrong or can have conflicts of interest; rely on peer-reviewed research in mainstream publications -- it helps ensure scientific accuracy; do your homework -- examine the detail behind the data; read the footnotes -- they often contain assumptions and other details; and follow the money -- who funded the research, who will benefit. If everyone followed these simple ideas, we would make better decisions, the government would be more effective, and businesses would avoid fiascoes such as Enron.

♬ ♬ ♬

Although the phrase "American ingenuity" is not in our founding documents, it nonetheless expresses a fundamental American guiding fiction. The book *American Virtues, Values and Triumphs* cites ingenuity an American virtue along with freedom, perseverance, honesty, faith, courage, humor, loyalty, friendship, and compassion. The early settlers of this country had to creatively address the challenges they faced in a rough and undeveloped land. They were often on their own and had to solve problems with a "can do" attitude that came to epitomize the pragmatic American. When things didn't work or problems needed solving, Americans prided themselves on seeking constructive change. Today, we face the need to once again reinvent our nation. The global economy presents a new unfamiliar landscape that threatens the prosperity and culture of many communities. We need pragmatic solutions to the challenges that we face rather than blind adherence to ideological desires for privatization, deregulation, and globalization.

Chapter 11

Reforming the government

...a more perfect union...

♫ ♫ ♫

Whether you admire the physical beauty, the soaring music, or the romantic mystique of the violin, upon closer examination, one conclusion is unavoidable. The violin is a contraptionary collection of wood parts held together by wood glue. It must resist the tension of the strings as well as rather violent handling even though early violins contained virtually no metal parts with the exception of a few nails to help secure the neck to the body. In some ways, the design of the violin anticipates modern engineering. Lightweight panels create a violin body of great strength much like the box girders used in building construction. Its structure resembles the monocoque design used in the innovative designs of mid-20th century racing cars as well as today's most sophisticated aircraft and modern automobiles. The robust fragility of the violin parallels that of our own society -- a heterogeneous amalgam of individuals joined together in a complex society that is capable of producing great music.

The political opposition awakens

With the approach of the 2004 election, it became clear that our country was also beginning to awaken from, as described prior to the Iraq War by John le Carré, one of its periods of "historical madness." The political opposition, part of our societal immune system was finally coming back to life. One of the first strong indications of the change was in the early days of the Democratic presidential primary campaign when the candidates, emboldened by the vigorous campaign of Howard Dean, finally began criticizing the policies and actions of the Bush administration.

Numerous authors also published books critical of Bush and the direction that he was taking the country. At one time early in 2004, these books comprised seven of the top twelve nonfiction books on *The New York Times* bestseller list. The phenomenal success of the Michael Moore's documentary film *Fahrenheit 9/11* concerning the Bush administration and events surrounding the attacks of 9/11 added to the resurgence of the opposition.

Various organizations, such as *MoveOn.org, The Media Fund,* the *AFL-CIO,* and others, began organizing huge numbers of supporters, raising large amounts of money through the Internet, and running aggressive advertising campaigns challenging the policies of the Bush administration. A national conference on media reform in Madison attracted nearly 2000 people pursuing ways to reverse the trend towards a media dominated by a small number of corporations controlled by a few individuals. A follow-up conference called for specific actions in support of needed media reforms. Former presidential candidate Al Gore returned to the public scene with strong criticism of the Bush administration including its decision to go to war in Iraq, its attack on our civil liberties, and its use of fear and manipulation for its own political gain.

The Democratic Party nominee for president in 2004, Senator John Kerry, spoke out repeatedly and with growing strength against the lack of leadership and flawed policies of the Bush administration. The vice presidential nominee, Senator John Edwards, used his charismatic personality and ability to speak plainly about his concerns over the way in which our country has evolved into "two Americas -- one for the rich and one for the rest of us." The political opposition was finally beginning to find its voice after the shock and depression following the controversial ending to the 2000 election and the subsequent 9/11 attacks.

The polls began to reflect the changing political climate as well. Following the 9/11 attacks according to a Time/CNN poll, the president's popularity soared from just under 60% in the summer of 2001 to over 90% in late 2001. By May of 2004, his overall approval had dropped to under 50%. When evaluated on specific issues, his ratings were even lower: 46% thought he was doing a good job handling the situation in Iraq (as the situation in Iraq continued to decline amidst violence in the streets and prisoner abuse by our forces), 42% gave him a good rating handling foreign policy, and only 39% gave him a good rating handling the economy. The country had returned to the evenly divided, highly partisan state reflected in the 2000 presidential election results.

Following these national trends, the mass media gradually increased its coverage of the large and growing opposition to the administration. Journalists, economists, and political commentators seemed to have finally found their voices. They may have recognized the dangers in being perceived as too one-sided in their coverage. Perhaps, they wanted to improve their ratings. In any event, the growing coverage had the appearance of leading by getting out in front of where you see the crowd is going. *The New York Times* even published an apology for its journalistic failures during the pre-Iraq war period acknowledging that it should have been more skeptical before publishing stories in support of the administration's positions. Witnesses at hearings held by the 9/11 commission repeatedly described an administration obsessed with Iraq and slow to respond to terrorism threats before 9/11.

In the summer of 2004, the situation in Iraq continued to deteriorate. Despite no credible evidence linking Iraq to the support of terrorism or any weapons of mass destruction, the administration still alluded to both as justifications for our war in Iraq, along with an ever shifting laundry list of other explanations for the quagmire that we found ourselves in. Bush went to the United Nations in an effort to obtain help from an organization that he had spurned when he decided to invade Iraq without its approval. Foreign leaders were skeptical, while European newspapers criticized what they described as mistakes and Bush's refusal to face the reality of what was actually going on in Iraq. Many in our own country also felt that the situation in Iraq was much worse than Bush described in his campaign rhetoric. Some commentators suggested that Bush's strategy for Iraq was to "pretend" that we were succeeding despite all evidence to the contrary.

James Fallows, in his article "Bush's lost year" in *The Atlantic Monthly,* reported the view of a senior figure at a military-sponsored think tank that our country was much worse off than it was prior to invading Iraq. His article further noted that the Iraq War distracted us from problems in Saudi Arabia and Pakistan as well as the search for Osama bin Laden and threats from Iran and North Korea. It consumed military resources, personnel, equipment, and supplies at a prodigious rate that were hard to replace and left us in a weakened condition to respond to military challenges elsewhere in the world. It also weakened our abilities to enhance domestic security in the fight against future terrorist plots. Fallows concluded that 2002 was a lost year for our nation during which Bush's choices left us weaker and more vulnerable.

As the election approached, John Kerry continued to speak more forcefully concerning the problems in Iraq and the misguided decisions that got us there. Evidence continued to surface of problems with both the administration's rationale for the invasion of Iraq as well as its management of that invasion and its aftermath. *The New York Times* ran an article discrediting statements made by the Bush administration during the buildup to the invasion regarding Iraq's purchase of aluminum tubes. Investigations revealed that these tubes were unsuitable for use in uranium centrifuges as the administration had claimed, but their properties were entirely consistent with their use in the production of small rockets as claimed by Iraq prior to the war.

Newspaper reports quoted Paul Bremer, the U.S. ambassador and administrator of Iraq after the invasion, as saying that we did not deploy enough troops in Iraq nor did we adequately contain the violence and looting that followed our invasion. In early October, a report from U.S. weapons inspectors stated that Saddam Hussein did not have weapons of mass destruction or plans to develop them when we invaded his country. The gap between Bush's "pretending" and reality grew larger every day.

Meanwhile, the situation was not much different on the domestic economic scene. The economic recovery was not creating the jobs that the administration had promised. During the summer of 2004, job creation not only fell far below expectations of both economic analysts as well as market traders, but the few new jobs paid much less that the manufacturing jobs that the country had lost to overseas suppliers. The federal budget had gone from a position of surplus to record deficits and our foreign trade imbalance soared.

Commentators were beginning to question the Bush administration's devotion to an economic policy focused on tax cuts for the rich and trickle-down economics. Nobel Prize winner, Joseph Stiglitz, in his article "The Roaring Nineties" in *The Atlantic Monthly,* cautioned against overselling American capitalism. He noted that there are other successful variations including the modified social welfare state in Sweden. In a similar vein, Ron Grossman's article in the *Chicago Tribune* suggested that just as communists such as Lenin and Deng Xiaoping found it useful to adopt some capitalistic measures, Bush should learn the value of government intervention to remedy some economic problems.

While a growing number of Americans had no health insurance, the administration touted Medicare revisions that favored the health care industry and threatened the long term future of the system. A report released by the nonpartisan Congressional Research Service in May of 2004 concluded that the administration's efforts to withhold the true costs of the Medicare legislation probably violated federal law in effect since 1912. According to a General Accounting Office report on the same topic, the Bush administration also violated two federal laws in producing videos to garner support for the Medicare changes. One law prohibits the use of federal money for propaganda, while the other prohibits use of federal money for unauthorized purposes.

Even in a Republican controlled Congress, the administration's new rules designed to modify overtime regulations for millions of workers encountered substantial resistance. Many observers realized that the proposed changes would allow employers to deny overtime pay to countless professional and higher level employees who earn more than a minimal salary, but are nonetheless earning middle class wages and should receive overtime pay for their extra hours. Others noted that some workers would gain the right to receive overtime pay, but would suffer professionally and lose pension and health benefits reserved for white collar workers. Most felt that the changes would result in little if any additional overtime costs for corporations while reducing their costs for benefits since hourly employees usually receive less comprehensive benefits than salaried workers.

In yet another setback for the administration, Congress managed to pass legislation that overturned the efforts of the Federal Communications Commission (FCC) to raise the allowable market penetration of television stations owned by a single corporation to 45% of the nation's households. Although the compromise measure still raised the allowable market penetration from 35% to 39%, it reflected a willingness on the part of Congress to deny administration requests that clearly favored a few giant corporations.

The judicial branch also began to reassert its power as federal judges ruled that parts of the Patriot Act were unconstitutional. These included sections making it a crime to give assistance to designated foreign terrorist organizations, which a judge ruled unconstitutional due to vague language that threatened First and Fifth Amendment rights, as well as sections that allowed secret and unchallengeable searches of Internet and phone records. In October of 2004, a federal appeals court ruled that the government had no right to search protesters at a rally simply due to fear of a terrorist attack. By the spring of 2005, opposition to the Patriot Act led several conservative and liberal organizations to join forces and seek the repeal of provisions of the Act related to obtaining records from businesses and libraries, secret searches, and the definition of "terrorist."

The courts also defended the rights of those imprisoned by the government. A federal appeals court ruled in December of 2004 against the Bush administration's argument that the president had the unilateral authority to declare U.S. citizens "enemy combatants" and to hold them indefinitely and incommunicado. Subsequently, the Supreme Court ruled that the prisoners held at Guantanamo Bay must receive certain basic rights and sharply limited the power of the Bush administration. A federal judge also found that trial procedures established by the Bush administration for the prisoners were invalid under U.S. and international law. There was increased willingness among attorneys to represent Guantanamo detainees as attorneys began to recognize that the real issue was maintaining the "rule of law" -- a long standing and essential guiding principle of our nation.

Judges also rebuffed attempts by the Bush administration to extend its power in other areas that had no connection to terrorism. When the Justice Department under Attorney General John Ashcroft adopted new guidelines calling for federal prosecutors to seek the toughest possible sentence, federal judges complained that the guidelines interfered with their ability to determine fair and appropriate sentences. The judges also urged the repeal of an earlier law that had limited their ability to impose lighter sentences. Some months later, a federal appeals court also ruled against Ashcroft's interference with Oregon's physician-assisted suicide law.

Efforts by the private sector to resist other policies of the Bush administration and the conservative Congress grew stronger. In April of 2005, the National Education Association, with 2.7 million teacher members, along with a collection of school districts and NEA chapters from across the nation joined forces to sue the U.S. Department of Education. Their lawsuit claims that the department forced schools to meet federal demands under the No Child left Behind act without providing adequate funding. Between 2002 and

2005, Congress authorized $122 billion and only appropriated $95 billion under the act forcing school districts to take money from other activities to comply with the costly and ill-considered mandates. Although numerous school districts and states had either sued or threatened to sue the Department of Education regarding the act, the NEA lawsuit was the first lawsuit with national support.

Charges and counter-charges

As the nation's political immune system began to recover, the political right recognized that they needed to take stronger action to stem both the cascade of bad news regarding the war in Iraq and the state of the economy. With the 2004 election drawing near, they crafted a counterattack that featured fear, innuendo, and distortions to draw support for Bush.

Political ads trumpeted Bush's strong leadership against terrorism even though the administration's war in Iraq had consumed vast amounts of resources in equipment and personnel without producing much improvement in our security. In fact, many of the administration's opponents complained that we had done too little to improve domestic security. They suggested increasing border patrols, inspecting more shipping containers, improving security on trains and buses, and securing the huge number of nuclear weapons available for potential use by terrorists.

In addition to their manipulation and domination of political machinery at both the state and national level, there were growing complaints that the Bush administration was also using the Department of Homeland Security's color-coded alert system for its own political purposes. For example, when the Department announced a highly specific alert concerning possible terrorist attacks on selected buildings in New York and Washington, many people questioned the motivations behind the alert. The limited scope of the alert as well as its timing, in the aftermath of the Democratic Convention, created the appearance of once again entangling politics with the fight against terrorism. It may or may not have been a coincidence, but the alert pushed the post-convention campaign tour by John Kerry and John Edwards off the front page.

The revelation that the information used to justify the alert, found on the computer of an engineer that authorities arrested a few days earlier in Pakistan, was anywhere from many months to several years old only served to fuel the controversy. What many found particularly upsetting was the way in which the Secretary of Homeland Security, Tom Ridge, used the announcement of the alert to praise the efforts of the Bush Administration in fighting terrorism.

Even more unsettling, when opponents challenged the facts behind the alert, senior officials quickly noted that they had additional intelligence that also supported their actions. Why they did not mention this in their initial announcement is unclear. The timing and form of their latest alert certainly created the appearance of political machinations. Whether or not these suspicions were true, the Bush administration had so politicized the climate regarding threats from terrorists that the country found it difficult to know whether or not they were crying wolf.

Meanwhile, reacting to strong images at the Democratic convention of Kerry surrounded by many of his shipmates from the Vietnam War, some conservatives with Vietnam experience even managed to find a way to tear into Kerry's military record much like had been done in the past to Republican Senator John McCain and Democratic Senator Max Cleland. Despite Kerry's three Purple Hearts, Bronze Star, and Silver Star, they managed to claim with a straight face that all three wounds were either minor, self-inflicted, or non-combat related and that he did not deserve his other medals. As with unethical officials and dictatorial regimes throughout history, it was easier to tell "the big lie" than to engage in meaningful debate, i.e. malign Kerry's distinguished service in Vietnam and trivialize his combat experience, heroism, and five (!) medals while refusing to examine the details, ambiguities, and uncertainties of Bush's military service in this country.

As the election drew near in mid-October, the Sinclair Broadcast Group ordered its 62 television stations to broadcast a one hour special that, despite some effort at a balanced presentation, nonetheless portrayed Kerry as a traitor and liar for the antiwar statements he made following his Vietnam service. Although most Americans have long since recognized the Vietnam War as a misguided and futile effort by the United States to impose its will on others, some still wanted to see it as heroic and resented those who opposed it. After more than 30 years, they still harbored resentment towards those, like Kerry, who rightly criticized our actions in Vietnam.

In our world of "sound bite" reporting of scandalous news, their claims received broad coverage that probably caused significant damage to Kerry's reputation among some voters. The media gave much less coverage to the fact that the leader of this effort had opposed Kerry for decades, not because of Kerry's record in Vietnam, but because Kerry had returned home from Vietnam as a harsh critic of that war. Many people also missed the reports of those who served alongside Kerry that contradicted the claims of those who were not even present at the incidents that they questioned.

Unfortunately, when CBS broadcast a story questioning Bush's service with the National Guard, they included references to documents whose authenticity CBS ultimately could not confirm. In the uproar that followed, little was said about the difficulty encountered by those seeking Bush's military service records as well as other information on the Bush administration under the Freedom of Information Act.

Lost in the controversy over these documents were more substantive questions concerning Bush's treatment and behavior during his service with the guard. As Roger Ebert noted in his review of *Going Upriver,* a powerful documentary on both Kerry's military service and his antiwar efforts, mistakes made by Dan Rather and CBS News in their reporting did not vindicate the irregularities and uncertainties in Bush's service record. However, as usual, form dominated content and Kerry, a bona fide decorated war veteran, had to defend his military record even as Bush, a favored son who appears to have taken full advantage of his privileged status, was able to avoid a full accounting of his actions.

Perhaps the humor weekly *the Onion* again provided the most fitting comment on the absurdity of the attacks on Kerry's swift boat service. In a satirical opinion poll concerning a possible military draft, one of the fictional respondents stated that, if drafted, he hoped he could serve on the swift boats since according to news reports, the swift boats are never in any danger.

During this brazen distortion of military records, Bush supporters continued to accuse Senator Kerry of "flip-flopping" on various issues. As with many thoughtful individuals, Kerry's positions did change over time for a variety of reasons. One of the most highly publicized so-called "flip-flops" involved Kerry's vote on an $87 billion bill for the war in Iraq. Initially, Kerry voted for the bill when it included a roll back of Bush tax reductions. Kerry later voted against the bill when the leadership removed this provision.

On the other hand, Bush often flip-flopped on issues before him including many times on questions concerning the Iraq War. He used well over a dozen different reasons to justify the war as each in turn became discredited. In one classic example of flip-flopping that received relatively little publicity, Bush stated in an interview that he thought the war against terrorism was unwinnable, only to reverse himself several days later and report that we were winning the war against terror. Later in the campaign, he changed his position once again and expressed uncertainty as to whether we would win the war against terror -- three different answers to the same question.

In May, an ad supporting Bush ran endlessly that criticized John Kerry's votes against various weapons systems and suggested that these votes left our troops without critical equipment. In reality, without analyzing the details concerning these votes, many of the weapons mentioned in the piece had little or nothing to do with the war in Iraq. If anything, our military forces in Iraq required additional troops, more tanks and armored vehicles, and more body armor, rather than sophisticated supersonic bombers and exotic weapons systems. These elements were in short supply not due to any decision by John Kerry, or even Congress as a whole, but due to ill-advised decisions and inadequate planning by the White House, the Secretary of Defense, and the Pentagon.

In fact, in December of 2004, 21 months after the invasion of Iraq, a soldier confronted Secretary of Defense Donald Rumsfeld about the lack of armored vehicles including trucks and humvees. Not only did he report that soldiers had resorted to scavenging to improve their vehicles, but we soon learned that the producers of armored humvees had unused production capacity that no one in the government had asked them to use. A number of analysts stated that this was just one more example of poor planning and execution in the war, including the use of too few troops and our failure to anticipate the extended violent resistance during our occupation.

Rumsfeld's matter-of-fact response that he would have asked the same question if he were a soldier in the same position didn't help the situation nor did the president's statement. For many Americans, the more important question was why the president hadn't asked the question before the war, or in the summer of 2003 when the problem became apparent.

In a final absurdity, Bush's campaign ads claimed that he didn't start the war with Iraq -- once again blithely combining and confusing the war against Iraq and the war against terrorism. Despite statements from members of his administration and other officials as well as the 9/11 commission report that there was no direct link between the 9/11 attacks and Iraq or between Al Qaeda and Iraq.

Despite the fact that political expediency motivated many of the Bush administration's statements following the 9/11 attacks, the administration was quick to accuse Kerry and the Democratic Party of playing politics whenever it mentioned the 9/11 attacks. Its political ads continually attacked Kerry in vague, fear inducing terms echoing the 9/11 attacks and warned of the dangers of failing to reelect Bush. One of its ads during the last week before the election featured wolves roaming through the woods as symbols of terrorists and noted that Kerry had voted against a bill related to intelligence even after the first terrorist attack. Of course, they didn't mean the attacks of 9/11 as the ad implied. In small print, the ad tersely noted that the vote occurred in '94 -- 1994, after the first bombing of the World Trade Center in 1993 -- who knows what that vote from the past entailed, but the ad certainly didn't want you to ask.

While endorsing a president that led our country into an unfinished, dangerous, and costly war in Iraq without the approval of most of the global community, the Bush ads had the temerity to suggest that Americans must reelect the president if they want peace. They continued to speak of our supposed success in Iraq while violence still raged throughout much of the country and the rebuilding program proceeded only with great difficulty.

The actual actions of Republican Congress and the Bush administration over the past four years received much less emphasis. The ads didn't say much about their tax cuts for the wealthy and large corporations, the false justifications they used to wage a preemptive war in Iraq, and their confusing Medicare drug card plan that most analysts say is of little value. Instead, the ads tried to paint a reassuring, though fuzzy, picture of how Bush and the Republicans would do all those things in the future that they should have already done to protect and strengthen our country.

Joshua Green, in his article on Bush's chief political strategist "Karl Rove in a corner" in *The Atlantic Monthly*, provides numerous examples of Rove's audacious, ruthless, and unscrupulous approaches to political campaigns. So it was not surprising that the use of misdirection, confusion, and fear came to dominate the 2004 Bush reelection campaign.

Sheldon Solomon, a psychologist at Skidmore College, published research results in the December, 2004, issue of *Psychological Science* that help explain why this approach may be effective. In their research study, Solomon and his colleagues asked several groups of college students to choose between three candidates, one who emphasized the achievement of goals, another who emphasized cooperation, and a third who emphasized the nation's greatness and victory over evil. A control group gave only 4% of its support to this third candidate. However, another group, who the researchers had previously asked questions related to death and their own mortality, subsequently gave 30% of their support to the candidate who emphasized greatness and victory. The results suggest that fear for the future and the need for reassurance may have generated support for Bush among at least some voters.

Little wonder that many people weren't sure what to think. The campaign for a sitting president, with a questionable record in military service, ever changing positions on a costly, unresolved war in Iraq, an economic program that generated record budget deficits, and tax programs that created windfalls for the wealthy, continued to claim that a senator with a distinguished record of patriotism and service throughout his life was a flip-flopping danger to peace.

Meanwhile, the candidate with three Purple Hearts had to listen to arguments about whether his wounds -- three of them -- were sufficiently serious to merit those medals and whether his personal actions during combat were indeed worthy of his Bronze and Silver Stars. Once again, as illustrated in a series of *Doonesbury* comic strips in March of 2003, up was down. We had entered a new and not very attractive political wonderland.

Down to the wire

By the end of September, unscrupulous, smear tactics appeared to have cost Kerry his modest lead in the national polls. Bush reclaimed the lead by a small margin as the candidates prepared for their first debate. However, in a reversal of his success in his debates with Al Gore in 2000, the first debate showed a disgusted, smirking Bush hunched over the lectern looking like a confused challenger. Often repetitive in his responses and unable to fill his available time,

Bush's campaign sound bites became simplistic and inadequate. His long standing pattern of avoiding tough questions in press conferences, or even to listen to those who disagreed with him, came back to haunt him.

Kerry, on the other hand, looked and sounded like the incumbent president. He was knowledgeable, relaxed, and fully in control of the situation. He condensed and sharpened his often lengthy, and sometimes overly complex, campaign responses into crisp and articulate answers. The most difficult subject for Kerry to address was probably the Iraq War. Despite obsessive charges by the Bush campaign of Kerry's "flip-flopping," Bush and his staff continued to change their stories regarding their justification for the war on almost a daily basis. In addition, because of the problems that Bush had created for our nation in pursuing that unwise war, none of the available options were particularly attractive -- another reminder of the later years of the Vietnam War.

Some of this confusion carried over to the vice presidential debate held the following week between Dick Cheney and John Edwards. As had become his custom, Cheney continued to claim "an established relationship" between Iraq and Al Qaeda that was at odds with most independent sources. Although he insisted that he hadn't claimed there was "a connection between Iraq and 9/11," many people got exactly that impression from his continuing comments regarding Iraq and Al Qaeda.

In addition to their broad disagreement on almost every issue, they also presented very different appearances and personalities: Edwards was often smiling and effervescent; Cheney was often scowling and disgruntled. The post-debate analysis provided another example of the weaknesses inherent in our current media. In an effort to be "fail and balanced," reporters must find parallel shortcomings in both candidates. This may be one of the reasons that some voters felt so confused. Every time a candidate made a questionable statement, the media offered a counter-example by the other candidate. However, these counter-examples were seldom equal and parallel.

For example, to balance Cheney's highly questionable statements linking Iraq, Al Qaeda, and 9/11, one report noted that Edwards had stretched the facts by claiming the war in Iraq had cost $200 billion. It turns out that although we had not yet literally spent the money, Congress had, in fact, authorized expenditures totaling that amount through the end of the fiscal year starting on October 1, 2004 -- not much of a stretch, particularly in light of still greater expenses to come. Cheney also challenged Edwards' claim that 90% "of the coalition casualties" were Americans. Cheney insisted that the number was about 50% if you include Iraqi deaths -- but the coalition did not include Iraqis and there was no reliable data on Iraqi deaths.

Beyond these details, the emphasis by Kerry and Edwards on the need to work with others, to give more attention to domestic safeguards, and to address problems of jobs and health care for the middle class provided a clear and positive alternative to the policies of the Bush administration.

Most observers, including many Bush supporters, felt Kerry won the first debate. Although Bush was more effective in the second and third debates than he had been in the first, most observers felt that Kerry had won all three encounters. National polls suggested that the race had again returned to a virtual dead heat.

Five days before the election, my wife and I attended a massive rally for John Kerry in downtown Madison. A crowd of 80,000 supporters filled the broad street leading westward from the state capitol building. A hopeful spirit filled the air. Both major candidates spent the remaining days before the election flying back and forth to attend similar rallies in important "swing" states such as Wisconsin, Florida, and Ohio.

In the final days of the campaign, the lead news story was the discovery that hundreds of tons of high-grade explosives were missing in Iraq. The initial and all too typical reaction of the Bush administration was to suggest that the explosives may not have been in the storage bunkers when we invaded the country. However, subsequent news footage from a Minnesota television news crew confirmed that our troops had inspected the explosives cache soon after our occupation of Iraq began. Despite warnings from the United Nations' International Atomic Energy Agency, we had failed to secure it against theft. The incident provided yet another example of our mismanagement of the invasion and occupation of Iraq.

In light of foreign opposition to the Bush administration, it's not surprising that many Europeans expressed frustration over their inability to influence an election in a country that holds so much power over the rest of the world. Most Europeans favored Kerry by a wide margin, including Britain, one of our allies in Iraq. They preferred Kerry's multilateral perspective and worried over what one commentator called Bush's "messianic message."

Kerry also received support from unusual quarters in the United States. A few days before the election, Gary Comer, the founder of Lands' End in Wisconsin, personally paid for a full page newspaper ad opposing Bush's reelection. Comer stated that although he had voted Republican for most of his life, he felt that the Bush administration was taking the country in a dangerous direction. A number of newspapers that generally endorsed the Republican candidate echoed similar comments and decided to endorse Kerry.

Despite the uncharacteristic opposition in the media to a president who had failed the country in so many ways, the former mayor of New York City, Rudolph Giuliani, in a statement of towering hyperbole, favorably compared Bush with Abraham Lincoln. He claimed that Bush had an "overarching vision" much like Lincoln. Of course, Giuliani didn't note that Lincoln's vision was of a government "of, by, and for the people," while the Bush administration too often adopted policies viewed by many as "of, by, and for the rich and powerful."

As the nation counted down the final hours to the 2004 election, a chasm divided supporters of Bush and Kerry. Many Bush supporters saw Bush as a spokesman for their particular moral and religious values. Others endorsed his unqualified embrace of global capitalism, deregulation, and privatization. Still others saw a strong leader who had taken the reins following the 9/11 attacks and led our nation forward in its fight against terrorism.

Kerry supporters endorsed his distinguished military record, his willingness to confront difficult issues, and his experience in Congress. In contrast to Bush, they saw Kerry as a knowledgeable leader who brought an ability to handle complex problems, who emphasized multilateral approaches, and whose policy proposals reflected an understanding of the problems of middle and lower income Americans. Contrary to Bush's campaign rhetoric, they saw Bush as a president who had flip-flopped his positions on an almost daily basis regarding Iraq, the war on terrorism, and many other subjects, while serving the rich and powerful.

Even more than in 2000, there were real and substantive differences between the candidates in the 2004 election. And just as in the 2000 election, polls suggested that going into the election support for each was about equal.

♫ ♫ ♫

"In order to form a more perfect union" is another goal of our government according to the Preamble to the Constitution. At a time when many of our political leaders worry more about their own power and control than any commitment to unifying our people, it is a good time to recall this phrase. We need to pay more attention to restoring and maintaining our democratic processes. The 2004 election offered a choice between an incumbent who had repeatedly demonstrated a willingness to intimidate the media, dominate the judiciary, suppress any opposition, and distort our elective system and a challenger with a distinguished record of service and commitment to our democratic processes throughout his life.

Chapter 12

The 2004 presidential election

...persevering under adversity...

♫ ♫ ♫

The beginning student sometimes finds it difficult to even produce a sound on the violin. With a bit of practice most students are soon able to pass this hurdle, but it remains a challenge to produce strong, clear notes. Even intermediate students struggle to maintain a good sound while playing complex slurs and string crossings. They must apply a subtle combination of precise pressure and fluid movement to produce a beautiful tone as they guide the bow through ever more complicated motions. The need to incorporate vibrato to produce the quavering note that adds interest to music presents yet another challenge for students. It takes a strong commitment to continue in the face of these many difficulties, not unlike the perseverance required to accomplish any worthy goal. As with life itself, the violin is impossible to master, but offers moments of sublime beauty that make the effort worthwhile.

The 2004 election

November 2, 2004, was Election Day. Much had changed over the past two years. The United States had engaged in what many saw as its first preemptive war against a nation that had neither attacked nor posed an immediate threat to our country. We remained embroiled in the chaotic aftermath of our invasion with no end in sight to the ongoing violence to Iraqis, Americans, and other nationalities. The economy was struggling to emerge from recession, and the nation had seen a net job loss over the past four years. The sharp divisions in the country were evident at many local polling places. In some cases, election officials had moved the voting stations to larger spaces to accommodate the expected crowds. Observers from various political groups monitored the voting.

The early election returns suggested that the race would be just as close as that between Bush and Gore, four years earlier. The same red states for Republican wins and blue states for Democratic wins began to slowly fill the presidential map. By the early morning hours of November 3, Bush had 254 electoral votes, while Kerry had 252 including Wisconsin, with 270 required for victory.

Three states still appeared too close to call -- New Mexico with 5 electoral votes, Iowa with 7 votes, and, most importantly, Ohio with 20 votes. Both candidates needed Ohio to win the presidency. As the morning wore on, it became clear that Bush's margin in Ohio was holding at about 130,000 votes. Despite questions concerning various provisional and absentee ballots, about midday, Kerry decided there weren't enough votes available to make a difference and conceded the election to Bush. Additional details on the numbers surrounding the election are in the Appendix II.

As mentioned earlier, in the days and weeks that followed, numerous reports came forth of election abuses and irregularities at Ohio polling stations including long lines that discouraged many voters from voting. Many Kerry supporters believed that once again the election results, much like those in Florida four years earlier, did not reflect the will of the Ohio people.

Nonetheless, the lengthy and rancorous presidential election campaign had finally ended. An incumbent president who had used multiple, ever changing, reasons to justify a preemptive invasion of Iraq, who had delivered massive tax cuts to his wealthiest supporters, who couldn't provide a clear accounting of his military service in the air national guard, and who had a hard time thinking of any mistakes that he made, won reelection to the presidency of the United States.

A challenger who attacked Bush's costly mistakes in Iraq, who supported real improvements in domestic security, who criticized Bush's tax cuts for the wealthy and favoritism towards corporations, who supported middle class Americans, and who had a distinguished military record, lost the election under a smothering blanket of fear and unfounded accusations.

Fear was an important theme in the minds of many voters. Many Americans live their lives under a cloud of fear. They fear another terrorist attack, they fear they may lose their jobs, they fear they may lose their medical insurance, they fear the wrath of God, and they fear death. Bush's standard practice was to translate his own political agenda into language, often religious, that spoke to the fears rather than the hopes of these Americans. He spoke of an "endless" war against terrorism driven, presumably, by endless fear; told Americans that homosexual unions threatened the sanctity of the sacrament of marriage, even though for many people marriage is a state-sponsored secular ceremony. Out of fear, many people voted for a candidate who supported programs and policies that were often not very appealing, went against long standing American traditions, and often harmed the very people who supported him.

Many took offense at political rhetoric that used a specific brand of Christianity as a wedge between not only the political right and the political left, but also between Christian conservatives and Christian liberals. Bush frequently drew an identity between his personal views on moral issues and the views of Christian people, even though many Christians disagreed with his actions and policies. Some of his Christian opposition responded to this continued rhetoric with a campaign that noted "God is not a Republican."

Nonetheless, the religious right had little doubt that he was their candidate. After the election, one commentator suggested that some evangelical conservatives may even have a mystical belief that the reelected President was God's anointed representative. A post-election letter from a conservative Bush supporter to evangelicals, quoted by Hanna Rosin in *The Atlantic Monthly,* claimed that "God is indeed a Republican" who had helped reelect President Bush.

The result was what playwright Tony Kushner described in an interview as an "unholy alliance between theocracy and plutocracy" -- those who want to impose their religious beliefs on the nation and an elite who believe their wealth entitles them to a privileged role in our society. Ironically, there probably is relatively little overlap between the two groups -- good for building a winning coalition, but not necessarily a relationship that will last. The views of both groups have little to do the guiding fiction of "liberty and justice for all" that has inspired our country since its founding.

The aftermath

In the days following the 2004 election, many of those who had supported Kerry felt a deep sadness and depression. The extraordinary effort that they put into the race combined with the extreme closeness of the result made Bush's second victory almost intolerable. It did not help when Bush again vowed to unite the nation and in the next breathe claimed a mandate for action. He claimed that the election had given him considerable political capital and that he intended to spend it. The evangelical right demanded a political reward for their support during the election.

The Democratic Party had run a strong campaign with adequate funding to compete strongly at all levels. New grass roots organizations had enrolled supporters who worked for the campaign and raised money for advertising. Despite corporate control of much of the print and broadcast news media, a succession of best selling books and popular movies such as *Fahrenheit 9/11* and *Going Upriver* had informed the electorate about the failures of the Bush administration and the strengths of the Democratic ticket.

John Kerry and John Edwards had proven to be articulate, knowledgeable, and effective campaigners. They both excelled during their four televised debates with Bush and Cheney. The

Democratic ticket received support from many moderates, including Republicans, and endorsements from newspapers that had rarely, if ever, supported Democratic candidates. Although Kerry and Edwards made some mistakes, so did Bush and Cheney.

Nonetheless, the Democrats lost not just the presidency -- albeit in a race that was again very close in electoral votes, somewhat less so in the popular vote -- but across the nation in the majority of races for Congress. The sweeping success of the Republicans startled many observers. The Republicans won reelection to the White House for an incumbent whose first term was most notable for failure on almost every front. Already enjoying a 5-4 conservative majority in the Supreme Court on many decisions, the Republicans were in a position to appoint new conservative justices to replace those who might leave the court over the next four years. They solidified their control of the Senate, where they defeated the Senate Minority Leader, Tom Daschle. They also increased their control of the House thanks, at least in part, to the aggressive redistricting efforts linked by some to Republican congressional leader Tom DeLay.

A few weeks after their sweeping election triumph, the House Republicans voted to change their rules to allow DeLay to remain Majority Leader even if a grand jury indicted him. DeLay's colleagues claimed this rule change, loudly opposed by some Republican representatives, was necessary to protect DeLay from opponents who might conjure up charges anywhere in the country. In reality, they acted out of concern that a Texas grand jury investigating fund raising activities for a political action committee with close connections to DeLay might indict DeLay, as it already had three of his associates.

Most analysts attributed the redistricting plan in Texas, passed by a new Republican majority in the state house, as causing the defeat of at least four veteran Democratic congressional representatives from Texas. It is also likely that the new Republican representatives in both the Texas state house and the U.S. Congress owe some measure of their electoral success directly or indirectly to the political action committee being investigated by the grand jury. Unfortunately, actions by the new Congress will remain in effect no matter how many political operatives face indictment and whether or not the courts convict them.

The day after House Republicans approved this rule change, they passed an extension of the national debt limit without any restrictions on further tax cuts or spending by a vote of 208-204. Ten Republicans joined the Democrats in a losing effort to kill the measure. In the new Congress, such measures will be even more difficult to defeat due to the increased Republican majorities in both the Senate and the House.

A few days later, some of the dangers facing our country when extremists from one party dominate our government became quickly apparent. The House and Senate passed a $388 billion spending bill that included a highly controversial anti-abortion provision. Almost no one had read all of the 3000 page bill that many Democrats and Republicans had opposed. The effects of haste and limited review became embarrassingly apparent even to the bill's supporters when they learned that the bill also authorized the House and Senate Appropriations Committees to have access to federal income tax returns. The Republican leadership quickly decided to withhold the passed bill from the White House for the president's signature until Congress repealed this provision. No one knows for certain how many other bad ideas still remain in this massive bill.

Even with their almost complete control of all levers of the federal government, the White House moved quickly following the election to ensure that the president's cabinet for his second term would serve him without question or opposition. Senator Russ Feingold of Wisconsin spoke on the floor of the Senate about his concern that the appointment of Condoleeza Rice as Secretary of State sent the message that "the modest moderating influence of the State Department will disappear."

Other problems occurred with nominees who the administration did not properly investigate prior to announcing their nomination. For example, Bush's nominee for Secretary of Homeland Security, former New York City Police Commissioner Bernard Kerik, withdrew his nomination in light of questions concerning his employment of a nanny and other issues including a possible conflict of interest associated with a $6.2 million windfall from stock options in a stun gun manufacturer where he served as a director.

Continuing the administration's policy during Bush's first term of ensuring that he will see no opponents and no opponents will see him, officials announced security provisions for his inaugural parade that required every person attending the parade to pass through metal detectors. Fencing created a large security zone around the parade route and surrounding streets. Although some provision for security is obviously necessary, these measures did more to create a controlled environment for the inauguration than provide any significant additional improvements in security. As in Bush's campaign appearances, they muted or eliminated any possible political protests during the parade.

The Republican leadership in both Congress and the White House clearly believed that they had all of the answers and saw no need to consider alternative viewpoints even from those within their own party. Less than a month after the election, Speaker of the House Dennis Hastert reified this philosophy when he announced that Congress would only consider those bills that had the support of a majority of the House Republicans. Little more than 25% of the House members could block any legislative proposals. Even bills sponsored by individual House Republicans would not reach the floor for debate, much less balloting, if they did not have the support of a majority of Republican members. Neither the Democratic minority nor moderate Republicans who are a "minority of the majority" would have much influence over the content or progress of proposed legislation. Not surprisingly, Charles Babington reported in his analysis that senators from both parties as well as leaders of the September 11 commission strongly criticized the new policy.

This rule by a majority of the majority runs contrary to American traditions of fair play and respect for minorities. It also will prevent bills that have bipartisan support from a majority of both houses of Congress from even being debated on the floor of the House. Once again, up becomes down and even members of the majority may find it difficult to achieve their goals and move their legislation ahead.

This is far from idle speculation. Congress failed to pass an intelligence bill with broad bipartisan support in both the House and the Senate because of opposition by a majority of House Republicans. Conservative Republicans had been on the boundaries of real power for so long that they did not know how to function when they gained control of all three branches of government. We often speak of the need to be a good loser, but in some ways, it is more difficult to be a good winner.

Strategies for the minority

Despite their close loss in the presidential race, Democrats did not fare well in the 2004 election. In light of this harsh reality, one needs to question whether the Democratic losses across much of America were due to the weaknesses of their campaign tactics and candidates or simply due to the fact that many American do not agree with their values and policies. The reality, of course, is that there some truth to both statements. Nonetheless, it is important to remember that Kerry came very close to winning the election. Contrary to both Bush as well as some of the mass media, the election was no mandate for Bush and his conservative policies.

In fact, polls suggested that the election may have come just in time for Bush. By May of 2005, his ratings on specific issues had declined further, and a USA Today/CNN/Gallup poll found that his overall approval rating had fallen to just 46 percent. In June of 2005 as this book went to press, an AP-Ipsos poll found that only 43 percent approved of the job Bush was doing and only 41 percent supported the war in Iraq.

Despite this glimmer of hope, progressive liberals in our country will, for at least the next few years, have to learn how to function as a minority bloc in national politics. Throughout the ages, minorities have survived by functioning on the margins. By being adaptable and innovative they have often been able to achieve their goals even when strong majorities oppose them. They searched for opportunities in the nooks and crannies of the monolithic power structure of the majority. Rather than taking on fights that they are sure to lose, they looked for common ground with the majority or even a minority of the majority -- that is, they created new coalitions and redrew the political map.

Direct confrontation will not achieve their objectives. Instead, progressives will have to nudge the opposition in various ways and avoid reducing decisions to simple votes which they cannot win. Progress will only occur through the use of coalitions on specific issues and other creative approaches. Incremental change may also be achievable by working through committees and subcommittees. Additional opportunities to pursue progressive change exist at the state and local level where Democrats still retain considerable power. Independent agencies and institutions outside of government provide other alternatives. It may be necessary to compromise more and settle for less.

An early opportunity for Democrats in Congress may come as the Bush administration and its supporters attempt to privatize part of the Social Security system. Projections that show that the Social Security surplus will last until either 2042, according to the Social Security trustees, or 2052, according to the Congressional Budget Office. Even then, ongoing revenue from payroll taxes will sustain 75% of current benefits, even after adjustments for wage inflation. Relatively small adjustments in benefits, retirement age, or taxation levels could handle any projected funding problem. In fact, the Medicare program faces much more pressing financial problems.

Shortly after his reelection, Bush proposed allowing all but the oldest participants to set aside a portion of their Social Security contributions for their own private investment accounts. This proposed change would reduce the long term benefits that Social Security would have to pay, reduce the short term receipts that Social Security would collect (in the process, generating $1-2 trillion additional debt for the government), and provide a windfall of additional revenue for the investment industry. There is serious doubt whether the average worker would see a net benefit, and an unknown number would likely lose money due to poor investment decisions.

In order to garner support for this radical change in a fundamental societal contract with all working Americans, many expect the Bush administration to resort to its usual campaign proven techniques to manipulate public opinion. An article by Mike Allen and Jim Vandehei predicted that the Republican strategy would include bombarding Americans with a tightly scripted message that created and exploited fear. It came as no surprise that Bush was soon warning of the "crisis" in the Social Security system and its looming "bankruptcy" despite facts to the contrary. Whether the Republican goal is to help their friends in the financial community or simply to dismantle the Social Security program, bit by bit, is unclear. In either case, the problems with this radical and unnecessary proposal should provide ample motivation for a strong coalition to join in opposition.

It will not be easy. An administration that had outrageous success in painting John Kerry as a "flip-flopper," while President Bush changed his position on virtually every topic on a weekly basis, will not hesitate to do the same over Social Security. For example, despite the description by many politicians including the president, as well as the news media, of the administration's proposals as attempts to privatize Social Security, the administration began admonishing everyone not to refer to their proposals as privatization or creating private accounts. This is because polls indicated much less support when using these words. They insisted on labeling these accounts as "personal" accounts rather than "private." Once again, the label was more important than the content, which stayed the same.

In early 2005, House Democrats demonstrated how to be effective as a minority by passing a rule requiring their leadership to leave their positions if a grand jury charges them with a felony. Not wishing to allow the Democratic minority to gain any political advantage, the Republicans quickly followed suit. They rescinded the rule they had passed in November that would have allowed Senate Majority Leader DeLay to retain his position even if a grand jury in Texas indicted him. Meanwhile, Democrats remained opposed to Republican changes in the membership and rules of the House ethics committee that make it easier to obtain a dismissal of ethics complaints. As a result, Democrats have blocked work of the committee insisting that the Republicans reverse these changes.

Senate Democrats, virtually ignored by the Republican majority, also announced that they would be holding oversight hearings under the auspices of the Democratic Policy Committee, a policy and research arm of the Senate Democrats that is not under the control of the Republican majority. Although it does not have subpoena powers, it can still hold investigative hearings with willing whistleblowers and others who wish to provide public testimony on issues that they believe are important. Clearly, the Democrats had finally found the means and the desire to assert their rights and those of their supporters in the halls of Congress.

There are other approaches that the minority can pursue when the majority blocks their path. The decision in November of 2004 by California voters to fund stem cell research at the state level provides one example. In his first term, Bush had placed severe restrictions on federal funding of stem cell research. Because of these restrictions, many researchers and investors were concerned that our country may lose its leadership position in this emerging technology. California, with an economy larger than many nations, has now taken a big step towards remaining an important player in this field.

Surprisingly, in May of 2005, there was also encouraging news regarding stem cell research from Congress. The House passed legislation that would allow federal funding of stem cell research using discarded embryos from fertility clinics by a margin of 238 to 194 with substantial bipartisan support. Although the margin was large, it was not sufficient to override an expected Bush veto -- it would be his first -- if the legislation also passes the Senate. Nonetheless, this was very good news both scientifically and politically. It likely will encourage alternative funding sources for additional stem cell research. It may also slow down efforts by conservative forces to criminalize certain areas of embryonic stem cell research which would only increase the flight of researchers to Europe and elsewhere to pursue their research.

Perhaps most significantly, the bipartisan support that this legislation received, despite strong opposition from both the House leadership and the White House, revealed an important crack in the current conservative coalition. If moderate Republicans and Democrats can work together to support stem cell research, there may be other opportunities for them to work together without the blessing of the ideologically extreme party leadership.

Another encouraging example occurred in the debate over Democratic use of the filibuster against Bush judicial nominees. The Republican leadership threatened to use the so-called nuclear option, discussed in Chapter 8, to change the long-standing rules of the Senate if the Democrats used the filibuster. Despite the controversy over Republican use of the nuclear option, it seemed that this was a battle that the minority Democrats could not win. However, at the eleventh hour, a group of 14 senators -- 7 Republicans and 7 Democrats -- reached agreement that the group would oppose any rule changes and would allow a vote on three of the Bush nominees opposed by the Democrats.

The driving spirit behind the agreement appeared to be a shared desire to preserve the rules of the Senate. Nonetheless, the agreement did an end run around the leadership of both parties. Democratic

Senate leader, Harry Reid seemed little concerned since he noted that the agreement resembled many of the offers that he had previously made to Republican leader Bill Frist. However, despite trying to put the best face on the situation, Frist's desire to break the filibuster had failed. Consequently, at least for the time being, the filibuster remained available for potential use in the much more important debate over the next Supreme Court nominee.

It remained uncertain whether the agreement would hold and whether the group of 14 would be able to tackle other thorny issues before the Senate. Without the votes of the 7 Republican senators in the group, the remaining Republicans have only 48 votes -- not enough to pass anything by themselves. Clearly, the group of 14 could constitute a new moderate coalition that could control the Senate if they desired. Most importantly, whether or not they choose to remain together at least for some purposes, their success in resolving the filibuster crisis revealed a weakness in the conservative leadership that remains for others to exploit.

Reflections on the election

Besides having to learn how to function effectively as a minority bloc over the next few years, progressives must also identify paths to strengthening their political power. Former president Bill Clinton issued a call for Democrats to do a better job of letting small town and rural America know that the Democratic Party believed in "faith and family...work and freedom." This should not be difficult since many Democrats and liberals in our country are, in fact, among our most active church members. As we look to the future, it is important to remember that the religious right is simply one voting bloc, among many in our country, that does not even speak for all Christians.

Thomas Frank, in his book *What's the Matter With Kansas?* notes that conservatives have virtually erased economic and business issues from the political agenda. Perhaps unwittingly, Clinton and the so-called New Democrats in the 1990s contributed to the problem by taking economic positions that were often nearly indistinguishable from those of the Republican Party. In order to be successful, Democrats and liberals need to bring economics back into the national political debate. They need to emphasize the real differences that exist in the priorities of Republican and Democrats regarding economic and business issues.

John Podesta, a former Clinton White House chief of staff, noted in a *Time* magazine article by James Carney that the election was less about John Kerry, the person, than about the direction of the country. The political movement that opposed Bush is unlikely to collapse just because its candidate lost. As a consequence, the upcoming years are likely to be extremely contentious. Columnist Bob Herbert and others called for Kerry supporters to get back to work at the nuts and bolts level of politics -- supporting good candidates, running for office, attending meetings, raising money, and so on.

Finally, some well-meaning commentators suggested that it was time to bury the hatchet and give Bush a chance. Andy Rooney in a commentary following the election on CBS' *60 Minutes* called for us to support our president. In his call to support Bush, Andrew Sullivan, in *Time* magazine, lumped Michael Moore and MoveOn.org into the same category as the Swift Boat Vets. Recognizing the widely divergent views of all three, it is difficult to deny that the Swift Boat Vets moved far beyond mere partisan arguments of the sort used by Moore and MoveOn. The Swifties resorted to smear tactics against Kerry that were often absurd and motivated by hatred that went back more than 30 years.

These calls to support Bush and his administration fail to take seriously his consistent lack of interest in compromise or working with others. Should we support Bush as he threatens other countries? As he continues to place our country outside the laws and conventions of the international community? As he proposes more help for the wealthy while dismantling the safety net for middle and lower income taxpayers? As he proposes costly, unnecessary, and risky changes to Social Security? As he pursues new reductions in environmental protections? As he weakens our constitutional rights through his appointments of judges favoring the evangelical agenda and a new attorney general with questionable views on the treatment of prisoners? As he fails to support women, homosexuals, and minorities in their continual battle for fair treatment?

This is not a new president. This is a president with a proven track record, even if he and many voters paid little attention to it during the 2004 election. There is little reason to give this president the benefit of the doubt much less a new "honeymoon" when he has made his divisive views so clear. In his second inaugural address, President Bush spoke in high sounding rhetoric about liberty, freedom, and human rights. However, the Bush administration's endorsement of the repressive Patriot Act, its unilateral decision to invade Iraq, and its treatment of our prisoners in Iraq and Guantanamo Bay fell far short of his stated ideals. Rather than inspiring, many saw his comments as simply one more attempt to put a better face on our misguided invasion of Iraq -- yet another example of packaging over substance.

Not surprisingly, Bush followed up his inaugural address with a State of the Union speech in which he returned to form and, as one headline stated, failed to tell the whole truth. According to that article, Bush failed to note that his Social Security proposals will include smaller Social Security checks for future recipients, neglected to report that despite some recent job gains there had been a net job loss over the preceding four years, and once again linked the invasion of Iraq to the war on terror despite little, if any, justification.

From this speech, it sounded like Bush's second term will continue the same shopworn themes of his first four years in office. By June of 2005, public opinion polls showed continued slippage of support for his actions in Iraq, his Social Security proposals, and his overall approval rating. More than 1600 U.S. troops had lost their lives in the Iraq War along with a much larger number of Iraqi soldiers and civilians. Total expenditures and funding requests for the war exceeded $300 billion.

About the same time, the so-called "Downing Street memo" triggered widespread discussion over the statements of the Bush administration prior to its invasion of Iraq. The memo, believed by many to be authentic as of this writing, contains the minutes of a high level British meeting in July of 2002, at which a British official reported on his meetings with U.S. officials in Washington. It notes that military action by the U.S. in Iraq was seen as "inevitable," "Bush wanted to remove Saddam," and that "intelligence and facts were being fixed around the policy." Michael Smith, who writes for the *Sunday Times of London,* also suggests that the U.S. increased bombing in the no-fly zone in the summer of 2002 -- the "spikes of activity" in the memo -- to provoke Iraqi retaliation and justify full scale bombing. Many believe that the memo and related documents, if valid, further demonstrate the lies and deceptions of the Bush administration during the prewar debate.

The White House quickly modified its knee-jerk reaction that the claims in the memo were "flat out wrong" when the high level source of the memo became apparent -- yet another flip-flop. British officials did not challenge the validity of the memo and simply stated that it contains nothing new. Nonetheless, although the full impact of the memo remains uncertain, the issue refused to go away.

Facing these unpleasant realities, Bush gave a speech to the nation on June 29, 2005, that once again shifted the focus in Iraq. Rather than democracy, he returned to the alleged connection between Iraq and the September 11 terrorist attacks despite lack of evidence of any substantial connection between the 9/11 terrorists or Al Qaeda with Iraq. Nonetheless, Bush invoked the 9/11 attacks five times in his speech saying that "Our mission is clear. We are hunting down the terrorists," attempting to return to the issue and time that brought him his greatest popular support.

However, Stephen J. Hedges in his analysis in the *Chicago Tribune* quoted even U.S. commanders as saying that the Iraqi insurgency is only partially composed of Islamic terrorists. Hedges characterized Bush's efforts as "rebranding" the war in Iraq, which was beginning to resemble a difficult guerilla war rather than conventional warfare.

Iraq held elections at the end of January, 2005. Members of the Sunni minority virtually abstained from the election in which a Shiite coalition won the most votes. It remained unclear where the Shiite coalition would take Iraq, how the Sunnis would react, and how long violence would continue to disrupt Iraqi society.

Following the 2004 presidential election, the Bush administration and its ideological partners declared that they had received a mandate from the people. However, champions have always found that it is at least as hard to stay on top as it is to get there. Jared Diamond in his book, *Collapse,* noted that civilizations often begin a rapid decline shortly after the apogee of their success and power. Success creates problems and is often not sustainable -- a disturbing thought for the Bush administration as well as our nation.

♫ ♫ ♫

"Perseverance" is another American guiding fiction mentioned in the book *American Virtues, Values and Triumphs.* The United States has a long tradition of priding itself on its willingness to do whatever it takes to accomplish its goals. This attitude was a necessity for a people comprised primarily of immigrants who had left their past behind them, and whatever security it offered, to live in a new land. They had to succeed in their new lives; they didn't have any attractive alternatives. And so, they persevered. Perseverance brought this nation success in such varied efforts as its war for independence, the building of the first transcontinental railroad, its pursuit of victory in World War II, and its race to the Moon. It will take perseverance to overcome the political and economic challenges that we are facing today in order to achieve a "new birth of freedom."

♫ ♫ ♫

Interlude three

Transformations

♬ ♬ ♬

Change and personal identity

...on letting go

♫ ♫ ♫

The bow plays a critical role in creating a rich, beautiful tone from the violin. It is not unusual for the bow used by a serious musician to cost a significant fraction of the cost of their violin. Learning how to properly use the bow is extremely difficult. It resembles making a wine glass "sing" by lightly running a moist finger tip along edge of the wine glass. Although the glass may feel smooth, your finger is actually creating minute vibrations by sticking and sliding as it moves around the rim. In the same fashion, the hairs of the violin bow, coated with a layer of rosin, slide across the strings in a series of microscopic sticking and sliding movements. This "sticktion" -- sticking friction -- causes the string to vibrate at a pitch determined by its length. The pressure on the bow cannot be too heavy, nor too light. When the pressure is just right, the string "sings" to create the beautiful sounds that we all enjoy. In the same way, our lives and the life of our nation depend on the proper balance between freedom and control.

The need for control

Today, many people in our nation have an obsessive need for control. The terrorist attacks of 9/11 have reinforced their fear that life will turn chaotic if it is not subject to tight controls. In their attempts to achieve a sense of security, they try to control whatever they can. They seek to criminalize any activities of which they disapprove, support harsh punishment for those who break the law without much regard for the circumstances, and accept the need for more prisons, while resisting efforts to build new schools. They support political candidates who will place legal constraints on their neighbors' social behavior, while accepting economic policies that benefit the elite few at their expense.

The alternative to control is cooperation. Those who seek cooperation rather than control see a need for more schools and fewer prisons. They see drug addiction as a disease not a crime. They see religious questions in shades of gray rather than black and white. They see birth control education and reproductive health programs as reducing the need for abortions and avoiding illness. They see the community and its government as responsible for all member of our society, for protecting our personal freedoms, and for ensuring a fair and level playing field in our economy.

Today, we need to "let go" as a nation: let go of our need for power and control, let go of our pride and arrogance, let go of our need for easy answers. We need to let go of our embrace of simplistic patriotism and religious clichés. We must learn to live with ambiguity, faith, and trust. Absolute answers are not always possible. Our national values and spiritual ideals are strong enough to survive uncertainty and change.

Letting go

As a freshman at Northwestern University, I was a conservative youth possessed of all of the idealism typical of that age. I grew-up in a middle-class family that had never sent anyone to college. Children of immigrants, my parent's generation worked hard and believed in the so-called old fashioned virtues. My father was a rugged individualist and staunch Lutheran. My grandparents raised my mother as a Roman Catholic, but she converted to the Lutheran faith when she married my father. The members of our family were active participants and leaders in our local church.

I was the obedient, overachieving, perfectionist, always trying to please my parents and teachers. I lived within the boundaries and assumptions that they presented to me. In 1964, I accepted the Bible as the literally inspired word of God and was a radical individualist who supported Barry Goldwater for President. I agreed with Goldwater that "Extremism in the defense of liberty is no vice. And...moderation in the pursuit of justice is no virtue." My world was black and white, good and evil. Clear as crystal -- simple.

During my freshman year at Northwestern University, I encountered students, professors, and a minister at our Lutheran student center who did not see the world in such primary colors. Shades of gray filled their worlds. They challenged my politics, my belief in a literal Bible, my basic assumptions about life. I learned theological distinctions and nuances that were new to me. My economics class presented new ways of viewing business, government, and the market economy. Every way I turned, I saw a very different world than the world I thought I understood.

At first, I strongly resisted these challenges to my personal beliefs. I was a successful debater in high school and enjoyed a good argument. However, as time went on, I found it increasingly difficult to reconcile my early beliefs with my rapidly evolving knowledge of the world. For awhile, I felt trapped between either having to forsake what I regarded as my essential identity or closing my mind to what I was learning.

When I least expected it, a transformation occurred. Late one night, while walking back to my dorm, it suddenly occurred to me that I *could* change my views without losing my personal identity. My spirituality did not depend upon a literal interpretation of the Bible. My individuality did not depend upon ignoring the needs of the community. My patriotism did not require blind support of the government. It was like a cloud had lifted. From that evening forward, the world was a different place.

Amazingly, I went to college to get an education and that's what I got. I could grow in new directions and consider new ideas. My world suddenly changed from black and white to a multicolored rainbow. Diversity, pluralism, and ambiguity emerged from a one-dimensional world of simple answers that were no longer adequate. I did not need to force my education to fit some preconceived view of the world. The result was liberating. I could move on.

Life resembles a helix more than a circle or straight line. When we meet old friends or colleagues, we often find that we still have many things in common. It feels like we have come full circle. However, we soon discover that the ends don't quite match. We have changed and so have they. Like a helix, we find that we have returned to a different place than where we were before.

Education works much the same way. When we encounter books, ideas, and experiences from our past, we often react to them as if they were new -- and they are for we are no longer the person we were. Similarly, when we return to the hard questions, we will often find that we have changed. If we grow, we will see them from a different perspective than before. Our answers will often change. Rather than being concerned, we need to see these changes as a fundamental element of being alive.

Violins and golf

For many of us, a rigid set of religious or political beliefs provides the foundation for the way in which we view the world. We are reluctant to leave the security of these beliefs due to fear that our world might collapse without them. We think that rigidly holding onto our beliefs is the only thing separating us from utter chaos and confusion. Ironically, the reality is quite the opposite. It is only by letting go that we are able to face reality and fulfill our potential as human beings.

I have enjoyed playing an occasional game of golf since I was a young boy. When I learned to play the violin, I saw surprising similarities between the violin and the game of golf. When I strike a golf ball, the harder that I try to hit the ball, the poorer the result. The more things that I think about as I swing, the more likely I am to hit a bad shot. My best shots occur when I swing in a smooth relaxed fashion without focusing too much on anything.

Similarly, the harder that I hold the violin bow, the more difficult it is to play well. When I try too hard to avoid making mistakes, my tense muscles make it harder to move the bow properly and create a good tone. I sometimes even forget to breathe. I do my best when I worry less about making mistakes, or even dropping the bow, and simply relax.

Part of the appeal of golf and the violin is in the way in which they are both a metaphor for life. Many of us hold our golf clubs and violin bows too tightly out of fear that we might lose control. We cling to the assumptions and beliefs in our lives in much the same manner. If we let go, we fear that life will go "out of control."

When I resigned from the corporate world, I found it hard to let go of the relationships, responsibilities, and activities of my position. I welcomed the new opportunities and freedom that my new lifestyle presented, but I worried about leaving the security of a regular paycheck and all of the other perks that come with being a corporate executive. I was fearful and reluctant to let go of the past. Gradually, I came to realize that it was time to move on. Only by letting go of the past was I able to create a new future.

When my mother and grandparents left Europe, a place to which most of them would never return, they had to let go of an entire lifestyle and culture. They did this to seek a better life for themselves as well as their children. Today, in much the same way, we must let go of old assumptions and misconceptions for the sake of our children and grandchildren. Fortunately, our children and grandchildren can help us in the process. They are experts at experiencing the new and learning from it. They do not cling to the past; they learn from it. As infants, they encounter the new by tasting, touching, listening. If they like it, they try it again; if they don't, they try something else. Their rate of learning and growing is prodigious.

This is the way that America once worked. We boldly experimented with new approaches to governing and living. Today, we have too often abandoned this adventurous spirit in favor of efforts to preserve a past that never was. It is time to learn from our past, not worship it. This will require us to abandon some of our old beliefs and accept some that are new. We may drop the bow a few times, but we can always pick it up again.

♫ ♫ ♫

As we let go of old assumptions and misconceptions, answers to questions that may have once satisfied us will often lose their appeal. When I talk to my grandchildren, they ask many of the same questions that we think about as adults. However, they have limited knowledge and experience. They do not expect the same level of detail that I might provide to an adult. I don't lie to them, but I also don't tell them the whole story. They will seek and receive more complete answers as they mature into adults. In the process, they will let go of the simplicity of those early explanations.

Part IV

♫ ♫ ♫

Religion, democracy, and the future

...liberty and justice for all...

♫ ♫ ♫

Chapter 13

From exclusivism to pluralism

...the blessings of liberty...

♫ ♫ ♫

Many musicians create sounds by pushing air, striking hammers, or plucking strings, but violinists usually create sounds using a bow. In addition to bowing techniques such as legato (smoothly connected notes) and staccato (sharply separated notes), they can also play martellato (hammering the strings with the bow), spiccato (bouncy strokes with the middle of the bow), richochet (throwing the bow at the strings) or pizzicato (simply plucking the strings without using the bow). The almost endless variety of musical instruments and playing techniques reflects the rich diversity of ways in which we live our lives. However, despite these differences, we share a common love of music with our neighbors. Music provides a link between the physical world that we encounter and the feelings that we experience. It inspires in us a sense of beauty and compassion enabling us to see new connections in our lives.

Religion in America

For some, an enduring image of our nation, found in an early 17th century sermon by John Winthrop, is that of "a city on the hill." Others speak of the United States as the new "promised land." These images presume a special place in God's plan for our nation. The nationalistic mixture of church and state underlying this presumptive and muddied theology is not only arrogant, but also dangerous.

The founders of this nation knew the limitations of humanity all too well. They recognized that people make mistakes. This is why they engineered a system of checks and balances among the forces within the government. Rather than heaven on earth, they saw our nation as "a great experiment" in freedom and liberty.

They also had a diversity of views on the role of religion in national life. Perhaps for this reason, the Declaration of Independence opens with the parallel construction of "the Laws of Nature and Nature's God." After affirming that "men" are "endowed by their Creator with certain unalienable Rights," it describes a great many grievances against the British king, and concludes with "a firm reliance on the protection of Divine Providence."

The limited number of oblique references to God in the Declaration of Independence reflects the struggles of the authors to find words that were acceptable to delegates with a wide range of beliefs. Similarly, the Constitution makes virtually no reference to religion or God until the First Amendment of the Bill of Rights which directs that "Congress shall make no law respecting an establishment of religion, or prohibiting the free exercise thereof" -- a broad guarantee of religious freedom.

Despite the conflicted beliefs of our founders over religion and God, Dean A. Murphy, in a 2004 article in *The New York Times,* discusses how some extremists insist that religion has always played a central role in out country. In reality, from the earliest days of the Republic, the role of religion and the exact degree of separation between church and state has remained blurred. We accept such practices as the presence of chaplains in various units of government and the use of the Bible when administering oaths of office. Our coins and currency include the phrase "In God We Trust." In the 1950s, the nation's concern about "Godless" communism led to the addition of the phrase "under God" to the Pledge of Allegiance.

However, despite these public references to God and religion, there has always been a strong belief in the separation of church and state. While I was growing up in the fifties and sixties, there was a line, even though sometimes fuzzy, between what went on at church and what happened at school. Most of us did not know much about the religious beliefs and practices of our classmates unless they were among the relative few who attended our own church.

From 1900 to 2000, the percentage of Americans who claimed to be Christians, though still very high, has declined from about 96% to 84%. The percentage of Americans belonging to a mainstream Protestant denomination declined from about 46% to 23%. The growth of more conservative, independent churches not affiliated with any mainstream denomination has partially, though not completely, masked this dramatic decline. The percentage belonging to these independent churches increased from about 7% to 28%. The diverse membership of the Roman Catholic Church has increased more moderately from about 14% to 20% of all Americans.

Oddly enough, as overall support for religion has gradually declined, religion in public life has significantly increased, perhaps due to the more activist stance of many remaining adherents. Today, it has become customary for presidents from either party to close their speeches with the phrase, "...and God bless the United States of America." There are regular demands for the inclusion of public prayers in schools, the issuance of vouchers for private schools, and the posting of the Ten Commandments in public buildings.

The Declaration of Independence states that governments derive "their just Powers from the Consent of the Governed," but an article on the display of the Ten Commandments quoted Justice Antonin Scalia stating that "the government derives its authority from God" -- this may be his personal belief, but it is inconsistent with our founding documents. The same article quoted the disturbing suggestion by Justice Anthony Kennedy that "if an atheist walks by, he can avert his eyes and think about something else."

Despite the generally more conservative era of my youth, we could not have imagined that the government would ever move so close to direct endorsement of specific religious beliefs. Today, more than a few politicians draw a virtual identity between the United

States and fundamentalist Christianity. In June of 2005, a chaplain at the Air Force Academy expressed her concern that a report by a task force responding to complaints of religious harassment of cadets by evangelical Christians failed to address the misuse of power and position at the academy to promote “a certain religious ideology.”

Some religious leaders are also taking a more active role in the political arena. When I was young, many people scoffed at accusations that religious pressures might influence the decisions of President John F. Kennedy, a Roman Catholic. However, over forty years later, before the 2004 elections, a Wisconsin bishop of the Roman Catholic Church sent letters to several Roman Catholic state legislators stating that their spiritual future depended on their opposition to any legislation supporting abortion rights. Local priests received instructions to deny access to Holy Communion to those political leaders who failed to comply with his demand. Similar restrictions apparently applied to those who supported legislation related to euthanasia or the use of birth control.

One legislator subsequently asked whether the bishop’s ban would also apply not only to legislators, but also to those Catholics who vote for legislators who support abortion rights and so on. Another Roman Catholic bishop in Wisconsin gave a partial answer when he told voters to base their votes foremost on opposition to abortion and same-sex marriage. Another church leader, during an interview on *Fresh Air* on National Public Radio, stated that voters could vote for someone who supported abortion as long as they did not cast their vote primarily on intentional opposition to the church’s teachings, whatever this exactly meant in practice. This speaker’s notable use of the word “man” in reference to elected officials and his confrontational description of pro-choice individuals as “anti-life and pro-abortion” -- two terms that few, if any, in the pro-choice movement would accept for themselves -- certainly made his personal feelings crystal clear.

Along the same lines, an article by Richard N. Ostling following the installation of Pope Benedict XVI noted that during the 2004 presidential election campaign, the former Cardinal Joseph Ratzinger wrote that a bishop has the right to deny Communion to those who disagree with the church after meeting with them to issue a warning. Needless to say, many conservative Christians in the U.S. welcomed the new pope as an ally in their efforts to impose their religious views on society as a whole.

Much like Pope Benedict XVI, many conservative religious leaders, in addition to their opposition to abortion, homosexuality, and in some cases, birth control, also oppose stem cell research, particularly if it involves embryonic stem cells. As is so often the case, the Bush administration tried to have it both ways. It announced a "compromise" in which the federal government would support research using existing stem cell lines, but not research involving the creation or use of new lines. Due to the small number of available stem cell lines and questions concerning their long term viability, this position was hardly a compromise. It severely restricted current and future research activities. Opponents to the administration's position included much of the scientific community as well as former first lady Nancy Reagan and such well known figures as Michael J. Fox.

The unfortunate battle over Terri Schiavo, a woman in a persistent vegetative state, was another example of the clash between the supporters of personal freedoms and medical science, on the one hand, and the advocates of state controls and rigid religiosity, on the other. Ideologues and evangelicals insisted that Terri Schiavo was conscious and that her condition could improve. Senate Republican Majority Leader Bill Frist even questioned the medical diagnosis that she was in a persistent vegetative state, though he only observed Terry Schiavo via videotape. After she died following removal of her feeding tube, an autopsy revealed that her brain was half the normal weight, she was blind, and the damage to her brain was irreversible. Evangelicals and their political leaders virtually tripped over themselves trying to justify or reverse their previous comments.

Evangelicals and moderates also battle over evolution. Some school boards seek to attach disclaimers regarding evolution to their textbooks to the dismay of most scientists as well as many moderate religious leaders. They inaccurately argue that evolution is simply a theory that many scientists do not support. In fact, the vast majority of scientists consider evolutionary theory a well-documented explanation of the development of species. Although the details are subject to continued refinement as new knowledge accumulates, the theory of evolution has no competition in mainstream science.

Scientists use "theory" to describe much of our scientific knowledge -- the theory of relativity, quantum theory, solid state theory, and so on. This does not mean they are just guesses. We use these theories to build bridges and fly airplanes. Virtually all scientists accept them as reasonable descriptions of how the world works. The continuing attacks on evolution from fundamentalist Christians, most recently under the guise of "intelligent design," are simply attempts to impose their religious beliefs on society. Their efforts undermine our constitutional rights, detract from the spiritual insights of others, and threaten our future health and prosperity by suppressing scientific knowledge and research.

The founders of our nation favored tolerance over endorsement when it came to religious questions. The United States has a long history, with only a few exceptions, of allowing its citizens to think, believe, or be guided by whatever they desire. However, the Constitution does not allow us to impose our religious beliefs on others by codifying them into law. It is the desire of activist religious fundamentalists to impose their particular version of morality on the nation as a whole that lies at the heart of the intense political disputes that are dividing our nation. Rather than simply expressing their beliefs through their lives, religious fundamentalists also wish to control the lives of others.

In his essay in *The New York Times Book Review,* Mark Lilla suggests that the focus of American religion is moving from the reality-based faith that thinkers of the Enlightenment envisioned towards a faith-based reality. Today, many fundamentalists not only simply see reality through the filters of their personal beliefs, but they are attempting to make this reality conform to these beliefs. Some commentators, including retired Episcopal bishop John Shelby Spong in a 2005 essay in the *Chicago Tribune,* worry that fundamentalist religious leaders and politicians are attempting to change our nation from a democracy to a theocracy. These religious zealots justify their political views simply by invoking the name of God.

Ironically, the religious beliefs of fundamentalists in our country have many similarities with the extremist religious beliefs of those who carried out the 9/11 attacks. They share an opposition to the separation of church and state, have a low tolerance for opposing views, dismiss the findings of science, and distort history to conform to their beliefs. Both groups also claim an exclusive relationship with God: they believe that God is on their side.

Many conservative voters saw their vote in the 2004 election as an endorsement of their Christian values in a world threatened by both secular Americans as well as non-Christian foreigners. However, when Bush and his supporters speak of their moral values and concerns, you won't hear much about the Sermon on the Mount. As suggested by Brett Hulsey in his column in *The Capital Times,* our invasion of Iraq, our abuse of prisoners, and our tax cuts for the wealthy do not go well with blessings for the peacemakers, the merciful, and the meek, loving your enemies, and laying up treasure in heaven rather than earth.

Following Bush's reelection in 2004, public support for the Iraq War among Americans began a steady decline as the number of lives lost continued to increase along with the level of violence and financial costs. A Gallup Poll at the end of April, 2005, indicated that the percentage who thought that it was worth going to war in Iraq had declined to 41 percent from 50 percent only a year earlier.

With little good news from Iraq and with his justifications for the Iraq War discredited, Bush tried to refocus attention on spreading democracy throughout the world. Apart from questions regarding the wisdom of telling other peoples how to run their countries, his new theme was not very credible considering the views of Bush and his evangelical Christian supporters. A liberal democracy, such as the United States, depends on the protection of individual rights and a spirit of tolerance, reform, and progress. Unfortunately, these are the very qualities that are missing among ideological and religious extremists who believe that they have all the answers. As expressed by Mark Lilla in the conclusion of his *New York Times* essay, a successful liberal democracy requires religious believers to incorporate liberal elements into their thinking.

Religious fundamentalists who view a country as more theocracy than democracy virtually erase the line between the personal and political. Azar Nafisi, in her book *Reading Lolita in Tehran,* explains that the personal and political in our lives, though interdependent, are separate and distinct. One of the primary goals of a democracy is to protect our rights in our personal lives. We do this by working together through our government. The consequence of blurring the line between the personal and the political, according to Nafisi, is to destroy both the personal and political. In such a world, rather than protecting our personal lives, the government intrudes on them. Rather than providing individuals a means for collective action, the government functions in isolation and secrecy.

Long before the war with Iraq became a public issue, Dominique Moisi, an analyst with the French Institute for International Relations, noted, in an article by Peter Ford in *The Christian Science Monitor,* that Bush's blurring of the line between religion and politics might not only threaten the international coalition against terrorism, but could also lead to a dangerous religious clash between civilizations. After the 9/11 attacks, many people urged restraint concerning our feelings towards Middle Eastern people or followers of Islam. They did not want "the war against terror" cast in religious terms of Christianity versus Islam. For this reason, Bush's reference to a "crusade" against terrorism generated criticism throughout the world.

James Carroll, in his article "The Bush crusade" in *The Nation,* discussed the parallels between "crusade" and "jihad." Both have strong religious connections to what Carroll describes as "apocalyptic conflict between irreconcilable cultures." Carroll further warns that wars against outside enemies often lead to persecution of those within. The original crusades led to persecution of the Jews in Europe. Similarly, we now see not only suppression of the rights of foreigners from the Middle East and elsewhere, but also of American citizens who participate in protests, attend public gatherings, or simply use their libraries.

On a larger scale, Carroll suggests that Bush's religious rhetoric places the war against terrorism on a cosmic scale as an ultimate battle between good and evil: the United States versus the "axis of evil." Such a perspective transcends traditional issues of public policy and diplomacy. As we respond to the "will of God," military sanity is an early casualty. We are free to attack whoever, wherever, and whenever we wish. Our aggressive stance drives others, friends and foes alike, to acquire their own weapons of mass destruction to protect themselves against our unpredictable actions. The world moves ever closer to Armageddon as the line between heaven and earth vanishes in the minds of those who would destroy the world in order to save it.

Legalists and progressives

As described by Hanna Rosin, in her *Atlantic Monthly* article "Beyond belief," the divisions within America are not simply between those who take a secular view of life and those with a religious perspective. Within the Christian tradition, there exist significant differences of belief. Rosin's traditionalists (religious legalists, fundamentalists) oppose abortion, gay rights, and stem cell research as violations of God's law. Rosin's modernists (spiritual progressives, religious moderates) see all three as acceptable and consistent to varying degrees with their Christian beliefs. Virtually all mainstream Christian denominations include members of both groups. In many ways, Catholic legalists have more in common with Lutheran legalists than they do with Catholic progressives.

Religious legalists and spiritual progressives bring quite different perspectives to the Bible. The religious legalists see the world as primarily flawed, a malevolent place. They consider all people as sinful beings, victims of original sin. Their focus is on God's harsh judgment for those who violate the Law. Drawing on images from the Old Testament, they often consider their own group or country as "God's chosen people" and prefer to think that God is on their side. They emphasize the need for control and often support tough law and order measures.

An alternative Christian perspective is that of the spiritual progressives who see creation as primarily good, a blessed place. They consider all people as part of God's creation. They don't believe that God chooses sides. Spiritual progressives focus more on the New Testament teachings and parables of Jesus, particularly the Sermon on the Mount. They emphasize the role of the community and a spirit of cooperation more than control. They favor hope over fear, grace over law.

Religious legalists are more likely to say that "God helps those who help themselves." This homily encourages individual initiative, but can be harsh and also discourages the spirit of neighborliness that is an American core value. Spiritual progressives are more likely to look to the Gospel directive to "love your neighbor as yourself." This directive encourages personal caring, but is not always possible and can allow your neighbors to avoid accountability for their actions.

Despite the sharp distinctions that I have drawn between religious legalists and spiritual progressives, the religious beliefs of church members in the United States fall on a continuum. There are many variations on these two primary themes that occupy different places on a line between the most extreme expressions of either perspective.

For many people, it is a question of emphasis. Most religious legalists also subscribe to the teachings of Jesus in the Sermon on the Mount and appreciate the need for compassion. Most spiritual progressives also appreciate the wisdom of the Old Testament and the need for law and order. This common ground provides a basis for discussion between individuals in both groups.

Sexuality and politics

The early Christian church evolved into a patriarchal and hierarchical structure that stressed power, control, and exclusivity. A small number of men wrote and selected the various books of the Bible as described by Elaine Pagels in her books *The Gnostic Gospels* and *Beyond Belief.* Despite the prominent role of women in many of the Gospel stories and throughout Jesus' ministry, the acceptable roles for women in the religious community became and, in many cases, remain sharply limited. While most mainstream Protestant denominations now ordain women as ministers, few serve as bishops, and the Roman Catholic Church, despite a serious shortage of priests, does not allow women to serve as priests.

Today, some evangelical politicians use sexuality as a wedge issue to sharpen divisions between groups. They speak of preserving the "sanctity" of marriage, despite the fact that marriage is not a sacrament for most Protestants and that the government has long performed secular marriages. They seek to restrict access to contraceptives and condemn their use even as population growth remains one of the most critical problems facing the world. They oppose abortion, even in cases when the woman's life is in danger, often while supporting cuts in social services and education for our children. They oppose research on stem cells that holds the promise of life and health for millions. They believe that life begins at conception, while ignoring the long tradition in Christian churches of not baptizing or holding funeral services for fetuses.

What is the common denominator in the opposition of religious extremists to birth control and abortion as well as the opposition of evangelical politicians and conservative extremists to minimum wage laws and improved access to health care? They most directly affect women. It is women who bear our children, who often take the primary role in raising them, who receive substandard wages for their work, who bear the brunt of restricted access to health care, and who are mostly absent from the halls of power, whether it is in business, government, or the church.

Many men have an obsession with achieving and maintaining power over others. Keeping women in their place is a key part of their philosophy. A few months before the 2004 election at the Republican National Convention, Arnold Schwarzenegger, the governor of California, spoke, perhaps jokingly, about economic "girlie-men" -- an amazing example, even in jest, of sexism, ageism, and arrogance in one brief phrase. Later, speaking at a reception, Tommy Thompson, secretary of health and human services and former governor of Wisconsin, reportedly said that if you don't vote for Bush "you truly are a girly man." Both comments, whether or not said in humor, suggest an obsession with masculine power and control. They also imply a fear of the feminine side of life that some men ridicule, but many do not understand.

No wonder that some men see homosexuality as a threat to the male dominance that underlies our culture. For them, seeing men or women in a homosexual relationship challenges their view of the dominant role of men in our society. Elayne Rapping, a professor of women's studies and media studies, suggested in a film commentary by Douglas Rowe that the relative lack of male nudity in films compared to female nudity is due to men's fear of the "male gaze" for homophobic reasons. People fear and suppress that which they don't understand, and for some men this includes homosexuality. We might add that many people oppose women's rights for similar reasons.

Homosexuality has become a touchstone for many of the conflicts between religious legalists and spiritual progressives. The Bible says very little about homosexuality. Those opposed to homosexual behavior point to a few isolated verses that appear to support their position. Others, point to ambiguities or inconsistencies in these verses that weaken the case against homosexual behavior.

For example, amidst pages of rules concerning our sexual nature and other often archaic matters in the book of Leviticus in the Old Testament of the Bible, the 18th chapter contains one verse that some interpret as prohibiting homosexual behavior between two males -- there is no comment regarding homosexual behavior between women. As a result, both sides endlessly debate how to parse the content of one brief sentence. Neither side mentions, much less follows, the many other obscure and obsolete prohibitions also contained in Leviticus. They don't provide grist for efforts to suppress the freedom of others and achieve political advantage.

There are a wide variety of family structures in our society including partnerships and marriages between young adults, middle-aged adults, and retired seniors. They may involve heterosexual or homosexual relationships and may or may not include children, adopted or biological. Many children live with single parents, whether unmarried, divorced, or widowed.

Spiritual progressives accept our sexuality as a good and natural part of God's creation. They support all relationships that are expressions of love and commitment between human beings regardless of their gender composition. They recognize that heterosexuals as well as homosexuals in loving, caring relationships express their human sexuality in a variety of ways.

Same-sex relationships that are loving and caring need the acceptance and support of society in the same way that it supports other healthy relationships. Spiritual progressives oppose discrimination based on gender or sexual orientation. They support an active and equal role for woman in the church, including ordination. They seek healing for abusive and dysfunctional relationships, regardless of the age, socioeconomic status, and gender orientation of those involved.

Religious legalists often see our sexuality in light of the Genesis story where Adam and Eve become aware of their nakedness in the Garden of Eden. For some, sexuality never escapes this early association with evil. They view sexuality as something to suppress and control. Despite abundant evidence to the contrary, they publicly acknowledge a narrow definition of acceptable sexual behavior and feel compelled to control the sexual behavior of others, regardless of their own personal behavior.

As a result of the limited discussion of homosexuality in the Bible and the divergent view of sexuality among progressives and legalists, arguments rage in many Christian denominations regarding same-sex unions and acceptable roles for homosexual or bisexual members and clergy. The American Episcopal Church's installation of a gay bishop brought forth strong objections from many members. Several congregations have already left the Episcopal Church, U.S.A. and either have or are in the process of aligning themselves with Anglican Churches in Uganda, Bolivia, and Kenya.

During the 2004 election, voters in 11 states approved constitutional amendments prohibiting same-sex marriages. Despite this opposition to same-sex marriage, polls have suggested that many Americans believe that same-sex couples should receive the legal benefits of marriage and be able to unite in civil unions. Unfortunately, 8 of the 11 amendments that passed also banned civil unions. In addition, some amendments could also endanger existing access to partnership benefits for same-sex households, even without same-sex marriage. A small minority will bear the economic and health costs of a politically expedient wedge issue.

These were far from the first efforts to restrict the rights of others on the basis of their sexual orientation. In 1996, as some states moved towards allowing same-sex marriages, Congress passed the Defense of Marriage Act (DOMA) to deny federal recognition of these marriages and to ensure that other states did not have to recognize their validity. However, as discussed by Steve Chapman in the *Chicago Tribune,* when the Massachusetts Supreme Court struck down that state's ban on same-sex marriages, conservatives also tried to pass an amendment to the U.S. Constitution banning same-sex unions across the nation. Curiously, despite the obsessive pursuit by conservatives of national uniformity in banning same-sex unions, there is no such uniformity regarding the marriage of first cousins -- about half of the states allow first cousins to marry and half do not.

After the failure of this effort in the Senate, the House passed the Marriage Protection Act in July of 2004. This act includes a provision banning any federal court from hearing challenges to state laws against same-sex unions -- an example of the growing popularity of the highly controversial and constitutionally uncertain practice mentioned earlier of "court stripping." Conservatives wanted to reserve to the states the authority to prevent such unions without judicial review. Ignoring constitutional issues concerning the division of power between the states and the three branches of the federal government, they continued to pander to the ignorance and fear of their supporters. Ironically, despite his campaign rhetoric, Bush announced soon after the 2004 election that he would not push the Senate to approve the stalled constitutional amendment banning same-sex marriage.

Much of the opposition to same-sex unions is particularly mean spirited. Not only does it fail to recognize successful, loving, same-sex relationships that have endured for years, but it occasionally harms those in heterosexual marriages as well. In December of 2004, an article revealed that the Social Security Administration was rejecting all marriage certificates for Social Security purposes from four cities that had performed gay weddings earlier in the year. At least temporarily, these heterosexual couples had no way of proving their marital status in order to get new Social Security cards or to draw benefits.

In an interesting footnote considering the concern of conservative voters for the "sanctity of marriage," an article by Pam Belluck following the election noted that many blue states have among the lowest divorce rates. The lowest rate is in liberal Massachusetts, while some of the highest rates are in states like Kentucky, Mississippi, and Arkansas that went strongly for Bush and supported constitutional bans on gay marriages. Many suggest that the lower divorce rates in blue states are due to higher educational levels, higher income levels, and greater stability in their communities, certainly positive characteristics. Perhaps conservatives should focus more on developing these characteristics rather than passing unnecessary laws to supposedly protect marriage.

Submission to authority

The Bible is a great spiritual text. Many Christians see the Biblical story of creation as a metaphorical description of the creative action of God. In the hundreds of pages that follow, powerful insights and wisdom coexist with stories filled with death, violence, and injustice, endless irrelevant genealogies, obsolete cultural beliefs, and often contradictory, impossible to understand verses. Most Christians recognize the need to apply some degree of interpretation and selectivity to their reading of these ancient writings.

We don't limit our selective reading of the Bible to the Old Testament. Jesus speaks of the difficulty that a rich man will have in finding heaven. Nonetheless, even religious fundamentalists rarely take a vow of poverty. Paul teaches that women should be submissive to their husbands. Most Christian churches in the United States rejected this admonition long ago.

Despite the important role of the Bible for virtually all Christian traditions, few church members accept its words without some qualification. They avoid or suppress what they don't like or agree with and follow, in some cases obsessively, what they believe to be correct. When the Bible appears to endorse their own views, they place it at the center of the debate with little desire to compromise. When the Bible does not endorse their own views, they closely analyze the syntax, language, and context in an effort to minimize the impact of the apparent content.

Whatever view one might take of the role of God in inspiring the Biblical texts, it is clear that it contains countless inconsistencies, inaccuracies, and misguided thoughts. It is our responsibility to use our collective intellect and experiences to discern the wisdom within the many distractions and irrelevancies that fill its pages. Most importantly, we need to let go of our use of the Bible as a "proof text" to support our personal prejudices and discriminatory beliefs.

Many Christians no longer depend on the literal interpretation of the Bible that has fueled so many arguments concerning evolution and scientific knowledge. Rather than using the Bible to fill the ever narrowing gaps in our scientific and historical knowledge, they see the Bible as a collection of powerful and evocative stories about life and spirituality.

Dietrich Bonhoeffer, a German Lutheran theologian who the Nazis executed at the close of World War II, suggested, in an outline of a book he would never be able to write, that using God as a "stop-gap for our embarrassments" was superfluous at a time when humanity had "come of age" -- that is, humanity had conquered nature with scientific knowledge and no longer saw a need for God or religion. In such a world, Bonhoeffer called for the church to follow the example of Jesus in the Gospels and live for others. Ironically, fundamentalist religious forces in the United States continue to deny what was so clear to Bonhoeffer sixty years ago. Rather than helping and serving through lives of patience and humility, they practice a religiosity that instead seeks to control the lives of others.

The literalism, absolutism, and legalism that cause so many conflicts among religious minded Americans may have their roots in the dysfunctional relationship that the early church had with the Roman authorities. Rome "simply" demanded complete submission to its rule in exchange for its protection. The church suffered persecution and abuse when it refused to give this "simple" obedience to Rome. Ultimately, much like its treatment by Rome, the church developed a theology that "simply" required complete submission to its exclusive views. It proceeded to persecute for two millennia those who refused to submit to it just as the Roman authorities had persecuted the early church.

Submission finds its political expression in countless totalitarian or dictatorial regimes throughout the world. Abusive personalities, leaders, empires, and ideologies demand submission. They do not seek cooperation or compromise, but focus on their own needs and desires without concern for others. They typically try to minimize their demands by claiming that they "only" desire obedience and respect. Their common response when confronted by their victims is to insist that their demands are "for your own good." Demands for submission typically lead to anger, conflict, and violence.

The response of an Anglican panel to the consecration of an openly gay bishop in the United States is highly instructive in this regard. The panel asked the American Episcopalian Church to apologize for its action and to not do it again without permission. Notably, it did not ask for the resignation of the gay bishop nor did it call for the expulsion of the American Episcopals from the worldwide Anglican communion. The panel focused its response on the need for the American church to submit to its authority rather than follow any moral or ethical imperative.

American political history contains similar evidence of the importance of submission to political leaders who bring this religious perspective on authority to their secular responsibilities. Jay Winik in his book, *April 1865,* quotes Abraham Lincoln's statement to Generals Grant and Sherman in March, 1865, regarding surrender terms for the Confederacy. Although Lincoln's terms, now known as the *River Queen* doctrine, were very generous, he also added the words, "I want submission" -- the demand of all those who, above all else, insist on imposing their authority over others.

As Winik notes, Lincoln held a mystical devotion to the idea of the Union. Maintaining the Union held a higher priority for him than questions regarding slavery or war and peace. In his Second Inaugural Address, Lincoln displayed his eloquence in rationalizing the bloodiest war in our nation's history through a combinations of dazzling rhetoric about the Union and fatalistic views of God's role in history. Despite the often quoted generosity of its final paragraph ("With malice toward none..."), Lincoln failed to acknowledge that the length of the Civil War was at least partially due to his demands for complete submission from the Confederacy -- not unlike the demands of the British Empire for submission by the colonies to its rule that led to the Revolutionary War.

For these reasons, it was not surprising to learn from John Dickerson in his article in *Time* magazine that George W. Bush took comfort from his reading of *April 1865.* Fond of fatalistic and religious rhetoric as was Lincoln, Bush wrote to Winik that he would stay the course, just like Lincoln. Unfortunately, Bush's obsession with loyalty from his staff and intolerance of any opposition also suggest parallels with Lincoln's demand for submission from the Confederate leadership. Many see Bush's obsessions and intolerance as shortcomings rather than strengths.

It is ironic that Bush, speaking at the dedication of the new Abraham Lincoln Presidential Museum in Springfield, Illinois, also compared his desire to spread liberty throughout the world to Lincoln's desire to emancipate the slaves in the Civil War. In fact, Lincoln was clearly willing to tolerate slavery as long as he could preserve the Union, didn't issue the Emancipation Proclamation until it seemed politically expedient, and only freed the slaves "in areas still in rebellion," rather than the entire country. Similarly, Bush belatedly found his desire to spread liberty when he couldn't find any weapons of mass destruction in Iraq, still maintained close relationships with many repressive foreign regimes, and showed little concern for the rights, liberties, and freedoms of Americans in his own country, particularly if they opposed his policies. There are parallels between George W. Bush and Abraham Lincoln, but they are not necessarily appealing.

Listening

This book, and particularly this chapter, focuses almost entirely on the role of western Christianity in our nation's political life. This is partially due to my own personal experiences and knowledge, but it also reflects the dominant place of western Christianity in the United

States, both today and in the past. As mentioned earlier, some of the most intense debates occur today between Christians with differing religious and political beliefs. However, the United States is, and has always been, a diverse country. There are thoughtful, caring people within many other religious traditions in this country as well as elsewhere in the world who also have important insights to offer.

As we move forward, we need to do a better job of listening. We need to pay more attention to what our critics are saying. We need to listen to our enemies. Following the 9/11 attacks, Diane Perlman, co-chair of the Committee on Global Violence and Security of Psychologists for Social Responsibility, noted that the media and our government treated the statements of Osama bin Laden out of context as unconditional threats, rather than conditional warnings. In the three examples that she presented, bin Laden warns of the consequences *if* we should use nuclear weapons, *if* we continue our oppression and aggression against Muslims, or *if* violence continues against Palestinians and Iraqis. Perlman noted that the media rarely included the full quotations with their conditions in its reports.

In addition to our opponents, we need to listen to those who have special knowledge. This includes scientists with professional knowledge and experience in such critical areas as global warming, oil reserves, missile defense, nuclear weapons, and biological research. Contrary to popular opinion, scientific opinion, though rarely unanimous, is often in strong agreement on such issues. Groups such as the National Academy of Science, the National Academy of Engineering, Union of Concerned Scientists, Physicians for Social Responsibility, among many others, often speak with a unified and authoritative voice on critical public policy questions. It is invariably possible to find individual experts who may disagree, but isolated voices on controversial topics should not outweigh the combined views of the vast majority of the scientific community.

Terry Eagleton, a professor of cultural theory, suggests, in his book *After Theory,* that we need to reexamine the foundations of our civilization. He noted that liberation theology and feminist theology may be useful starting points as we begin this process of reexamination and renewal. Liberation theology sees the Christian message as providing a voice for the poor and oppressed while feminist theology reinterprets Christianity to provide a voice for those outside of the centers of power in our patriarchal culture.

Many of the poor and powerless in this nation as well as the Third World are women. We need to listen more closely to their views and experiences. Ursula Le Guin, in her widely acclaimed speech at Mills College "A Left-Handed Commencement Address," noted the reality of failure in our success driven society. Women bring a unique perspective on loss. They must daily deal with the dark side of life that includes caring for the weak and sick, accepting the irrational, and cleaning up the dirt. Many men also live their lives under the clouds of defeat and loss. They have much to gain by listening more closely to the voices of women.

We also need to listen to others at the margins of our society. This includes the minorities, the poor, and the powerless in this country as well as the Third World. They provide experiences and insights that are out of reach for those of us empowered by the developed world. For example, Senator Ben Nighthorse Campbell, writing in the *Smithsonian* magazine, noted that American Indians are unique compared to other minority communities in that they lost what they once had. Many lost family members, their language and culture, and an entire way of life. Other immigrant people came to this country in search of gaining success -- they wanted to move up the economic and social ladder. American Indians are trying to regain what they once had and then lost.

The theologian Douglas John Hall once spoke of his perspective on the United States as a Canadian living at the "edge of empire." From this location, he could be both close and yet separate. In the same way, the poor and oppressed, whether women, children, or those living in the Third World, are both members of our global society and yet separate. Throughout the stories of the Gospels, Jesus listens to outcasts at the edge of society. He takes time to talk with the women, the poor, the sick, the outcasts, and others who are not rich and powerful. There are many prophetic voices today. We only need to take time to listen.

♫ ♫ ♫

The Preamble to the Constitution lists "the blessings of liberty" as one of the goals behind the formation of our new government. Among these blessings are the First Amendment prohibitions against any laws that favor or restrict the free exercise of religion. The founders of our country saw the United States as a diverse country with a plurality of religious views. They did not want the government to endorse any particular religion to the exclusion of all others. Those who try to connect the values of this nation with those of a particular brand of Christianity fail to recognize the religious diversity that existed at that time and continues to this day. The separation of church and state is a cornerstone of a free and democratic society.

Chapter 14

From conflict to consensus

...the new democracy...

♫ ♫ ♫

After attaining some degree of proficiency, many student musicians begin playing duets or in small ensembles, bands, or orchestras. Playing with others introduces a whole new world of complexity. Students must simultaneously listen to other musicians while also playing their own instrument. If they listen too closely to others, they will fail to properly perform their part. If they don't listen closely enough, they will fail to harmonize with the other musicians. Playing together requires a delicate balance between the individual and the group, between listening and performing.

Split decisions

The founders of our nation believed in the principle that the collective actions of individuals living in a free society are more effective than the decisions of the few. For this reason, we have preferred juries over judges, free markets over planned economies, and elections over dictatorships. Research has shown that the collective wisdom of many individuals is more likely to produce good decisions than those of any single individual. We vote on referendums, legislative initiatives, candidates who will make our laws, judges who will decide judicial questions, and officers of the executive branch who will administer our government.

In much the same way, we believe that the collective decisions of many independent consumers provide better guidance for the economy than unilateral decisions made by the few, whether in corporate boardrooms or the offices of a centralized government. In fact, our enthusiasm for economic voting has grown so great that many would like to submit virtually all societal questions to a market-based decision-making process. They want to privatize government functions in order to force all activities to work for economic votes in order to survive.

However, there are many pitfalls in our often unquestioning embrace of economic voting to make our decisions. Economic voting presumes a free and open marketplace with large numbers of customers and suppliers with comparable levels of power and information. Today, our markets are far from free and open. It is very difficult for small suppliers to penetrate the barriers that large government and large corporations have established. The difference in power and information between customers and suppliers is often very large. Marketplace decisions take a limited quantitative view of the world that does not reflect many societal costs and benefits as it counts dollars to determine the direction of our society.

Although many people today are debating the limitations of economic voting through the marketplace, there is less often discussion of the problems associated with our use of voting to make political decisions. The use of voting to make public decisions is an American tradition. Whenever a group gathers together and faces a difficult decision, there is usually a call for a vote. On simple questions with relatively little impact, our instinctive desire to vote generally works well. Acceptance of the results is usually not a question. Majority rules. However, on more complex and important issues, conflict often increases and voting may not necessarily be the best way to proceed.

Despite its popularity, voting is simply an expression of our democratic belief that the people should control the government. It is not the only or perhaps even the best way to express the people's power in a democracy. In our winner-takes-all voting system, a 51% majority can oppress a 49% minority. Too often, voting enables the majority to ignore the minority. The results often divide us, produce poor decisions, and fail to reflect a balanced view of the community's desires.

In a homogeneous society united by a common culture, religious heritage, and shared values, there usually are no great differences in opinion. However, we are increasingly becoming a bimodal society of rich and poor, religious and secular. Deep divisions are emerging on questions related to religion, culture, and economics. In such a culture, our heavy reliance on voting is destructive to the spirit of unity and cooperation that lie at the heart of a democratic society. It also discourages adequate consideration of the complexities and nuances of many societal questions.

Many of our most contentious issues today have no clear and simple answer. Unfortunately, voting does not make provisions for ambiguity and complexity; it forces us to reduce complicated questions to simple "either-or" decisions. We either ban abortion or we do not. We either go to war or we do not. We either raise taxes or we do not. After the forming of the question, often through a series of legislative votes, alternatives or compromises are no longer possible. Voters often find themselves faced with a choice between two equally unattractive alternatives. This may be one of the reasons that voter turnout percentages are usually so low.

For some years, California has led the way in the use of referendums and direct legislative initiatives. These efforts by-pass the traditional analyses, extended debates, and thoughtful compromises that should occur in the legislative and executive branches of government. The replacement of a recently elected second term governor of California through a truncated election campaign dominated by money and celebrity provides an example of how excessive reliance on voting can produce decisions of questionable merit. Voters had to select from a long list of candidates without the benefit of a primary to narrow the field.

Unfortunately, democracy depends upon an informed electorate, and many people lack the information necessary to cast a responsible ballot. In addition, with a relatively small number of corporations and individuals controlling much of the mass media, many people find it difficult to obtain reasonably objective, independent information. Even worse, those in control of the media are able to bend the views of voters for their own benefit by selectively presenting and sometimes distorting the news, particularly ay a time when many people look to figures of authority to make their decisions for them.

Sources of authority

In his book *Stages of Faith,* James Fowler presented a model that draws on the work of Erik Erikson and his "eight ages of man" to describe the ways in which people relate to the content of their religious beliefs. His model is also useful for describing how people relate to other areas of their lives. In particular, it can help inform our understanding of how people view authority.

As we live our lives, many people pass through a series of distinct stages. At first, to fulfill our need for personal identity and meaning, we search for authority figures, such as parents, teachers, or other leaders, to follow. This perspective corresponds to Fowler's stage 3 of development. Some adults never stop being followers. Throughout their lives, rather than examining the facts for themselves, they accept the teachings of trusted leaders.

However, others come to recognize that there are many authority figures with differing views in the marketplace of ideas. They realize that as independent individuals they must examine the data, study the arguments, and come to their own conclusions. They no longer depend on external authorities to make their decisions for them. Autonomy replaces allegiance to authority. This view of reality corresponds to Fowler's stage 4 of development. At this stage, individuals carry out their own personal search for the answers to life's questions and often become leaders themselves.

Eventually the ambiguities and complexities of the real world drive some people to move beyond this "either-or" view of reality. These individuals recognize that many of life's most important questions simply do not have black and white answers; the answers depend upon the context. Moreover, Kurt Gödel has shown that there are even mathematical questions that we cannot answer. Thus it should come as no surprise that life in all its complexity presents us with many questions whose answers are complex or unknowable.

Rather than accepting the views of authority figures or finding their own answers from a wide array of alternatives, they adopt a more nuanced and paradoxical view of reality. They accept the need to develop relationships with others to develop workable solutions to life's problems in the face of conflicting and incomplete information. They see life as a process rather than a product and recognize ambiguity, complexity, unpredictability and disorder as unavoidable.

This process or partnership perspective resembles Fowler's stage 5 of development. In this stage, individuals realize that reality has many layers and looks different as you change your perspective: depending on the circumstances -- light can behave as a wave or a particle. They accept paradoxes and contradictions as inherent features of the world in which we live.

Dependent stage 3 followers as well as confident stage 4 leaders often this stage 5 perspective as intolerable relativism. However, opening ourselves up to a multiplicity of views is not the same as accepting mindless relativism in which nothing matters. We need to avoid the exclusivist view that "there is only one right answer" as well as the relativist view that "all answers are the same." Some answers are indeed better than others, but complex questions rarely have a single "right" answer. We must make our decisions based on our own knowledge, experiences, and feelings as well as those of others in our community. This is not easy, but it is better than relying on simplistic formulas or obsolete dogma.

Fowler's life stages can help illuminate our understanding of political decisions. Looking to outside authorities to form your beliefs, though a useful process that we all follow to some extent, is especially common under repressive regimes and dictatorships. Making one's own personal determination of how to live as an individual forms the philosophical basis for democratic societies. Elections or elected representatives allow individuals to directly or indirectly express their opinion on various questions.

David Brooks, in his article "Bitter at the Top" in *The New York Times,* suggests that the current polarization within our society is due to a division in the educated class between the "aristocracy of money" that produces products and the "aristocracy of mind" that produces ideas. Building on the preceding discussion of stage theory, Brooks' description of the aristocracy of money portrays leaders who know the answers and are comfortable making decisions for others -- the characteristics of many stage 4 corporate leaders. Brooks' description of the aristocracy of mind portrays those who are less sure of the questions, much less the answers, and seek out partnerships and collaborations -- the characteristics of many stage 5 knowledge professionals.

And so, the civil war that Brooks describes is not so much between those concerned with producing products and those concerned with producing ideas, but between two very different views of authority and beliefs. Regardless of educational level, those oriented towards authority see the world in straightforward, black and white terms -- which they will happily state, often in a sound bite. Those oriented towards relationships see the world as a labyrinth of possibilities in a kaleidoscope of colors -- which they will happily discuss, often for hours. The brief responses of George W. Bush and the more expansive answers of John Kerry in the 2004 presidential election campaign presented the two approaches in sharp contrast.

Another perspective on these issues is in Thomas Frank's book *What's the Matter with Kansas?* Frank notes that people often vote their cultural interests rather than their economic interests. To some extent, this may be due to their perception that since, as discussed earlier, there is little difference between the current economic positions of the Democratic and Republican parties, economics is no longer a meaningful issue. However, they may also be responding to very different views of authority.

Many voters are followers who, while busy making a living and raising a family, look to leaders to help them understand the world and form their beliefs -- priests and ministers, teachers and doctors, labor leaders and business executives, talk show hosts and presidents. From this perspective, rather than supporting their cultural interests over their economic interests, they are actually choosing authority figures. Rather than analyzing life's many questions in detail, they look to authority figures in the various sectors of their lives to provide them leadership. In an ever more complex world, it is one way to deal with life's challenges.

Hanna Rosin described an interesting example of this phenomenon in her article in *The Atlantic Monthly*. She noted that Orthodox Jewish communities that strongly supported Al Gore in 2000, reversed direction and gave equally overwhelming support to George W. Bush in 2004. Prior to the election, the Bush campaign had made a great effort to gain the support of Orthodox rabbis based on religious issues and support for Israel. Orthodox rabbis received invitations to Hanukkah parties at the White House and the Bush campaign held a special event during the Republican convention aimed particularly at Orthodox Jews. Rosin suggested that the huge swing in the Orthodox Jewish vote from Gore to Bush, which increased Bush's overall share of the Jewish vote from 19% to 25%, was due to the loyalty that Orthodox Jews feel towards the views of their rabbis, many of whom had shifted their support to Bush.

Many individuals are followers who look to the "president" as a legitimate authority figure. If the president says that same-sex marriages threaten the "sanctity of marriage" and that the economy is strong, they will support his statements even if they disagree with their personal experiences. As followers, they would rather ignore or deny their personal knowledge than abandon their devotion to their leader and the security that it brings them.

It will require a fundamental shift in their view of authority before individuals can assume the role of stage 4 leaders who form their views based on their own personal knowledge, experiences, and judgment. It is not easy to "let go" of the comfort that following a respected leader brings. Even more wrenching is the shift towards a stage 5 partnership perspective that accepts the limitations of all answers. Many people want answers to life's questions. It indeed requires considerable faith to live our lives in a complex and often paradoxical world in which answers are often difficult to find. Although many of us sense this reality of life, we often find it too disturbing to acknowledge.

Building consensus

As we deal with increasingly complex questions, the use of simple majority voting is not necessarily the best way to reflect our democratic ideals. Many questions require more sophisticated and individualized answers than simplistic, "one size fits all" solutions suitable for voting. Rather than simply attempting to gain the support of 51% of the voters on a particular issue, we need to find solutions that come closer to receiving unanimous support.

Although this ideal is often difficult to achieve, it is usually possible to craft solutions that receive substantially more support than a bare majority. In order to do this, it is necessary take all views in a discussion seriously rather than simply those of the majority. Rather than counting votes and declaring winners, we need to make greater use of consensus approaches to decision-making. Consensus decision-making encourages tolerance and recognizes the values that are usually present in the views of the minority.

Joan Chittister, in her book *Heart of Flesh,* writes that a commitment to consensus rather than control underlies feminist spirituality. She suggests that feminists prefer consensus approaches because they give decisions credibility and unify rather than divide.

There was a time when consensus decision-making was a natural part of public life. When I was young, bipartisan efforts in Washington crafted compromises to resolve many difficult problems. There was a willingness on the part of politicians from both parties to work cooperatively for the good of the country. Today, it is difficult for political parties to craft a consensus even within the membership of their own parties. In Congress, the voting process itself has virtually replaced debate as a way to obtain support for controversial measures. Roll call votes continue for hours as the leadership brings extreme political and personal pressure on representatives to change their votes. The willingness to gain a razor-thin victory at any cost has destroyed any spirit of thoughtful analysis and compromise. The views of even substantial minorities mean nothing. As with so much else in American political, economic, and public life, winning is the only thing that matters -- and coercion has replaced consensus.

Consensus decision-making is more popular than many people might recognize. Some private organizations use "approval balloting" in selecting their leadership. In this approach, voters cast votes for all candidates that they find acceptable. The candidate with the most votes wins the election. Approval balloting avoids dividing votes between two equally attractive candidates and tends to elect those who have broader support than a simple plurality. The City of San Francisco uses "instant-runoff voting" in which voters rank the candidates in order of preference and if no candidate receives 50% of the votes, the process uses second and third-choice votes to determine a winner. As with approval voting, this system tends to elect candidates with broad support. Although no system is without its problems, approval voting or instant-runoff voting are examples of building consensus into the election process.

In Madison, Wisconsin, Advent Lutheran Church, where I am a member, and Community of Hope United Church of Christ have formed a partnership named the Madison Christian Community. Through this 35 year old partnership, they jointly own and operate their church building, conduct joint educational programming, and cooperate in their respective ministries.

Both churches place a high value on inclusivity, diversity, and caring. In order to build community and reach harmonious decisions, they have a decentralized organization and employ consensus decision-making processes. Small task forces and committees carry out many of the functions of both churches. These groups make their decisions based on a consensus approach. There are very few votes. Discussion continues until a course of action receives broad, often unanimous support. This procedure is sometimes more cumbersome than a simple vote, but through careful consideration of all alternatives points of view, it produces better decisions, greater support for decisions, and increased harmony following the decision.

The scientific community provides an example of the use of consensus decision-making on a global scale. Richard Rhodes, in *The Making of the Atomic Bomb,* describes how scientific progress flows from a network of distributed authority without any absolute leaders or voting. Drawing on the work of Michael Polanyi, he notes that this network of scientists forms its decisions through a process that emphasizes the opinions of those closest to the question at hand. These scientists, in turn, use a combination of theory and experiment to analyze, evaluate, and, hopefully, replicate the new results. Gradually a consensus emerges as to the accuracy and usefulness of the original finding.

Consensus decision-making recognizes the ambiguity present in many issues. Rather than eliminating minority positions through majority rule, it takes all positions seriously. It is clearly easier for builders of relationships to accept the consensus approach to decision-making. They recognize the complex and paradoxical nature of many questions. They are more willing to compromise with the views of others.

After early years of sometimes violent conflict, labor and management learned to work together to reach consensus decisions on labor problems or production practices. However, in recent years, exacerbated by Reagan's dismissal of the nation's air traffic controllers in 1981, these efforts have collapsed as labor and management have adopted a confrontational, adversarial relationship. Many corporate managers and political leaders want to destroy the union movement. Their efforts along with the impact of globalization and the availability of cheap labor have caused a continued decline in union membership. Remaining union members have often become understandably hostile to those in power.

Similar hostility to those in positions of power is even evident within the Christian community. During the 20th century, there was a trend towards church mergers and increased ecumenical activity. The Second Vatican Council opened up the Roman Catholic Church to a variety of progressive reforms. Protestant denominations sought closer working relationships. Tolerance for alternative views and diversity increased.

However, the papacy of John Paul II slowed or reversed many of the changes brought forth during the time of John XXIII and many believe that Pope Benedict XVI will continue the rigid policies of John Paul II. Conservative branches of Protestant denominations have distanced themselves from more progressive branches with little desire for reconciliation or consensus. Conflicts over homosexuality and same-sex unions have brought forth threats of schism within some denominations.

In most, if not all, of these examples, there seems to be little willingness to discuss issues with an open mind, to listen to the respective positions, and to develop a consensus approach to the problem. Instead, the tendency has been to use hierarchical authority and political power to impose one position over another without regard to individual consciences or alternative views. In fact, a desire for power and control often drives some leaders to seek out controversial issues and present them in as divisive a manner as possible that leaves little room for compromise.

On the other hand, some organizations try to resolve controversial questions without resorting to votes that divide their members into winners and losers. During a long and highly charged study of homosexuality, some members of the Evangelical Lutheran Church in America (ELCA) searched for a middle road between either outright approval or disapproval of officially blessing homosexual relationships or allowing homosexuals in a committed relationship to serve as ordained ministers.

In January of 2005, the Task Force for ELCA Studies on Sexuality issued a report that included three recommendations. First, it recommended that the ELCA find ways to live together despite disagreements on these issues. Second, it recommended that the ELCA "continue to respect" the 1993 statement from the Conference of Bishops that did not approve creating an official ceremony for the blessing of homosexual relationships, but expressed their trust in pastors and congregations who minister to homosexuals and affirmed "...their desire to explore the best ways to provide pastoral care for all to whom they minister." Finally, it recommended that the ELCA continue its policy against allowing congregations from calling homosexuals in a committed relationship, but stated that the "...church may choose to refrain from disciplining..." those who make or accept such a call.

The recommendations are a highly nuanced response to these divisive questions. They adopt a typically Lutheran stance that manages to both condemn and tolerate the actions under question. However, the recommendations do avoid outright division, attempt to articulate a consensus position out of seemingly irreconcilable views, and perhaps most importantly, move decisions somewhat closer to the local level -- an approach that holds promise for other questions on which Americans hold sharply divergent beliefs.

Small and local

Large governmental agencies, corporations, universities, and churches find it difficult to maintain democratic principles of equality and justice. They use voting to make a few carefully crafted decisions in an effort to create a facade of democratic processes. This does little to change the reality that most large organizations are oligarchies with decisions made by an elite few.

The Soviet Union provides a vivid example of the futility of large, centralized organizations. As with so many empires in the past, this large and powerful country collapsed under its own weight. Similar dangers exist for other countries and large organizations. Giant corporations such as Enron, one of the largest corporations in our nation, can disappear virtually overnight. Dioceses of the Roman Catholic Church suffer from a shortage of priests, closing of local parishes, and even threats of bankruptcy. In June of 2005, the summit meeting of the leaders of the European Union (EU) collapsed in disarray following the rejection of the proposed EU constitution by French and Dutch voters as well as the inability of the leaders to agree on the EU budget. Size is no guarantee of success or even survival in a world of rapid change.

We need to place greater emphasis on the value of smallness and less emphasis on growth and the creation of super-sized organizations. Large church bodies should give serious consideration to dividing into smaller denominations in order to get past divisive disagreements and focus more effectively on their primary missions. Communities should provide increased support for smaller, locally based organizations and businesses.

Interestingly, even during a time of continuing corporate mega-mergers, some corporations are recognizing that their various units are worth more as separate businesses than as part of a single corporation -- the parts are more valuable than the whole. For this reason, these companies are spinning off some of their business units to increase overall shareholder value and often create more tightly focused and nimble businesses.

Similarly, we need to consider new approaches for restructuring government. We need to think creatively about changes that would enable our nation to function more effectively. Some of these changes may require modifications or extensions to our Constitution.

The Constitution has proven to be a remarkably useful and flexible document. However, after more than 200 years, we need to be open to changes in the fundamental structure and administration of government to meet today's needs. In order to move from ineffective and sometimes divisive reliance on simplistic decisions made through voting at the national level in the legislative or the executive branch, we need to drive decisions down to smaller units. We need to decentralize the power and authority within our institutions.

The decision following the 9/11 Commission report to centralize all national intelligence and security activities under a single agency is exactly contrary to this vision. Decentralized power and control provide more flexible and effective ways to manage the activities of large organizations. The armed forces have long recognized that the mass confusion that often results in battle requires small units capable of functioning rather independently using a few basic guidelines for their actions. They know that large, centralized bureaucracies are lethargic and slow to respond. They are not suitable during times that require fast and flexible action. One oft-cited example is the way in which the crew of an aircraft carrier adopts an adaptive, interactive process in lieu of its traditional hierarchical organization during the launching and recovery of aircraft. There is no time for the inefficiencies of bureaucracy.

Effective managers have long recognized the virtues of moving a decision closer to those who are most familiar with the problem and the impact of any proposed solution. In much the same way, we should allow individual states and local communities increased autonomy in governing the lives of their citizens. On many divisive social questions, the only way to approach a consensus is at the state or local level. The cultural differences between many of the blue states and red states are too great for their citizens to comfortably coexist within uniform national rules. In the past, successful empires responded to similar problems by allowing local control in virtually all areas excepting those related to loyalty and support of the empire.

On many issues, there is little reason to insist on broad uniformity. The city where I live, Madison, Wisconsin, is one of the most liberal in the state. Recently, it has attempted to increase the local minimum wage in the city above the state level as well as broaden its ban on smoking in restaurants to include bars and taverns. Some Republican state legislators have opposed both actions and are trying to impose uniform state laws that would supersede local laws in both areas. There appears to be little justification for such a move. If anything, Madison's new minimum wage and expanded smoking ban may weaken its competitive position with other communities in the state. However, the local community has decided through its elected officials that just wages and cleaner air are worth whatever economic costs may result. There is little need to impose uniform standards on such local issues.

♬ ♬ ♬

Democracy is a system of government by people. Voting is a tool of democracy. This chapter has challenged the desire of some to not only use majority rule for all political decisions, but to allow voting with dollars to make our economic decisions. In both cases, poor decisions often result due to inadequate information, unequal power, intimidation, lack of alternatives, and failure to respect minority views. Consensus processes can produce better decisions that garner more support and better reflect our democratic ideals better than simple voting. Although often more cumbersome and time-consuming, they are more likely to result in political decisions and economic decisions that are "of, by, and for the people."

Chapter 15

The role of the left

...recovering the past, building the future...

♫ ♫ ♫

Most musical instruments require a subtle balance between technical virtuosity and artistic brilliance. Technical skills create the desired notes. Artistic ability produces those notes in a musically pleasing manner with the proper dynamics, tempo, and interpretation. For some instruments, technical skills develop rather quickly and the student can almost immediately begin to develop their artistic skills. However, the technical skills required to play the violin take a long time to acquire making it is difficult to develop the artistic skills that change mere sounds into music. In much the same way, it takes more than simplistic rhetoric and ideology to bring life to a democracy.

Reagan's "evil empire"

The signers of the Declaration of Independence rejected their role as dutiful followers of the king of England. They were no longer willing to accept his authority over their lives. In forming our nation, they sought to make their own decisions for their communities. After considerable discussion, they reached a consensus that enabled most of them (though not all, some fled to Canada or England) to endorse the Declaration of Independence and some years later, the Constitution. Despite these agreements, our founders remained an independent group of individuals who wanted to lead and worked hard to persuade others to see things their way.

Most of the leaders of our country maintained this independent leadership style until World War II. Following that catastrophic conflict, the victorious allies came together and formed the United Nations. The underlying presumption of that organization was that no single nation has all the answers. After two horrific world wars, the world's leaders were not even sure what were the right questions. They acknowledged that the nations of the world did not agree on many issues. For this reason, they saw a need for a forum where countries could discuss these differing views, rather than immediately resorting to violence and war.

The United Nations was a major step towards using international relationships to resolve problems between nations. In many ways, this is a very different perspective than a leadership style that believes that it has all the answers. It requires a recognition that your answers might be incomplete or not persuasive and leads to a partnership leadership style. This style of leadership emphasizes meeting with others, exploring alternatives, and building relationships -- listening, thinking, cooperating. Athletic coaches, corporate managers, and leaders in many other fields often use it with great effectiveness.

Many of our presidents had experiences that enabled them to see the value of partnerships and to use them effectively. Some had served in Congress where it was difficult to accomplish anything without working cooperatively with others. Others gained similar experience elsewhere: Dwight Eisenhower as Supreme Allied Commander during World War II and Jimmy Carter as a naval officer and businessman. Following World War II, U.S. presidents established a variety of partnerships with other nations. In addition to the United Nations, they formed international agencies and organizations, signed international treaties, created multilateral alliances, and developed many other relationships.

The election of Ronald Reagan as president brought a sudden halt to this partnership style of leadership and replaced it with a more combative independent leadership style. Reagan "knew" that he had the answers. He expressed them in simplistic aphorisms that appealed to our "sound bite" culture. These aphorisms did not leave much room for thoughtful responses or continuing dialogue. Following Reagan, political debate in our country deteriorated. Many Americans adopted the role of the dutiful follower who followed instructions from their chosen leader. For them, there was no need to consider alternative views.

One of Reagan's most well known aphorisms came from a sermon(!) that he delivered on March 8, 1983, to a meeting of the National Association of Evangelists in Orlando, Florida. In the context of an ongoing discussion regarding talks with the Soviet Union on nuclear freeze proposals, Reagan warned the audience near the end of his sermon not to ignore "the aggressive impulses of an evil empire." He further demonized the Soviet Union, by quoting Whittaker Chambers' description of "Marxism-Leninism," not as a political or economic philosophy, but as the second-oldest faith, first proclaimed to Eve in the Garden of Eden by the serpent.

This description from Chambers, which muddies the waters by deftly combining the social philosophy of Marx and Engels with its political implementation by Lenin and Stalin, enabled Reagan to turn a flawed Soviet government into the iconic example of communism and socialism. Reagan then claimed the source of our strength was not material, but spiritual, and turned his objections to a socialist ideology, formed as a pragmatic economic response to real economic problems, from economics to religion. In the process, Reagan transformed communism from an economic system to a religious faith in opposition to Christianity. Quite a sleight-of-hand, particularly since most readers of the New Testament see considerable evidence of socialist ideals in the teachings of Jesus and the actions of the early church.

Nonetheless, Reagan and his speech writers set up a dichotomy between essentially two theocracies: the United States as a Christian nation and the Union of Soviet Socialist Republics as an evil empire whose values hearkened back to the devil in the Garden of Eden. As a result, Reagan reduced the differences between the U.S. and the

U.S.S.R. to a fight between good and evil, God and the devil -- foreshadowing by 20 years George W. Bush's "either-or" pronouncement following the 9/11 attacks.

Ironically, in a speech just a few months earlier on June 8, 1982 to the combined Houses of Parliament in London, Reagan had emphasized the economic problems of the U.S.S.R. including the failure of its agricultural programs, its lack of economic growth, and the burden of its large military expenditures. Despite his upcoming demonization of the Soviet Union, Reagan concluded that it was facing a crisis, not due to shortcomings in its morality or values, but due to its failure to meet the needs of the economic order.

A moral snapshot of the United States

How well does the United States meet the high standards that Reagan's religious vision suggests? Clearly, the United States has much to be proud of: its democratic processes, its recognition of the need for individual rights and freedoms, its military successes with its allies against aggression in World War II, its contributions to peace through initiatives such as the United Nations and the Marshall Plan, its technical innovations, its material prosperity.

In a commentary on the CBS news magazine *60 Minutes,* Andy Rooney noted that our country has had many great moments. He mentioned winning our independence, beating Hitler, and going to the moon. We might add many others, like the successful return of the Lewis and Clark Expedition, the opening of the Panama Canal, and Charles Lindbergh's solo flight across the Atlantic Ocean.

However, these accomplishments lose some of their luster when we also consider some of the shortcomings of our nation: its tolerance of slavery for nearly one hundred years, its destruction of Native Americans and their culture, its frequent resort to "gun boat" diplomacy, its tolerance in the midst of prosperity of homelessness, poverty, and inadequate health care for its citizens, its continued acceptance of discrimination in many forms throughout our society, and its unqualified embrace of an economic system driven by greed and materialism.

Sadly, since the attacks of 9/11, our nation and many of its citizens have responded with fear and anxiety. Despite the confident statements by our leaders that we would not allow these terrorist attacks to change our way of life, it has changed. We have accepted broad new restrictions on our civil rights. We have backed away from our allies and the international community. We have waged preemptive war in Iraq without the support of the United Nations that we host and helped create. Too often, our citizens have tolerated lies, deceptions, and fraud by our government and business leaders. Meanwhile, we have been too quick to criticize those who question the direction taken by the leaders of our country.

In his *60 Minutes* commentary, Andy Rooney also focused on the dark day when our abuse and torture of Iraqi prisoners became known around the world. Despite the many positive accomplishments of our nation, this incident particularly bothered him. At the conclusion of his commentary, he noted that even though he was an old man, he had never before had the sense that the America he had known seemed to be slipping away.

The United States is a great nation and has much to be proud of, but it is not what Reagan's high flying rhetoric would want you to believe. In the history of any nation, we need to place the list of its achievements alongside the list of its failures. It is a reality of the human condition that both lists will usually be quite lengthy.

A moral snapshot of the U.S.S.R.

On the other hand, how well did the former Soviet Union mirror the demonized image of Reagan's vision? Once again, it is easy to find many aspects of the U.S.S.R. to condemn: its totalitarian government, its suppression of individual rights and freedoms, its ruthless treatment of its opponents, its periodic purges during the Stalin era, its domination of satellite countries, its failure to provide adequately for the material needs of its citizens. In many ways, it is not a record that inspires pride or admiration. Even its supporters have found much to criticize in the former Soviet state.

Nonetheless, despite its shortcomings, the U.S.S.R. did have substantial accomplishments during its relatively brief and turbulent history: its transformation of a virtually medieval state into a modern nation in a matter of decades, its embrace of progressive social ideals, its improvements in the living conditions of its citizens, its heroic contributions to the defeat of Hitler during World War II, its pioneering efforts in outer space, and its recognized excellence in other fields including science, engineering, athletics, and the arts. Perhaps the most notable of its achievements occurred during its collapse, when it dissolved into a collection of independent republics with minimal violence. Rather than pursuing an extended period of civil war, the central regime transferred control of the country to the governments that emerged in its former republics.

As summarized by Howard Zinn, in his book *Declaration of Independence,* the Soviet Union was a blend of appealing ideals and accomplishments within a totalitarian regime. Despite the many failures of its repressive government, the ideals remain attractive. The Soviet Union embraced the vision of Marx and Engels who saw how the industrial revolution was benefiting the few and often causing hardship for the many. Edmund Wilson in his classic book, *To The Finland Station,* noted that Marx and Engels wanted to restore the idea of the "complete" man in a society that increasingly treated him like a machine. Today, as much as ever, their concerns remain relevant in a globalized economy of shuttered plants and unemployed workers replaced by foreign sweatshops filled with regimented workers receiving minimal wages.

One of the guiding fictions of communist societies like the Soviet Union is "from each according to their ability and to each according to their need." This central ideal, far from being demonic, has long inspired charitable institutions, religious bodies, and even individuals and families throughout the world. On the other hand,

Robert Heilbroner, in his book *The Limits of American Capitalism,* noted that, despite its economic success and central position in our society, capitalism with its acquisitive and materialistic nature does not generate much appeal as an idea.

Writing in the 1960s, Heilbroner saw science and technology as better able to inspire us and capture our imagination due to its "altruism" and "purity." However, this optimistic vision soon faded into cynicism and suspicion as many people began to see technology as creating new problems as quickly as it solved old ones. In addition, many of our most pressing problems involved social, political, and economic issues for which scientific and technological approaches were often inadequate.

In the third millennium, the cooperative ideals of socialism appear more relevant to solving our problems and creating a more just and humane society. In fact, socialist ideals continue to inspire even countries with capitalist economies to create programs to help the most needy members of their societies. Unfortunately, with the collapse of the Soviet Union, support for these programs has diminished, both due to the loss of the Soviet Union as a voice for the worker as well as the elimination of the competitive alternative that the Soviet Union posed for capitalist nations.

The movie *Goodbye, Lenin* illustrates the impact of the collapse of the Soviet Union and the end of communism on workers in East Germany. It portrays in a humorous manner the idealized hopes, stark failures, and limited successes of East German leaders and professionals, probably not unlike those in the Soviet Union and other communist countries. When western style economics and democracy took over, the people traded socialist idealism for capitalist materialism -- on balance, probably a good trade for many, but not without its downside.

Similarly, for her introduction to *Above the Clouds,* a collection of writings by Anatoli Boukreev, a Russian native who was one of the world's great mountain climbers, Linda Wylie wrote an excellent overview of the impact on professionals of the collapse of the Soviet

Union. Having grown up in the former Soviet Union, Boukreev was well aware of its shortcomings and problems, but he also recognized its positive accomplishments. It was not totally without merit and certainly something other than the "evil empire" that Reagan had demonized.

Boukreev was a commercial guide on Mount Everest during the 1996 tragedy that cost the lives of a number of climbers on other expeditions. After the event, he wrote that although climbers may pay substantial sums to become members of guided expeditions to the world's tallest mountains, the world of high altitude climbing is not subject to the laws of commerce. Contrary to the belief of many American capitalists, there are some things that you cannot buy. Guaranteed safety on Mount Everest is one of those things. Perhaps only someone, like Boukreev, who had grown up in the Soviet Union could express this simple truth with such eloquence. Those who issue unending calls for privatization and treat the omniscient market as God should heed his warning.

Reagan, Churchill, and Bush

When Reagan took office, the forces that led to *glasnost* (openness), *perestroika* (restructuring), and the ultimate dissolution of the U.S.S.R. were already gathering power. By 1978, China had moved towards closer ties with the west and by 1980, Polish shipyard workers gained the right to form labor unions and strike. Nonetheless, following the breakup of the Soviet Union in the early 1990s, Reagan's supporters claimed that the extreme rhetoric of his speeches at the beginning of his presidency was a major factor in its collapse.

They increasingly described Reagan as a political heir of Winston Churchill. They admired Churchill's opposition to Stalin and especially his famous speech at Westminster College in Fulton, Missouri, on March 5, 1946, in which he described an "iron curtain" that had descended across Europe. Reagan himself greatly admired Churchill and had a portrait of Churchill hung in the White House

Situation Room. However, in recent years, Churchill's reputation has declined as historians have analyzed his actions more closely.

Churchill provided powerful leadership for Britain during the dark early years of World War II, but his contributions to the postwar era were at best uneven. As occurred at other times in Churchill's long life, events evolved very differently than he had imagined. Even Churchill said later that if he could live one year of his life over again, it would be 1940 when the goals were clear and he promised "sunlit highlands" rather than the tense Cold War era that emerged after victory.

In the minds of many conservatives, Roosevelt gave Stalin too much at the end of the war as Churchill stalwartly resisted Stalin's advances. In fact, prior to the celebration in Moscow of the 60th anniversary of the defeat of Nazi Germany by the Soviet Union, George W. Bush gave a speech in Riga, Latvia, in which he stated that no good is served by stirring up the past and then proceeded to do just that. He criticized the actions of the United States, and by implication President Roosevelt, in signing an agreement at Yalta that gave the Soviet Union control of Eastern Europe.

The reality is quite different. Franklin Roosevelt felt that the allied victory presented a unique opportunity to craft a new approach to international relationships. As described by Warren Kimball, in his book *Forged in War,* Roosevelt was groping at the time of his death towards a new global structure built around a loose array of "open spheres" in which the great powers would influence, but not control their neighboring countries. He may have seen these open spheres as a pragmatic alternative to the rigid control of the British Empire and Stalin's totalitarian regime. Roosevelt apparently presumed that the openness of his approach would encourage the spread of American democratic ideals.

Churchill, on the other hand, worked hard in the final years of the war to preserve the power and reach of the British Empire. According to Kimball, he negotiated with Stalin on the percentages of influence that Britain and the Soviet Union would have in Central and Eastern Europe on a country-by-country basis. These negotiations encouraged the emergence of effectively "closed spheres" of influence, ultimately brought to fruition by the iron curtain. Kimball also noted that Churchill, again seeking to protect British interests in Hong Kong and elsewhere in the Far East, outlined a Far Eastern Settlement with Stalin that ultimately gave the Soviets rights in northern China. Rather than consistently resisting Stalin, Churchill often saw him as a negotiating partner who could assist Churchill in maintaining British power in the postwar era. Not surprisingly, Churchill and Stalin, with their past record of negotiating their own understandings, were present at Yalta and signed the accord along with Roosevelt.

In addition to these diplomatic efforts to protect British interests, Churchill also resisted various proposals to place atomic weapons under international control. New knowledge about the nucleus of the atom had encouraged virtually all of the major combatants of World War II to explore the development of a new type of bomb possibly more powerful than anything imagined in the past. However, the Manhattan Project in the United States used tremendous human and physical resources to proceed much more rapidly than any other nation. The United States became the first nation to create and use nuclear weapons.

Recognizing the danger posed by these uniquely powerful weapons, some of the scientists involved in the development of atomic weapons expressed grave concern over their future control and use. In particular, the great Danish physicist, Niels Bohr, as described by Richard Rhodes in *The Making of the Atomic Bomb,* tried to convince Roosevelt and Churchill of the need for international cooperation among the allies to control nuclear weapons and technology.

Churchill's hostility to Stalin and desire to preserve these weapons for the exclusive use of the United States and Britain caused him to reject Bohr's proposal virtually out of hand. He even went so far as to suggest that Bohr ought to be confined out of concern that

Bohr might pass secret information to Russia. The strong support of others within Churchill's and Roosevelt's staffs enabled Bohr to avoid this ignominious end to his valiant, but futile efforts. And despite Churchill's rejection of Bohr's proposal, the subsequent development by the Soviet Union of nuclear weapons was almost inevitable due to the widespread availability of the required scientific and technological knowledge.

Rhodes notes in his book that Churchill's obstructionism cost the world a unique opportunity. Today, it seems possible that Bohr's proposal to impose international controls on nuclear weapons might have eliminated the need for the United States and the Soviet Union to assemble their massive nuclear arsenals, eliminated the need for other countries to acquire these weapons, and greatly reduced the danger of their use by terrorists.

Much like Reagan, George W. Bush, is also a great admirer of Winston Churchill. During his administration, he placed a bust of Churchill in the Oval Office. Similarities between Bush and Churchill abound, but they do not always reflect favorably on either. Churchill embraced the elitist idea of "greatness" as exemplified in his own life and the British Empire itself, much like the way in which the oligarchy composed of the Bush administration and its supporters views our own country.

Churchill often favored ideas and action over planning and analysis. One colleague suggested in a famous quip that Churchill had 10 ideas every day, but only one was any good, and Churchill didn't know which one it was.

The consequences of his poor planning and analysis almost brought an early end to Churchill's career in World War I. With their forces bogged down in trench warfare, British leaders were searching for alternative strategies that would avoid the continuing need to send new troops to the trenches. Churchill, as First Lord of the Admiralty, endorsed an attack through the Dardanelles and the adjacent Gallipoli peninsula. Due to poor planning and questionable strategy, the effort turned into a catastrophe with the combined British ground forces at

Gallipoli suffering great losses. Churchill lost his position in the admiralty and his reputation suffered greatly because of his role in planning the ill-fated attack.

Much like Churchill, Bush's critics also regularly attack his lack of planning and analysis. While Churchill faced the consequences of the tragedy of Gallipoli, Bush faced ongoing military losses and violence following the poorly planned and executed invasion of Iraq. Two years after the United States had invaded Iraq, it was unclear how long our forces would remain in Iraq, what the total costs would be for our country as well as Iraq, and whether the final outcome would justify the death and destruction of the conflict.

In his Westminster speech, Churchill mentioned the "grand simplicity of decision" -- suggesting that decision-making reduces the problem to a simple binary choice. Although there is a brief moment during which a decision does indeed strip away ambiguity and complexity, there is an almost immediate need to consider other decisions that may extend, modify, or even reverse the initial decision. Decision-making involves an unending series of interconnected actions; it is a continuing process. Only leaders like Churchill and Bush, with their stubborn resistance to changing their minds or admitting mistakes, could view decisions as removing complexity. In his Westminster speech, Winston Churchill spoke favorably of "constancy of mind," and "persistency of purpose"; George W. Bush prides himself on "staying the course."

Unfortunately, Churchill and Bush failed to understand that effective leaders often need to change their minds, change their purposes, admit their mistakes, and recognize the inherent complexity of many problems. The simple energy and optimism that Churchill displayed so effectively at the start of World War II may be your only alternative when you are losing. However, they are not sufficient when you are winning: a lesson that would have helped Churchill at the end of World War II, as well as Bush and his supporters after his election and reelection to the presidency. Rather than modifying their thinking and behavior after they won, Bush and his supporters turned to Churchill with his outdated views of greatness and empire to justify their regressive policies and interventionist tendencies.

Marginalizing the left

Like a teeter-totter when one person steps off, the collapse of the Soviet Union moved the center of gravity of the world's social, political, and economic systems to the right. The end of communism in the Soviet bloc along with China's evolving relationships with capitalist companies made the political views of the left in the United States appear more extreme and easier to criticize. Since the Soviet Union represented "leftist" politics and was the work of the devil, it was easy to similarly condemn all leftist political movements. Conservative politicians and religious leaders alike used distinctions drawn from religious images to oppose the political left. As a result, it was difficult for the left to present viable alternatives in the United States to a ruling government more concerned with serving corporations rather than people.

Communism in the Soviet Union had provided a useful counterweight against the most extreme proposals of aggressive capitalism. Ironically, Reagan's conservative supporters often came to emphasize the Soviet collapse as due to its inability to meet the demands of the economic order even though they had previously condemned it ostensibly for moral and religious reasons. When convenient, they reintroduced economics to justify their belief that the political order existed to serve the needs of the economy rather than the other way around.

With the collapse of the Soviet Union, there were an unending stream of proposals in the United States to downsize government and privatize virtually every aspect of our lives. Conservatives saw an unregulated, uncontrolled, totally "unplanned" economy as justified by the demonstrated failures of the centralized, planned economy of the Soviet Union. Of course, their proposals did call for their own form of planning. They called for a state organized around the needs of corporations and business with decisions made by the market or management, rather than through democratic processes .

It is no accident that the aggressive form of free enterprise that many of our leaders embrace has led to a litany of abuses and scandals. These include the boom and bust cycle of the stock market beginning in the early 1990s, the numerous corporate scandals discussed earlier in this book concerning Enron and many other companies, and the push towards globalization that abandoned local communities as it exploited Third World workers. In the past, the electorate would have shown its displeasure with these events at the polls. However, in the society that the United States is becoming, economics has simply ceased to matter for many people. Despite the many examples throughout this book, these voters fail to perceive any significant difference between the economic policies of the Democrats and Republicans.

After World War II, it was unacceptable to be a communist. Then socialism fell out of favor, and with the fall of the Soviet Union, it became undesirable to be a liberal. Many liberals in the United States resorted to the more politically acceptable "progressive" label. Others, like Bill Clinton and the so-called New Democrats began embracing the economic world view of conservatives. This included supporting international trade agreements that led to the loss of domestic jobs, damaged local communities, and weakened the ability of our country's governments at the state and local level to do their job.

Following the election of George W. Bush and the events of 9/11, the White House as well as conservative leaders in Congress believed that they had all the answers. They rejected the concept that there might be other approaches that were equally compelling among the political opposition or our allies throughout the world. They did not see any reason to discuss or compromise with others. Most notably, they turned their backs on the United Nations and many of our closest allies in their pursuit of war in Iraq. Unfortunately, the aftermath of the invasion of Iraq demonstrated that their answers were often far from accurate.

The election of 2004 presented a choice between an arrogant candidate who had all the answers and a more reflective candidate who emphasized the building of relationships. Unfortunately, Bush's reelection meant that, at least for the immediate future, the United States would continue to speak in a monologue rather than engage in constructive global dialogue.

Reclaiming the initiative

In order for the left to reemerge as a political force, it must challenge the deceptive guiding fiction that the Soviet Union was an "evil empire." It must restore a more balanced view of both the United States and the Soviet Union. As discussed above, both countries have made valuable contributions in the past as well as committed great crimes. Only by facing the history of both countries clearly will we be able to move ahead successfully in the future.

The left also needs to challenge the fallacies of the theocratic perspective presented by Ronald Reagan. Even within the Christian tradition, people are not sinners or saints: we all have elements of both. Countries are not good or evil: they all have elements of both. The United States is not the "New Jerusalem," nor the "city on the hill." It is simply one more nation, probably better than some, perhaps not as good as others.

The left needs to reclaim the spiritual high ground in the debate. It is ironic that the political right has successfully marketed itself as the party for those concerned with religion and moral issues. In fact, the stories in the Gospels, the actions of the early church, and the traditions of Christian religious orders more closely reflect the beliefs and ideals of socialists than those of the political right. Jesus' description of the lilies of the field and the beauty of their raiment in the 6th chapter of Matthew doesn't suggests the materialistic world of American capitalism. His suggestion in the 10th chapter of Mark that it is easier for a camel to go through the eye of a needle than for a rich man to enter the Kingdom of God doesn't provide much comfort for the successful capitalist. The story in the 2nd chapter of Acts that describes early Christians as holding all things in common and selling their possessions to help the needy sounds more like socialism than Bush's "ownership society."

Taking a more recent perspective, many societies have embraced the cooperative ideals of socialist societies when facing a crisis. President Franklin Roosevelt, a member of the privileged class, lead our nation through the Great Depression with a series of initiatives that some condemned as dangerous socialism, but that most of us now embrace as central tenets of American life. According to Maureen Waller, in her book *London 1945,* even Winston Churchill's daughter, Sarah, pointed out to him the effectiveness of socialist policies of rationing and sharing in England during World War II.

The left brings important insights on the building of a world in which people matter, a world that seeks consensus rather than submitting every question to a vote, a world that recognizes the value of public ownership. The ideas driving the political left stem from ancient traditions of caring, sharing, and living in harmony with one another. American capitalism and the modern corporation are recent inventions whose strengths, despite their usefulness, are so great that they have distorted the social and economic fabric of our country. The left has much to offer in repairing this fabric and creating new structures to provide adequate public oversight of the actions of corporations in the global economy.

People invent governments and economies. The left needs to reintroduce economics into the debate. It needs to call for a world in which people and their government manage the economy rather than leaving all decisions to an amoral market or a small oligarchy operating behind closed doors. To do this, the left must stop apologizing for its ideals and not hesitate to speak out strongly in favor of a society in which the economy serves the people rather than the people serve the economy.

Perhaps we can learn from the experiences of gays and lesbians. They only began to make progress in their fight against discrimination and search for acceptance when they came out of the closet and expressed their views and desires. The left will only regain its political standing by speaking out for its beliefs.

In our 2004 holiday letter, my wife and I expressed our "anger, sadness, and depression" over the result of the presidential election. This letter brought more responses from our friends than any of our preceding holiday letters. Many wrote to say that they agreed and felt the same way. A few Bush supporters wrote back, one couple noting that now we knew how they felt about Clinton. Following Christmas, we had dinner together and had a good discussion about why they supported Bush as well as our concerns over the direction of our country. We didn't resolve our differences, but our comment opened the door to dialogue.

About the same time, I had breakfast with another friend who had always voted Republican, but decided to vote for Kerry in 2004. We had a thoughtful discussion about why he made this decision, and how we both felt about the issues. Another constructive step towards seeing each other at different points of the same continuum.

Investing in the future

The United States has always been a place where people can invest in the future. There are at least three dimensions to these investments. Our traditional investments include the houses, schools, factories, roads, and so on that comprise our physical infrastructure. Our human investments include the education, skills, and experiences of our people. Our social investments include the social relationships of our neighborhoods, schools, churches, businesses, clubs, associations, and so on that enable our society to function. Unfortunately, our investment in each of these areas is falling short of what a strong nation requires.

The inadequate investment in our physical resources is often quite obvious. Vacant plants and stores litter our landscape. Schools suffer from deferred maintenance. Highways and bridges need rebuilding. Water systems and sewage plants are often inadequate. Our electrical power grid is close to capacity. Viruses and spam are threatening to overwhelm the Internet. Landfills and waste disposal sites are running short of space. Environmental pollutants contaminate the air that we breathe and the water that we drink. The left must develop and present a new vision to respond to these needs.

The effects of the decline of investment in our human resources are harder to quantify. Although many believe that standardized testing programs are the answer to our educational problems, these tests are often a poor measure of educational success. In addition, goal setting is irrelevant if society is unwilling to make the investments required to improve the educational system. Instead, we expect our schools to do more with ever decreasing resources. We ask our colleges and universities to get by with fewer resources. As a result, we allow the cost of higher education to increase faster than wages, reducing access for lower income students.

Despite the widespread need for additional public investment in our physical infrastructure and human resources, we reduce taxes for the wealthier members of our society. As our schools suffer, the wealthiest members of society continue to build ever larger homes and purchase costly luxury vehicles. Overconsumption by the wealthy drains resources from the public sector and in the long run we will all suffer the consequences. The left needs to articulate forcefully its objections to the preferential treatment that we have given wealthy and high income Americans for the past quarter century.

Perhaps our failure to invest in our social capital is of greatest concern. Many people do not know or rarely see their neighbors. Church membership and attendance is declining. Schools, many of which are in dire financial straits, are eliminating or charging for activities such as music, athletics, and other extracurricular activities that help build social connections. Participation in clubs and associations is declining as two income families find it difficult to keep up with their responsibilities to their jobs and children. High levels of social capital, also known as civic culture, drive people to volunteer for community activities and participate in government. It often correlates with high voter turnout in elections. As it declines, we are in danger of losing the informed, active citizens that are essential in an effective democracy.

Part of the explanation for this decline is that deregulation and privatization have forced many Americans to devote too much attention to their jobs and personal finances. As a consequence, we are lacking the time and money to invest in our public infrastructure as well as our human and social capital. In order to make ends meet in a privatized, deregulated world, people work longer hours rather than taking time to build human capital by obtaining additional education or learning new skills. These financial pressures also get in the way of building social capital by preventing many people from volunteering for community activities, serving in churches or schools, participating in local clubs or associations, or simply enjoying their families. The left must lead the way to rebuilding our sense of community and helping all Americans fulfill their potential.

Renewing our nation

Ever since Bush pronounced Iran as part of the "axis of evil," many wondered whether or not Iran might be his next target after Iraq. During his 2005 post-election tour of Europe, he said that any "notion that the United States is getting ready to attack Iran is simply ridiculous" -- and then very quickly added, "...having said that, all options are on the table." Once again, who knows exactly what he meant by that worrisome postscript, but it sounded very much like military options are a possibility.

As the United States places ever more emphasis on militarism and privatization, it might be well to reflect on the history of

Dubrovnik, today a small town in Croatia on the eastern shore of the Adriatic Sea. For about 1000 years, Dubrovnik was the center of a tiny independent republic. Originally known as the Republic of Ragusa, it had few natural resources, a modest population, and no standing army. Nonetheless, it prospered for many centuries. The city lay at the intersection of a line connecting Venice with the Mediterranean Sea and a line connecting Rome with Constantinople. As a result, it developed into an important trading center and meeting place between east and west.

In order to prevent control of the government by a single dominant family, the ruling families installed a system of rotating rectors who only served one month at a time. They emphasized diplomatic solutions in order to survive at the boundary between powerful empires. Using wealth derived from its huge commercial fleet, larger than all but the fleets of Spain and the Netherlands, Ragusa provided its citizens health care and public schools. It constructed a public water system and adopted antislavery laws as far back as 1416. In cultural affairs, it developed into a city-state with collections of art and manuscripts that rivaled those of Venice. The admonition to "forget private business, care for public affairs" remains inscribed in Latin above a doorway at the Rector's Palace and provides a simple statement of one of their core values.

Ragusa demonstrates that it is possible to construct a successful society around diplomacy rather than militarism, public affairs rather than private business. Its leaders served the public good while creating a long lasting, wealthy and independent republic. Similarly, we need to restore our commitment to the inspiring guiding fictions, central myths, and collective ideals that form the foundation of our nation. We need to rededicate ourselves to principles such as liberty, equality, diversity, justice, and religious freedom.

As a nation, we need to become more comfortable with complexity and ambiguity. We need to move beyond simplistic clichés that reflect old prejudices and stereotypes. Multilateral programs, long term thinking, and political, economic, and cultural diversity do make our lives more complicated. They also enrich our lives and enable us to live cooperatively with others, both locally and globally.

For civilizations, the question is not so much how good they are, but rather the extent to which they are able to move beyond their failures and mistakes to a build a better society for their citizens. Success for a country, or an individual, is a dynamic process rather than a static condition. The United States needs to focus less on its past successes, and more on how it will deal with the future.

Rather than waging divisive struggles for power, we need to rediscover the spirit of George Washington when he turned away from power and established the tradition of a two term limit for the presidency. Power and control tend to destroy those who lust after them. We need to reconsider how to use the finite, but still great, political, economic, and military power that we have. As a nation, we need to stop acting like an impulsive teenager and start acting like the mature adult on the world stage that we should be. We must respect and shepherd our power so that we can constructively create a better world rather than contribute to its destruction.

We need to work with the leaders of other nations to develop global guiding fictions that can serve to unite the world in building a better future. Franklin Roosevelt's Four Freedoms, freedom of speech and religion, freedom from want and fear, provided an inspiration during World War II as we fought with our allies against the forces of tyranny. A strong sense of community and a recognition of the need for cooperation remain among many people of the world. We need to build on these principles and others to develop a set of guiding fictions at the global level. They would provide the guidance and inspiration that are lacking in trade agreements developed behind closed doors to serve the rich and powerful.

In our own nation, rather than imposing new controls on our own citizens through such misguided efforts as the so-called Patriot Act, we need to maintain a free and open society. Rather than resorting to religious rhetoric drawn from a particular religious tradition, we need to reemphasize the need for tolerance of all traditions. Rather than concentrating political power in one party and one branch of government, we need to recognize the value of minority views, political opposition, and decentralized power to our country for all of us.

We need to renew our system of checks and balances; separation of powers helps maintain a healthy government. A diversity of strong and independent institutions strengthens our societal immune system and protects us from the malignant growth of unfettered power. We need to provide everyone with the opportunity to participate fully in the political, economic, and social life of our nation. Discrimination on the basis of race, religion, gender, sexual orientation, age, wealth, or any other arbitrary and unjust basis weakens and divides our society. In order to bring harmony to a nation out of tune, we need to repair our broken strings and restore our missing notes.

♫ ♫ ♫

During the Civil War that tore our nation apart in so many ways, Abraham Lincoln returned to our guiding fictions in his address at Gettysburg speaking of "a new nation conceived in liberty and dedicated to the proposition that all men are created equal." He urged that "it is for us...to be dedicated...to the unfinished work which they...so nobly advanced" and closed by saying "that we here highly resolve...that government of the people, by the people, for the people, shall not perish from the earth." Lincoln as well as our country may not always have made the best decisions, but without our continued commitment to these guiding fictions and the spirit that lies behind them, the greatness of our country will, to paraphrase Lincoln, no longer endure.

Coda

The violin in your closet

...finding your path to the future

♫ ♫ ♫

There is a tradition that the emperor Nero played his fiddle while Rome burned. Although of questionable accuracy, this image has come to symbolize anyone who fails to act in time of great need. We are at a crucial time in our history. The forces of intolerance and repression are resurgent. They threaten our individual rights and freedoms as well as the stability of democratic governments throughout the world. Each of us needs to find our own way to create and sustain a world of peace and harmony.

Lessons from this story

One of the characteristics of most parables and stories is that they occur within a finite period of time. For instance, in the parable of the sower in the 13th chapter of the book of Matthew in the New Testament, the story does not consider how the uneven results of his sowing may have influenced his life. Did his family endure hunger because much of the seed did not survive due to birds, rocky ground, or thorns? Or, did he have a surplus of food since the seeds that fell on the good soil were so productive? Nonetheless, the basic lesson of the parable remains -- you reap what you sow.

In much the same way, we don't know precisely what direction the specific issues and events that this book discusses will take in the future. They will evolve in ways that we cannot predict with certainty. Nonetheless, the lessons from the past five years will continue to provide insights for all those seeking to build democratic societies based on liberty and justice for all.

The best of our guiding fictions will retain their power to inform and inspire. These guiding fictions have united us around a common set of values rather than a cult of personality, some abstract philosophy, or a desire for power as has often been the case in other less successful societies. Our guiding fictions have inspired us to renew and rebuild our nation in a constant search for a better expression of these values.

In order to act, and not just react, we need to become better informed; we need to accept personal responsibility for our lives and communities. Rather than engaging in either-or thinking as we look for the one right answer, we need to listen to others, seek consensus, search for a middle way. We need to think creatively, use our American ingenuity. We need to move decisions to the lowest possible level, to emphasize smallness over bigness, and to favor a long term perspective over short term gratification.

Most Americans across the political spectrum endorse some version of the Christian tradition. However, many do not support the views of religious fundamentalists who emphasize law over grace, regard the Bible as a religious relic, and seek to impose their particular interpretation of Christianity on others. They see a world in need of both law and grace -- restraints and forgiveness, tolerance and understanding, respect and cooperation. Our nation has always had room for a broad diversity of political views and religious beliefs. We must reject the leadership of those who would lead us down the path of intolerance and discrimination

In our religious lives, we should respect the beliefs of others and acknowledge the need to maintain a healthy, though sometimes uncertain, separation between affairs of church and state. This separation protects our political rights from religious interference and our religious beliefs from government interference. Rather than seeking to impose our beliefs on others, we need to build our lives around cooperation, harmony, and social justice. We need to care for the sick, the needy, the outcasts of society.

We need to recognize that we live in pluralistic world in which there are a multitude of ways of looking at life's perplexities. Some are more constructive and healthy than others, but all deserve a measure of our respect as we sort through the global labyrinth of ideas and beliefs. Every religious paradigm represents a minority view. Rather than confining ourselves within our own little box of beliefs, we need to expand our vision and make our box large enough to encompass the diversity that is the world. This will require a transformative change in the way in which we view authority. We will need to make room for other views and other authorities even as we practice our chosen beliefs; for many of us, this may require an uncomfortable combination of ambiguity, faith, and trust.

Although this book speaks from a liberal perspective, there is much to admire in the traditions of both the Democratic and Republican parties. Many Americans find it easy to endorse Republican concerns for personal responsibility, fiscal prudence, and a healthy economy. Many Americans also embrace Democratic concerns for helping the less fortunate, protecting the environment, and preserving our civil liberties. Unfortunately, the Bush administration and its conservative supporters have failed to honor not only the political concerns of traditional Democrats, but also those of traditional Republicans.

We need to regain control of our economic lives. The market is a human invention that is neither omniscient or omnipotent; it makes its decisions using incomplete and flawed data and based solely on short term profits without concern for their moral impact or long term consequences. We need to support small businesses and other alternatives to the corporate economic model; economic diversity helps build economic security. Appropriate regulations can encourage economic diversity as well as enhance accountability for the actions of individuals and corporations. To ensure that all individuals can participate in a fair and equitable manner in our economy, we need to pursue economic justice in such areas as education, employment opportunities, wages, benefits, and taxation.

As individuals, we need to take a longer term view of our lives. We need to accept personal responsibility for the vitality of our communities and to consider more than price in making our purchasing decisions. We need to live our economic lives in such as way as to support sustainability, fairness, and justice. We need to develop a new vision of success based on satisfaction rather than satiation, sufficiency rather than excess. This will take a significant change in our priorities, a spiritual renewal in our lives.

Globalization is making growing and often unreasonable demands on the lives of workers. These range from demands to relocate to demands to be available for work virtually around the clock. Some worker advocates have suggested that the current situation resembles the 1920s when the auto industry demanded assembly line "speedups." These demands alienated workers and contributed to the growth of labor unions in the 1930s. Scientists learn that for every action there is an equal and opposite reaction. A similar phenomenon in socioeconomic culture may encourage workers to seek new and unexpected solutions to the personal and economic problems that globalization is creating.

Our democracy requires continual nurturing and support. We need to become politically informed and involved in setting the priorities of governments at all levels. This may involve attending meetings, serving on committees, writing letters; it may involve supporting good candidates or running for political office yourself. Good government and strong communities evolve together. We need to strengthen the economic, social, cultural, and educational structures of our communities. Our political system is dependent on strong and balanced opposing political forces. We need to support the political organizations that help us express our own opinions and desires. We also need to respect the views of the political opposition; we should strive to understand, if not agree with, their perspectives on issues and problems.

Building and maintaining a free and democratic society is not easy. There are always new problems and challenges. Depending on your interests and skills, you may choose to work on economic issues, religious concerns, or political tasks. Whatever the area, we all need to contribute in an active way to the success of our communities and nation. Despite the growing fear and frustration among many Americans due to outside threats, economic uncertainty, and political divisions, this is not the time to throw up one's hands and quit. More than ever, we all need to find new ways of working together towards solving our problems -- and building a better tomorrow for our children and grandchildren.

Finding your path

How do we build a better tomorrow? How do we find the unique path that we should follow? As is often the case, we start with the past. We look in those places where those in power do not wish us to go. We think about our hopes and dreams. We talk to others about their experiences. We visit libraries and learn about a past that many want us to forget. We explore the dusty, half-forgotten corners of our lives.

In the past, many families stored unused or seasonal items in the attics of their homes. In fact, the Smithsonian Institution often refers to itself as the "nation's attic." Although newer homes sometimes do not have usable attics, we still have closets, basements, and garages filled with items from the margins of our lives. These spaces contain a strange mix of the familiar and the forgotten. They contain reminders of the past, new ideas for the future, and the space to allow them to grow.

In his morning feature on National Public Radio, *The Writer's Almanac,* Garrison Keillor described how author Michael Chabon came upon a box of comic books left over from his childhood. When he opened the box, the old paper smell brought back memories that inspired him to write a novel on comic books, *The Amazing Adventures of Kavalier and Clay,* that won a Pulitzer Prize.

In a wonderful essay some years ago, Ray Bradbury noted the important role of garages in the development of many of the 20th century's most important inventions and businesses. From the Wright brothers' pioneering aviation work and Henry Ford's development of his automobile to the formation of Hewlett-Packard and Apple Computer by the two Steves, Jobs and Wozniak, creativity seems to spring out of the humble garage. Bradbury suggests that we should ponder the question, what's in your garage?

The founders of the Nelson Muffler Corporation, where I worked for nearly 25 years, got their start in 1939 in the basement of a Buick garage in Stoughton, Wisconsin. In 1987, the first facility of Digisonix, a Nelson unit that grew out of my personal research activities, was a garage formerly occupied by a John Deere dealer.

Following the end of World War II, my father started his own tool and die shop in the garage behind our small house in a mixed residential and industrial area of West Allis, Wisconsin. This was the first of three businesses that my father founded during his life. Not long before he died, he talked to me while lying on a couch. He told how me how good it was to start new things later in life. He formed his final business when he was sixty years old.

If we search the corners of our lives -- our garages, our closets, our memories, our dreams -- we will find creative impulses and new possibilities for our lives, our businesses, and our nation. We may gain inspiration to serve others, to perform volunteer work, to return to school, or to learn new skills. We may become artists, musicians, or writers. We may see a need for a new product, a new business, or a new organization. We may change jobs or careers. We may become politically active by writing letters, visiting lawmakers, working on campaigns, or running for office.

Jimmy Carter, after serving as president of the United States, began a new career building houses through *Habitat for Humanity* and seeking peace through *The Carter Center*. His efforts won him the Nobel Peace Prize and perhaps even greater respect than he had achieved through his distinguished political career.

In Madison, former Police Chief David Couper retired from law enforcement and became an Episcopal priest. This career change enabled him to break through the darkness of police work and experience the positive side of humanity.

Robyn Davidson in *Tracks*, a book about her solo journey on camels across the Australian outback, notes that the first step towards any goal is often the hardest. We will face many physical, intellectual, spiritual, and emotional challenges.

For me, my father's violin contained echoes of the past and instilled hope for the future. The challenges of the violin demand a long term perspective. As I study the violin, I become aware of the many ways in which it serves as a useful metaphor for the problems that we are facing.

Perhaps the most important lesson that we learn from playing a musical instrument is that we can take a more active role in shaping our lives. We can take on difficult tasks. We can contribute to building a better world.

What's in your closet?

I found an old violin and a new way to look at life.

Who knows what you might find?

The future is open.

String Theory

a dark quiet night
the violin is silent
patiently waiting

the bow awakens
slowly moving back and forth
the music begins

soon moving faster
the bow crosses from string to string
in clouds of rosin

a blue glow appears
as ions accumulate
and the music builds

now sparks are flying
rivers of color and light
a cascade of stars

the night disappears
lightning arcs across the sky
filling the ether

energy from strings
creating light from darkness
as the bow moves on

sound and light spring forth
pushing the edge of the void
expanding the world

♬ ♬ ♬

Appendix I

On strings, violins, and music

♫ ♫ ♫

The Music of the Spheres

The success of the ancient Greeks in relating the length of a vibrating string to the notes of a musical scale caused them to look for similar numerical relationships elsewhere. This led to their belief that astronomical bodies such as the planets must vibrate, filling the universe with sound -- the music of the spheres. In the sixteenth century, Johann Kepler attempted to predict the radii of the orbits of the inner planets by viewing the Solar System as a nested set of alternating cubes and spheres. Unfortunately, the discovery of later planets did not fit Kepler's scheme, and his model is now just an interesting footnote to his famous laws of planetary motion.

Cosmologists have recognized for some time that there were sound waves -- variations in density of material -- present at the formation of the universe following the big bang. Even today, evidence of these sound waves from the far distant past exists in minute variations in the background radiation that permeates the cosmos. With the proper equipment, it is quite easy to listen to static that is like an echo from the creation of the universe -- the sounds that Bam, a character in Nadine Gordimer's novel, *July's People,* suggests when he notes that with the advent of modern science there no longer is any music of the spheres, only chaos.

Waves and vibrating strings are also central to research at the smallest scale of our universe. Wave mechanics describes the behavior of matter at the atomic level. String theory describes the behavior of subatomic particles using extraordinarily small, vibrating strings of energy. Individual biological cells produce pressure fluctuations or sound waves that scientists can measure with extremely sensitive atomic force microscopes. Sounds, waves, and vibrating strings permeate the world in which we live as well as our individual hearts and minds. Perhaps, as the Greeks suggested, there is indeed a music of the spheres at a far deeper level than we once thought possible.

The design of the violin

People have used stringed instruments such as the harp and lyre to create musical sounds for thousands of years. The use of a bow with stringed instruments was common throughout Europe by the year 1000. Eventually, bowed instruments such the fiddle, the rebec, and the *lira da braccio* evolved into the modern violin. By the early 18th century, makers such as Stradivari and others had fixed the basic design of the instrument that we know today.

Because of his fame, it has become quite common for violin builders throughout the world to attach the name Stradivari to their violins. My violin is no exception, but despite the Stradivarius label on the inside of the body, it remains simply a student instrument of no exceptional value. Nonetheless, it is attractive and probably at least seventy years old. Additional lettering on the label as well as the outside of the violin indicates that a company in Czechoslovakia made the instrument, perhaps in the early 1900s.

Other than the use of modern materials for the strings, violins have remained virtually unchanged since the time of Stradivari. It took somewhat longer for the viola and cello to evolve into scaled versions of the same basic design. Although the double bass may appear similar, it is quite different in design than the three smaller stringed instruments. Most noticeably, the body of the instrument tapers smoothly into the neck, and the pegs have threads to provide more force to tune its heavy strings.

In many ways, the design of the violin anticipates modern engineering. Despite its light weight construction with simple wooden parts, the violin possesses robust fragility. The complex structure includes a long wooden neck connected to a hollow body or soundbox that requires great strength to support the tension of the strings. It performs this difficult function even though early violins contained virtually no metal parts with the exception of a few nails to help secure the neck to the body.

The lightweight panels of the violin body possesses great strength much like the box girders used in building construction. Its structure resembles the monocoque design used in mid-20th century racing cars as well as today's most sophisticated aircraft and modern automobiles. These vehicles have bodies of great strength through the use of lightweight parts connected to form a unitized structure. It is the same concept utilized in the design of the former World Trade Center towers. They featured a large number of relatively lightweight wall structures assembled to form the strong, rigid, square tubes that defined the basic external structure of both towers and required minimal internal supports.

When we listen to a musician play a tone on a stringed instrument, the sound results from the response of the body of the instrument to a vibrating string excited by the bow. The pitch of the tone, also known as the frequency of the sound, is primarily determined by the length of the string. The string vibrates at the resonant frequency of the length that the musician selects. If you shorten the length of the string or the column of air, it will vibrate at a note of higher pitch or frequency.

The violin has four strings: the E_5 string, the highest string; the A_4 string (A above middle C); the D_4 string; and finally the heavy G_3 (G below middle C) string. The pitch of each string is a musical fifth from its neighbor. There are no frets to constrain the available pitches. The violinist can produce a virtually unlimited variety of pitches throughout its approximately four octave range beginning with G_3 (corresponding to an open G string, the lowest note possible on the violin).

By themselves, the strings of a violin produce very little sound. The bridge, an intricately shaped, thin piece of wood held in place on top of the violin body by the tension of the strings, supports the strings above the body of the violin and transmits their vibrations into the body and internal cavity of the violin. A long bass bar fastened to the top plate asymmetrically under the lowest string enhances low frequency vibrations. A sound post under the highest string connects the top and bottom plates of the body and enhances the transmission of vibrations into the bottom plate. Asymmetry and complexity underlie the superficial simplicity and symmetry of the violin.

When storing or transporting their instruments, violinists try to avoid extremes of heat and humidity. Violins are very sensitive to environmental changes. Variations in temperature and humidity can adversely affect the strings and wooden structure. In high humidity, the pegs can stick and become difficult to turn. In the winter, dry heated air can cause the pegs to dry out and loosen. Under such conditions, it can be helpful to store the violin inside its case with a device to add moisture to the air.

Tuning the violin

It is always preferable to properly tune a musical instrument to achieve harmonious results. The novel *The Piano Tuner* by Daniel Mason revolves around the journey of a London piano tuner to the jungles of Burma in the 1880s to tune a classic piano. During his journey and upon arriving in the jungle, he sees the world around him in new ways. He becomes aware of new possibilities for his life that he had not considered during his routine experiences in London. The story serves as a metaphor for the ways in which our musical instruments and lives can get out of tune. They sometimes need adjustments to restore them to harmony.

Most people tune their piano perhaps once or twice a year, sometimes less often, sometimes more. Unlike the piano, a violin needs virtually continual tuning. A violin that is out of tune is difficult to play alone and impossible to play properly with another instrument. Some notes will be either sharp or flat, and the musical result can range from mildly unpleasant to extremely annoying. If absolutely necessary, even in the middle of a piece, advanced players can adjust their fingering to account for the incorrect tuning, but the adjustment is often difficult and distracting.

A violinist needs to check the tune of the instrument before every practice session and even in the middle of especially long pieces. The tension on the strings of a violin will often change in unpredictable and sudden ways. Since the instrument is a tightly integrated structure, changes in the tension of one string can also produce changes in the others. These changes are particularly common during the winter when extremes of temperature and humidity can occur between the air outside and the air inside a warm, dry building. An instrument well-tuned at home can change substantially by the time of a performance or lesson.

A set of adjustable pegs at the end of the neck enable proper tuning of each string. Simple windings secure each string to its peg. The wooden pegs have a tapered fit into holes in the neck of the violin. They must move easily to allow the adjustment of the string tension and yet maintain their selected position against the strong pull of the tight string. Such conflicting and ambiguous requirements are common in the design of the violin. They lead to quite sophisticated compromises that have proven effective over centuries of use.

Tuning a violin is an art as much as a science, and there are many ways to do it. Perhaps the simplest way is to match the notes of the four strings to the same notes on a properly tuned piano. If a piano is not readily available, a common alternative is to match the sound of the A string to a tuning fork that sounds A_4 (with a frequency of 440 Hz). The violinist then tunes the other strings so their notes are a musical fifth apart.

A skilled musician can do this by bowing two strings at the same time and listening for the harmonious sound that results from the proper fifth spacing. The beginning student can achieve the same result by using the tune from "Twinkle, Twinkle, Little Star." The opening notes are a fifth apart and provide a basis for adjusting adjacent strings. Some electronic metronomes assist tuning by measuring how much flat or sharp each note may be.

Comparisons with the accordion

When I was a boy, I took accordion lessons for many years and became reasonably skilled at this now neglected instrument. The accordionist makes music using a contraptionary collection of keys, levers, and reeds arranged like the control panel of a machine. Both arms pump the bellows of the accordion while fingers push specific keys and buttons to produce the desired notes and chords.

The contrast between the accordion and violin is stark. On the violin there are no frets or guides to restrict either the position of the violinist's left hand or the placement of the bow by the violinist's right hand on the strings. On the modern piano accordion, your right hand plays a keyboard while your left hand selects from an array of buttons to play one or more chords. Tuning is not possible and virtually unnecessary. The internal mechanism and fixed number of predetermined notes and chords ensures proper tonality. Perhaps, it was not an accident that the accordion became so popular in the control oriented fifties. In today's world, the violin with its ambiguity and adaptability is a better metaphor for our life together.

Golf and the violin

There are a surprising number of similarities between the violin and the game of golf. The complicated movements for playing the violin or hitting a golf ball have both evolved over many years. Instructors carefully present them to new students, and they require considerable practice to master. The proper position of the hands, arms, and body are critical to both activities. The player must maintain fluidity, rhythm, and balance as they move the bow or club. In both cases, the required positions and motions feel unnatural at first and only with continual repetition can the player approach either task with any degree of confidence.

Perhaps due to the complexity of both activities, instructions for swinging a golf club or playing a violin include a large number of aphorisms. Golf instructors tell the student golfer to keep their head down, tuck their right elbow in, keep their left arm straight, keep their grip firm, but not too firm, and, of course, to relax. Similarly, violin teachers tell the beginning violinist to keep their left wrist straight, move their elbow under the violin, move their right arm from their elbow, apply firm pressure with the bow, but not too firm, and, most importantly, relax.

Despite the large physical movements that a player uses to hit a golf ball or a violinist to play the violin, both activities require a high degree of sensitivity and precision. Playing the violin and hitting a golf ball belong right up there with hitting a baseball as among the most difficult physical tasks ever devised. A well-struck golf ball or well-played note produces a satisfaction that is highly sensual. The sound of both echoes in your mind.

Both golfers and violinists value the traditions of the past. Much of the standard musical repertoire for the violin is hundreds of years old. Although most violinists play on modern instruments, often manufactured in a factory, their basic design remains almost unchanged from those produced centuries ago. Today, more accomplished musicians often use hand-crafted instruments and great violinists continue to play on instruments that are centuries old. John Hersey's novel *Antonietta* describes the journey of a violin as it passes through the lives of many owners over several centuries.

Golfers display a similar fondness for the old artifacts of their game. I began playing golf with an old set of hickory shafted golf clubs that my dad used as a boy. Today, hickory shafted clubs and wooden headed drivers have given way to clubs with new and exotic materials such graphite shafts and titanium heads. However, players often treat older wooden clubs as treasured relics and collect them for both their aesthetic and historical value. In the movie *Caddyshack,* a character resorts to a treasured putter for an important putt.

No two golf courses or concert halls are exactly alike. Each has unique characteristics that create its unique identity. Players approach famous golf courses as shrines to the game that they love. In a similar manner, musicians approach great musical venues with the reverence often reserved for a great cathedral. Skepticism and resistance greet any suggestions to modify or "improve" hallowed golf courses or concert halls.

Learning to play the violin

Over the years, I have attended many concerts featuring various solo violinists. During pauses in their playing, it was not unusual to see them lower their arms, while the violin remains clamped between their shoulder and jaw, cantilevered in space. I always thought it was a simply a flashy move and worried about whether their violin would come crashing to the floor without their left hand to support it.

My concerns were unfounded. While playing the violin, the left hand selects the desired notes on the strings. It does not support the violin. For this reason, it's not at all difficult to rest your arms, while leaving the violin under your chin. The only reason to lower the violin is to rest your neck muscles. Today, it has become the custom to clip a shoulder rest to the back of the violin to make it easier to hold the instrument between your head and shoulder.

The right hand holds the violin bow with a grip that feels both awkward and unnatural to the beginning student. The little finger rests on top of the bow, the others fingers wrap around the top of the bow, and the thumb curls around the bottom. Despite this strange grip, the right hand and wrist must remain relaxed, position the bow on the desired string in the proper location with the proper contact, and move the bow as required by the music.

The challenges for the left hand are just as demanding. The fingers of the left hand vary the length of the vibrating string. Since there are no frets on a violin, it takes time to learn how to position the fingers for each desired note. The hardest notes to reach and play for the beginning student are those requiring the use of the fourth finger. For most people, their fourth finger tends to be both their weakest finger as well as the finger over which they have the least control.

Changing notes on the same string is not too difficult and simply requires changing the position of the fingers on your left hand. However, when you want to play a note on a different string, the left hand must move quickly, while the right hand is rapidly changing the angle of the bow to reach the desired string. Multiple "string crossings" in quick succession are difficult to master.

Most songs for beginning violinists require one stroke of the bow for each note. As pieces get more complicated, this simple up and down pattern includes slurs where a single movement of the bow produces multiple notes. The speed of the bow must allow time to play all of the notes before reaching the end of the bow. The violinist must continually use both arms and the fingers of both hands to select the desired note or notes while moving the bow with the desired pressure, direction, amplitude, speed, and tempo on the appropriate string. It quickly becomes apparent why many consider the violin such a difficult instrument to play. In fact, researchers have found that the region of the brain associated with movement of the fingers on the left hand is significantly larger for violinists due to the demands of the instrument.

After just a few weeks, most students are able to occasionally bring forth a few good notes. At this point, their limited success offers them encouragement to continue. As they continue to improve, they gradually move on to more challenging pieces. Much like life itself, the violin is impossible to master, but offers moments of sublime beauty that make the effort worthwhile.

♫ ♫ ♫

Appendix II

Numbers and the 2004 presidential election

What do the numbers surrounding the 2004 election suggest?

- *American voters respect authority -- maybe too much.* Since 1932, only three incumbent presidents have failed to gain reelection: Gerald Ford in 1976, who had gained office by appointment; Jimmy Carter in 1980, who got caught up in the Iranian revolution and subsequent hostage crisis; and George H. W. Bush, the father of "W," who lost through a combination of unhappiness over taxes and an unusually strong opponent -- Bill Clinton. Otherwise, the incumbent president has won reelection 10 times since 1932.

- *Since Vietnam and the Civil Rights protests, Republican presidential candidates have been tough to beat.* Republican presidents and conservative policies have dominated the past 40 years of American politics. From 1968 through 2008, we will have had 28 years of Republican presidents and only 12 years of Democratic presidents. Despite the contempt of some Republicans for Bill Clinton, he was a moderate Democrat on most issues, certainly well to the right of many current Democratic liberals.

- *American voters are often wrong.* Robert McChesney, founder of Free Press, quoted results from a poll of the president's supporters that showed 72% thought there were WMDs in Iraq, 75% thought Iraq supported Al Qaeda, 66% thought Bush supported the International Criminal Court, and 72% thought Bush supported banning land mines. Of course, each of these beliefs is wrong.

- *So-called moral values, though important to some voters for a variety of different reasons, are only one of many issues that divide us.* Just a few days before the election, *Time* magazine suggested that moral values would not be a decisive issue for most voters. In fact, their poll results from mid-October showed that moral values was the most important issue for only 12% of those surveyed. The economy came in first at 26%. followed closely by terrorism, Iraq, and health care. Nonetheless, one post-election survey claimed that a leading 22% of the voters cited moral values as the most important issue for them. The economy came in second at 20%, followed by terrorism at 19%. However, according to the *Chicago Tribune,* a Pew Research Center poll taken following the election found that, using an open-ended question rather than providing multiple choice answers, the most important issue for voters in the presidential race was Iraq for about 25%, jobs and the economy for about 14%, and moral values for about 9%. It is likely that different views of exactly what moral values are important led some voters to support Bush and others to support Kerry. Interestingly, when the poll asked respondents to rank a specified list of issues, moral values were first at 27%, Iraq second at 22%, and the economy and jobs third at 21%. Clearly, the way in which you ask the question affects the result, and in recent elections, a number of different issues have become comparably important.

- *Southern states provide the cornerstone for Republican victories.* Beginning with the Civil Rights Act of 1964, banning discrimination in voting, jobs, and public accommodations, Democratic political influence in the south has declined. According to a report by Ronald Brownstein in the Chicago Tribune, Bush won 85% of the counties in 13 southern states. In 1964, Democrats held 22 of the 26 senate seats in these 13 southern states. Following the 2004 election, the situation had exactly reversed with Republicans holding 22 out of 26 southern senate seats. During the 40 years during which this political shift has occurred, the population of the south has grown and become more important in national politics. The 13 southern states (AL, AR, FL, GA, KY, LA, MS, NC, OK, SC, TN, TX, and VA) now control 168 electoral votes out of the 270 required to win the presidency, a little more than 60%.

- *It is difficult for a Democrat to win the presidency without any southern states.* In Bill Clinton's victory in 1996, he won Arkansas (his home state), Florida, Kentucky (narrowly), Louisiana, and Tennessee (Gore's home state, also narrowly) -- a total of 59 electoral votes from the south (in 1992, Clinton lost Florida, but won Georgia, both by narrow margins). Neither Gore in 2000 or Kerry in 2004 won any southern states. The candidacy of businessman Ross Perot may have helped Clinton in 1992 and 1996, while the candidacy of Ralph Nader almost certainly cost Gore his victory in 2000.

- *Nonetheless, the 2004 presidential election was a very close race.* Ultimately, Bush won New Mexico and Iowa by narrow margins to gain a total of 286 electoral votes compared to Kerry's 252 electoral votes. Bush also won the popular vote by a margin of about 3%, 51% for Bush versus 48% for Kerry. However, Bush's home state of Texas generated about half of his overall winning margin of 3.5 million votes.

- *Bush won many smaller states and counties by large percentages of the vote; Kerry won many larger states and counties by large numbers of votes.* As an end of the year newspaper story put it, Bush's winning margins were "more than 20 percentage points in the majority of the counties where he won the popular vote." The author clearly crafted this convoluted statement to emphasize the breadth and depth of the Bush win. Others have similarly noted Bush's large winning percentages in many states. For example, it is true that Bush won 22 states by victory margins of more than 10%, while Kerry only won 9 states (including the District of Columbia) by more than 10%. However, many of Bush's wins were in states with very small populations. Kerry won a number of states with huge populations by a very large number of votes. For example, Bush won his top 4 states (AL, GA, IN, and TX) by a combined victory margin of about 3.2 million votes (over half of which were from Texas), while Kerry won his top 4 states (CA, IL, MA, NY) by a combined victory margin of about 3.4 million votes. In addition, the victory margin in 18 states was less than 100,000 votes of which Bush won 10. Bush's victory, though broad in terms of number of states won, was not very deep or broad when viewing actual votes cast. This conclusion should be obvious considering Bush's narrow victory in both the popular vote and electoral college. The nation and many individual states remain evenly divided.

- *The election may have come just in time for Bush.* According to a Washington Post-ABC News poll in December of 2004, 70 percent of Americans believed that any improvements to our long term security from the Iraq War had come at an "unacceptable" level of military casualties. Since the summer of 2004, the number who believed the war was "not worth fighting" had increased from 48 percent to 56 percent. Fifty-seven percent did not approve of Bush's handling of the war, seven points higher than in September of 2004. The percentage of those who approved of his record on terrorism had fallen to 53 percent from 70 percent one year earlier. By May of 2005, his ratings on specific issues had declined further, and a USA Today/CNN/Gallup poll found that his overall approval rating had fallen to just 46 percent. In June of 2005 as this book went to press, an AP-Ipsos poll found that only 43 percent approved of the job Bush was doing and only 41 percent supported the war in Iraq. The results make one wonder how many of those who no longer felt he was doing a good job had voted for him just seven months earlier?

References by Chapter
(in approximate order)

Selected acronyms

CAFTA	Central American Free Trade Agreement
CDC	Center for Disease Control
CEO	Chief Executive Officer
CIA	Central Intelligence Agency
CPI	Consumer Price Index
CSA	Community Supported Agriculture
DFA	Dairy Farmers of America
EPA	Environmental Protection Agency
EU	European Union
FBI	Federal Bureau of Investigation
FCC	Federal Communications Commission
GDP	Gross Domestic Product
GOP	Grand Old Party (Republican Party)
IEEE	Institute of Electrical and Electronics Engineers
IMF	International Monetary Fund
NAFTA	North American Free Trade Agreement
NASA	National Aeronautics and Space Administration
NATO	North Atlantic Treaty Organization
NEA	National Education Association
PAC	Political Action Committee
QATT	Qualified Anti-Terrorism Technology
SAFETY	Support Anti-Terrorism by Fostering Effective Technologies Act
UCITA	Uniform Computer Information Transactions Act
WMD	Weapons of Mass Destruction (chemical, biological, nuclear)
WTO	World Trade Organization

Prelude

Fournier, Ron, "Something's wrong, but who to pick to make it right?" *Wisconsin State Journal,* April 25, 2004 (re AP-Ipsos-Public Affairs poll).

Lester, Will, "Bush ratings drop to new lows," *The Capital Times,* June 10, 2005 (AP-Ipsos poll).

Frank, Thomas, "American psyche: Analyzing the fractured national identity, through the prism of census data, economic plicy and red-blue clichés," *The New York Times Book Review,* November 28, 2004.

Chittister, Joan, *Heart of Flesh,* William B. Eerdmans Publishing Company, Grand Rapids, Michigan, 1998 (p. 12-13 re problems in U.S.).

Krugman, Paul, "Losing our country," *The New York Times,* June 10, 2005 (re decline of the middle class).

Gabler, Neal, "The last myth has been shattered," *Wisconsin State Journal,* Dec. 10, 2000.

Klein, Joe, "Where's the outrage?" *Time,* January 17, 2005 (re hearings on Alberto Gonzales, Bush nominee for Attorney General; quotes Republican Senator Lindsey Graham of South Carolina as suggesting during debate over use of torture that "...we have lost our way").

Roy, Arundhati, *War Talk,* South End Press, Cambridge, MA, 2003.
Kennedy, Jr., Robert, *Crimes Against Nature: How George W. Bush and His Corporate Pals Are Plundering the Country and Hijacking Our Democracy,* HarperCollins, New York, 2004.
---, "French 'no' vote buoys Dutch foes of EU push," *The Capital Times,* May 31, 2005.
Deutsch, Anthony, "Dutch vote deals 2nd blow to EU," *The Capital Times,* June 2, 2005.

I. Loss of harmony...of, by, and for the people

1) The role of guiding fictions...these truths to be self-evident

Shumway, Nicolas, *The Invention of Argentina,* University of California Press, Berkeley, 1991.
May, Rollo, *The Cry for Myth,* Norton, New York, 1991.
Barbour, Ian, *Myths, Models, and Paradigms,* Harper and Row, New York, 1974.
Keillor, Garrison, *The Writer's Almanac,* American Public Media, December 8, 2004.
Gordon, Mary, *The Shadow Man: A Daughter's Search for Her Father,* Random House, New York, 1996.
Isaacson, Walter, "A declaration of mutual dependence," *The New York Times,* July 4, 2004.
Baron, Robert C., ed., *Soul of America: Documenting Our Past,* Fulcrum, Golden, CO, 1989.
Agel, Jerome B., *Words that Make America Great,* Random House, New York, 1997.
Postrel, Virginia, "The eagle has landed," *The New York Times Book Review,* December 19, 2004 (review of *Liberty and Freedom* by David Hackett Fischer).
Fischer, David Hackett, *Liberty and Freedom,* Oxford University Press, 2004.
Brown, Martha Cluverius, Kauffman, Bill, and Morel, Lucas E., contributing editors, *American Virtues, Values, and Triumphs,* Publications International, Ltd., Lincolnwood, Illinois, 1996.
Drake, Ross, "The law that ripped America in two," *Smithsonian,* May, 2004 (on repealing the Missouri Compromise).
Safire, William, *Lend Me Your Ears: Great Speeches in History,* Norton, New York, 1997.
Sunstein, Cass R., "FDR vision worth recalling," *The Capital Times,* August 10, 2004.
Roosevelt, Franklin Delano, State of the Union Address, January 11, 1944 (see text at TeachingAmericanHistory.org).
Arneson, Eric, "Just out of reach," *Chicago Tribune,* April 25, 2004 (review of *The Working Poor* by David K. Shipler).
Shipler, David K., *The Working Poor,* Knopf, New York, 2004.
Miller, Alice, *For Your Own Good,* Farrar, Straus, and Giroux, New York, 1984.
Clinton, Hillary Rodham, *It Takes a Village,* Simon and Schuster, New York, 1996.
Simon, Julian L., "Bring on the wretched refuse," *The Wall Street Journal,* January 26, 1990.
Hoffman, Eva, *After This Knowledge,* PublicAffairs, New York, 2004.

2) The 2000 presidential election...the consent of the governed

Tackett, Michael, and Jones, Tim, "Some wounds of war have healed -- many others won't go away." *Chicago Tribune,* April 24, 2005.
Zeleny, Jeff, "Ballot woes went well beyond chads," *Chicago Tribune,* January 28, 2001.
Cauchon, Dennis, and Drinkard, Jim, "Florida voter errors cost Gore the election," *USA Today,* May 11-13, 2001.
Gabler, Neal, "The last myth has been shattered," *Wisconsin State Journal,* December 10, 2000.
Cockburn, Alexander, "A Republican coup d'etat: pondering the aftermath of an amazingly corrupt election," *Isthmus,* December 22, 2000.
Moore, Michael, *Stupid White Men,* ReganBooks, HarperCollins, New York, 2001.

Milbank, Dana, and Weisman, Jonathan, "Middle class gets tax hit under Bush," *The Capital Times,* June 4, 2003.
Doyle, Rodger, "Undercutting fairness: states and localities undermine tax progressiveness," *Scientific American,* July, 2004.
Larry J. Eriksson, "Economic Inequities and Corporate Accountability," published in *Resource Packet on Corporate Accountability,* Corporate Accountability Task Group, Wisconsin Network for Peace and Justice, February, 2002, Madison, Wisconsin.
---, "Reversal of fortune," *IEEE Specturm,* January, 2003, p. 74 (re salaries of engineers).
McManes, Chris, "Salaries for US IEEE members decline, according to survey," *The Institute (IEEE),* March, 2005 (also on decline in electrical engineering employment).
Krugman, Paul, "For richer," *The New York Times Magazine,* October 20, 2002.
Krugman, Paul, *The Great Unraveling,* Norton, New York, 2003.
Arneson, Eric, "Upshot of a revolution: a British journalist looks at the rise of conservatism and the growth of inequality in America," *Chicago Tribune,* September 5, 2004 (review of *More Equal than Other: America from Nixon to the New Century* by Godfrey Hodgson).
Hodgson, Godfrey, *More Equal than Other: America from Nixon to the New Century,* Princeton University Press, Princeton, 2004.
Hollings, Senator Ernest, "Worsening deficit ignored," *The Capital Times,* June 24, 2003.
Simon, Richard, "Report predicts $2.75 trillion deficit," *The Capital Times,* February 28, 2004.
Uphoff, Charles, "Profligate Republicans," *Isthmus,* June 18, 2004.
Fram, Alan, "U.S. faces record national deficit," *Wisconsin State Journal,* July 31, 2004.
Raum, Tom, "Bush will leave a mountain of debt," *Wisconsin State Journal,* March 20, 2005.
Lipman, Larry, "Bush delays, drops many regulations," *Milwaukee Journal Sentinel,* April 1, 2001.
Barcott, Bruce, "Changing the rules: How the Bush administration quietly -- and radically -- transformed the nation's clean-air policy," *The New York Times Magazine,* April 4, 2004.
---, "Bush team goes ahead with logging plan," *The Capital Times,* July 12, 2004 (note on plan to open up more national forests).
Conniff, Ruth, "God, guns and gays again dominate the state's legislative agenda," *Isthmus,* January 21, 2005. (re the Wisconsin legislative agenda).
Kennedy, Donald, "An unfortunate U-turn on carbon," *Science,* March 30, 2001.
Williams, Carol J., "Bush views on warming add to heat," *Milwaukee Journal Sentinel,* March 31, 2001.
---, "The climate leadership vacuum," editorial, *Scientific American,* March, 2004.
Easterbrook, Gregg, "There goes the neighborhood," *The New York Times Book Review,* January 30, 2005 (book review of *Collapse* by Jared Diamond).
McLemee, Scott, "Analyzing the interaction of society and environment," *Chicago Tribune,* February 6, 2005 (book review of *Collapse* by Jared Diamond).
Diamond, Jared, *Collapse,* Viking, New York, 2004 (re role of environmental change such as global warming on collapse of societies).
Longworth, R. C. "Allies diverge on world vision," *Chicago Tribune,* July 28, 2002.
---, "Missile defense ahead of schedule," *The Capital Times,* February 2, 2004.
Dupont, Daniel G., "Test drive: Will a planned defense shield defeat real missiles?" *Scientific American,* September, 2004.
Hendren, John, "Failed test postpones rollout of missile net," *Chicago Tribune,* Dec. 19, 2004.
Shorrock, Tim, "U.S. deploys missile defense system" *IEEE Spectrum,* February, 2005.
Struck, Doug, "Canada won't join missile defense plan, premier says," *Chicago Tribune,* February 25, 2005.
---, "U..S. told to get OK to fire over Canada," *Chicago Tribune,* February 26, 2005.
Rabadi, Dina, "U.S. drags feet on ratifying UN treaty on women's rights," *Chicago Tribune,* June 13, 2004.

Kessler, Glenn, and Lynch, Colum, "Sharp UN critic named as next envoy," *Chicago Tribune,* March 8, 2005.
Raum, Tom, "Europe sees Bush going to isolationism," *The Capital Times,* July 27, 2001.
Wright, Robin, "White House tries to fight isolationist label," *The Capital Times,* Jul. 31, 2001.
---, "What Bush had to say in Europe," *Wisconsin State Journal,* February 22, 2005 (re Mideast peace process).
Silva, Mark, "A kinder, gentler style on display," *Chicago Tribune,* February 23, 2005 (re Iraq as the dividing issue).
Ivins, Molly, "Many are coming to realize W is not up to the job," *The Capital Times,* July 16, 2001 (re Bush's low approval rating).

3) The power of corporations...regulate commerce

Hahn, Hilary, Foreword in cover notes with *Bach Concertos,* compact disc digital recording, Deutsche Grammophon, Hamburg, 2003.
Korten, David C., *The Post-Corporate World,* Berrett-Koehler, San Francisco, 1999.
Mostert, Noël, *Supership,* Knopf, New York, 1974.
Stiglitz, Joseph E., *Globalization and Its Discontents,* Norton, New York, 2002.
Miller, James P., "Problem child turns 10," *Chicago Tribune,* November 16, 2003.
Knutson, Kristian, "Free trade area would be worse than NAFTA," *The Capital Times,* April 16, 2001.
Dellios, Hugh, '10 years later, NAFTA harvest falls short," *Chicago Tribune,* Dec. 14, 2003.
Kinsman, John, "CAFTA's a new disaster," *The Capital Times,* January 26, 2005.
Adiga, Aravind, "Hanging by a thread," *Time,* December, 2004 (on global textile industry).
Lev, Michael A., "Sweater Town about to warm up," *Chicago Tribune,* December 31, 2004.
Iritani, Evelyn; Dickerson, Marla; and Marshall, Tyler, "Quotas go; breadwinner jobs likely to follow in poor lands," *Chicago Tribune,* January 30, 2005.
Prestowitz, Clyde, "Rethinking globalization: How much longer can the U.S. keep borrowing," *Chicago Tribune,* June 19, 2005.
Luttwak, Edward, *Turbo Capitalism,* HarperCollins, New York, 1999.
Eriksson, Larry J., *Business Decisions: the impact of corporate mergers and global capitalism on our lives,* Quarter Section Press, Madison, Wisconsin, 2002.
Lipinski, William O., "Where are the manufacturing jobs? Try China," *Chicago Tribune,* November 14, 2003.
Kirchoff, Sue, "U.S. manufacturers vs. China," *USA Today,* July 1, 2003.
Acohido, Brian, "Boeing rips a page out of Airbus' book," *USA Today,* October 22, 2003 (re outsourcing).
Singhania, Lisa, "Merger numbers rise with economy," *Chicago Tribune,* May 31, 2004.
Costanza, Robert, "When it comes to the GDP, what counts?" *Chicago Tribune,* Aug. 25, 2002.
Roach, Stephen S., "The productivity paradox," *The New York Times,* November 30, 2003.
Jones, Del, "How productivity is measured," *USA Today,* June 14, 2004.
Goolsbee, Austan, "The unemployment myth," *The New York Times,* November 30, 2003.
Burns, Greg, "Prices rising despite low inflation rate," *Chicago Tribune,* March 28, 2004.
Kadlec, Daniel, "It's worse than you think," *Time,* May 2, 2005 (re composition of the CPI).
Aeppel, Timothy, "An inflation debate brews over intangibles at the mall," *The Wall Street Journal,* May 9, 2005 (re hedonics and the CPI).
Burns, Greg, "Outsized, out of control?" *Chicago Tribune,* January 18, 2004.
Oneal, Michael, "Bank One exit revives the talk of Second City," *Chicago Tribune,* Jan. 18, 2004.
Manor, Robert, "Steel industry reducing to hard core," *Chicago Tribune,* February 2, 2003.

4) The decline of the middle class...promote the general welfare

Eriksson, Larry J., *Business Decisions: the impact of corporate mergers and global capitalism on our lives,* Quarter Section Press, Madison, Wisconsin, 2002 (see pp. 53-60 on externalized costs and pp. 117-125 on stagnation of wages for most Americans).

Greising, David, "Chinese firm wants Maytag," *Chicago Tribune,* June 22, 2005.

Oneal, Michael, "Small town's plant back on the bubble," *Chicago Tribune,* June 22, 2005.

Longworth, Richard C., "Buyer's market," *Chicago Tribune,* July 10, 2005 (re China's purchases of U.S. businesses).

Moberg, David, "Industrial evolution," *Chicago Tribune Magazine,* July 10, 2005 (impact of plant closings on Galesburg, Illinois).

Bloyd-Peshkin, Sharon, "Sugar Blues," *Chicago Tribune Magazine,* July 10, 2005 (impact of loss of candy-industry jobs on Chicago workers).

Martinez, Michael J., "Irrational exuberance, 5 years later," *The Capital Times,* January 13, 2005 (re bursting of stock market bubble, 1996-2005).

Lester, Will, "Half of Americans worry about debt," *The Capital Times,* December 21, 2004.

Earnest, Leslie, "Shoppers indulge their urge to splurge," *The Capital Times,* December 6-7, 2003 (re luxury stores vs. discount).

Miller, James P., "Yacht sales swell...," *Chicago Tribune,* March 21, 2004.

Welsh, Jonathan, "More cars sell for $100,000...," *Wisconsin State Journal,* March 21, 2004.

---, "GM may consider cutting weak brands," *The Capital Times,* March 24, 2005

D'Innocenzio, Anne, "A holiday divided: Retail cheer mostly limited to upscale stores," *The Capital Times,* December 18-19, 2004.

Handley, John, "Flying first class: The Glen takes shape as a sparkling and expensive place to live," *Chicago Tribune,* July 14, 2002.

Arneson, Eric, "Upshot of a revolution: a British journalist looks at the rise of conservatism and the growth of inequality in America," *Chicago Tribune,* September 5, 2004 (review of *More Equal than Other: America from Nixon to the New Century* by Godfrey Hodgson).

Hodgson, Godfrey, *More Equal than Other: America from Nixon to the New Century,* Princeton University Press, Princeton, 2004.

Zwingle, Erla, "Global cities," *National Geographic,* November, 2002 (re rich vs. poor).

Zackowitz, Margaret G., "A town of grave importance," *National Geographic,* October, 2003 (re loss of main street shopping diversity).

Steiger, David A., "The bottom line doesn't recognize national boundaries," *Chicago Tribune,* September 28, 2003.

Lok, Corrie, "Where's my job?" *Technology Review,* April, 2004, pp. 74-75.

Dinur, Esty, "Pharmacies struggle to make ends meet," *Isthmus,* November 28, 2003.

Tindall, Blair, "The plight of the white-tie worker," *The New York Times,* July 4, 2004 (music).

Jonjak, Stosh, "RIP? Pop musicians are making do without the icon of Americana," *Wisconsin State Journal,* January 2, 2005.

Broder, John M., "It's no longer an issue of class," *Chicago Tribune,* Dec. 8, 2002 (health ins.).

Kleiman, Kelly, "'We are unable to offer you coverage...' sometimes it doesn't pay to see a doctor when you're sick," *Chicago Tribune,* January 2, 2005.

Scheier, Lee, "Busted! Whether you're uninsured or underinsured, a serious illness can destroy you financially," *Chicago Tribune,* January 2, 2005.

Kaiser, Rob, "Health-care costs ranked No. 1 problem," *Chicago Tribune,* May 31, 2004.

Fallows, James, and Ganeshananthan, V. V., "The big picture," *The Atlantic Monthly,* October, 2004 (re effects of college "merit aid").

Neikirk, William, "U.S. economic growth slows," *Chicago Tribune,* July 31, 2004.

Neikirk, William, "Hiring fizzles in July," *Chicago Tribune,* August 7, 2004.

Oneal, Michael, "Jobs report stuns economists," *Chicago Tribune,* August 7, 2004.

Zweifel, Dave, "There's a method to Bush's madness," *The Capital Times,* June 23, 2003.

Boulard, Garry, "Rotting sewer, water lines tough problem in Big Easy," *Chicago Tribune,* July 7, 2002.
---, "U.S. infrastructure gets a grade of D," *The Capital Times,* March 9, 2005.
Stevens, Jane Ellen, "Bumpy road to Mars," *Smithsonian,* June, 2004.
---, "NASA basically needs to start from scratch," *The Capital Times,* January 9, 2004.
Hundley, Tom, "Concorde sings its swan song," *Chicago Tribune,* October 24, 2003.
Ferguson, Niall, "Clashing civilizations or mad mullahs: The United States between informal and formal empire," in *The Age of Terror,* edited by Strobe Talbott and Nayan Chanda, Basic Books, New York, 2001.
Ryan, Alan Peter, "Africa, top to bottom," *Chicago Tribune,* March 30, 2003 (review of *Dark Star Safari* by Paul Theroux).
Theroux, Paul, *Dark Star Safari,* Houghton Mifflin Company, Boston, 2003 (see particularly pp. 187-194, 305-332).

Interlude One - Missing notes

The importance of memories...our forefathers brought forth

Cooney, Eleanor, *Death in Slow Motion: My Mother's Descent into Alzheimer's,* HarperCollins, New York, 2003.
Frazier, Ian, "The Mall of America," *The Atlantic Monthly,* July-August, 2002 (on the "eternal present" in shopping malls).
Eriksson, Larry J., *Business Decisions: the impact of corporate mergers and global capitalism on our lives,* Quarter Section Press, Madison, Wisconsin, 2002 (see pp. 46-50 on corporations and time: suppressing the past, ignoring the future, focus on present).
Orwell, George, *1984,* Plume, Penguin Putnam, New York, 1983 (originally publ. in 1949).
Ivins, Molly, "Ineptitude, hypocrisy at home in Bush administration," *The Capital Times,* March 31, 2003 (re order to keep files secret).
Shenon, Philip, and Sanger, David E., "Clinton-era terror files kept in dark," *Chicago Tribune,* April 2, 2004.
Milbank, Dana, "Say nothing the rule for Bush, aides," *The Capital Times,* April 21, 2004.
Greenhouse, Linda, "Administration says a 'zone of autonomy' justifies its secrecy on energy task force," *The New York Times,* April 25, 2004.
Lucky, Robert W., "The impermanence of knowledge," *IEEE Specturm,* March 2004.
Goldstein, Harry, "The infinite archive: to preserve our knowledge base and cultures, we must find a way to save digital content for future generations," *IEEE Spectrum,* January, 2004.
Williams, Kent, "Do we still need libraries now that we have the Internet? The Library of the future: Can the bricks-and-mortar institution survive in the digital age?" *Isthmus,* December 17, 2004.
Wong, May, "Will libraries be commercialized?" *Wisconsin State Journal,* Dec. 26, 2004.
Faulkner, William, *Requiem for a Nun,* 1951.
Dowd, Maureen, "Unbearable lightness of memory," *The New York Times,* January 30, 2003 (on 9/11 memorial designs).
Howe, Robert F., "Monumental achievement," *Smithsonian,* Nov., 2002 (Vietnam memorial).
Nijhuis, Michelle, "Tribal talk: immersion schools try to revive and preserve Native American languages," *Smithsonian,* November, 2003.

II. America after September 11...certain unalienable rights

5) A time of division and discord...domestic tranquility

Kemper, Bob, " 'The hour is coming when America will act,' Bush says --- 'Every nation...has a decision to make: Either you are with us or you are with the terrorists,'" *Chicago Tribune,* September 21, 2001.
Rose, Don, "A tactic cannot be an enemy," *Chicago Tribune,* April 25, 2004.
Ringle, Ken, "Bush's first-strike policy breaks with U.S. tradition," *The Capital Times,* Nov. 30-Dec. 1, 2002 (on movies and not shooting first).
Finletter, Thomas K., "When Russia is ready," *The Atlantic Monthly,* September, 1954 (excerpt reprinted in September, 2004).
Postrel, Virginia, "The eagle has landed," *The New York Times Book Review,* December 19, 2004 (review of *Liberty and Freedom* by David Hackett Fischer).
Fischer, David Hackett, *Liberty and Freedom,* Oxford University Press, 2004.
Willing, Richard, "Anti-terror bill extends government's reach," *USA Today,* October 25, 2001.
Toner, Robin, "Civil liberty vs. security: finding a wartime balance," *The New York Times,* November 18, 2001.
Jardner, Jr., George, and Selvin, Peter, "Terrorism suspects won't get day in court," *The Capital Times,* November 14, 2001.
---,"Secret trials under attack," *The Capital Times,* November 17-18, 2001.
Ivins, Molly, "We can't swap civil liberties for freedom from terrorists," *The Capital Times,* Nov. 24-25, 2001.
Cassel, Doug, "A final toll: were rights also casualties of Sept. 11?" *Chicago Tribune,* June 23, 2002.
Conniff, Ruth, "The Patriot: Russ Feingold's opposition to President Bush's policies on war and terrorism makes him a target for Republicans -- and a model for Democrats," *Isthmus,* July 4, 2003.
Saemann, Karyn, "Let's all read '1984' to put terror law into perspective," *The Capital Times,* November 1, 2001.
Schmitt, Richard B., "Many having second thoughts on Patriot Act," *The Capital Times,* September, 3, 2003.
Holland, Jesse J. "Bush shuns 'Patriot Act' name...knows it is a sore point," *The Capital Times,* September 19, 2003.
---, "U.S. adds strings to research; foreigners are blocked UW says," *The Capital Times,* December 1, 2003.
Flatten, Amy, "U.S. visa difficulties are lessening, but more must be done," *Physics Today,* February, 2005.
Lappin, Elena, "Your country is safe from me," *The N.Y. Times Book Review,* July 4, 2004.
Romero, Anthony, "You too could be a suspected terrorist," *The Capital Times,* Aug. 19, 2004.
---, "Terror list snags Kennedy," *The Capital Times,* August 21, 2004.
Sinha, Anita, and Knight, Stephen, "Bill smears legitimate immigrants," *Wisconsin State Journal,* February 27, 2005 (re REAL ID Act).
Bluhm, Warren, "Disgrace at Guantanomo," *Door County Advocate,* October 21, 2003.
Eggen, Dan, "Report faults warrant use after 9/11," *The Capital Times,* June 27, 2005 (report by Human Rights Watch and ACLU re misuse of "material witness" warrants).
Holland, Gina, "International execution case goes to high court," *The Capital Times,* December 11-12, 2004.
Cassel, Doug, "U.S. has blown up rule of law and order," *Chicago Tribune,* March 23, 2003.

Geyer, Georgie Anne, "U.S. no longer plays by the rules," *Chicago Tribune,* March 21, 2003.
Longworth, R.C., "Why a unilateral America frightens its historical allies," *Chicago Tribune,* March 18, 2003.
Cronkite, Walter, "Truth not a Bush priority," *The Capital Times,* April 8, 2004.
Livingston, Gordon, "Bush's lying now routine," *The Capital Times,* June 4, 2003.
Chapman, Steve, "Lyndon Baines Bush and echoes of the 60s," *Chicago Tribune,* July 20, 2003 (re Bush and lies).
McGreevy, John T. , "Culture vs. faith: A sociologist sees the end times for traditional religion in the United States, *Chicago Tribune,* November 30, 2003 (review of *An Intellectual in Public* by Alan Wolfe).
Wolfe, Alan, *An Intellectual in Public,* University of Michigan Press, Ann Arbor, 2003 (see the essay "Idiot Time" re Bush administration and lying, p. 349).
Franken, Al, *Lies and the Lying Liars Who Tell Them,* Dutton, New York, 2003.
Sawyer, Jon, "U.S. might be heading for a fiscal train wreck," *Wisconsin State Journal,* July 20, 2003 (re misrepresentations).
Milbank, Dana, and Graham, Bradley, "Bush backtracks on Iraq combat," *The Capital Times,* Aug. 19, 2003.
Ivins, Molly, "If only President Bush would speak the truth," *Chicago Tribune,* Jan. 23, 2004.
Page, Clarence, "Bush leaves no promise behind," *Chicago Tribune,* January 25, 2004.
Milbank, Dana, and Morgan, Dan, "Bush praised programs and then cut them," *The Capital Times,* February 5, 2004.
Goldsten, David, and Hutcheson, Ron, "Bush plans cuts in programs he promotes," *Wisconsin State Journal,* February 8, 2004.
Herrndobler, Kristina, "Medicare overhaul under scrutiny," *Chicago Tribune,* March 20, 2004.
Holland, Jesse J., "Medicare actuary: We knew cost was a lie," *The Capital Times,* March 25, 2004.
---, "Medicare officials defend cost data," *Chicago Tribune,* April 2, 2004.
Graham, Judith, "Medicare card for drugs may be no bargain," *Chicago Tribune,* April 30, 2004.
Pariser, Eli, "Call CBS on Bush Medicare ads," email from *MoveOn.org* on CBS refusal to run *MoveOn* ad while broadcasting administration ads on Medicare changes, February 5, 2004.
Kurtz, Howard, "Feds pay pundit to tout law: he got $241,000, pushed 'No Child,'" *The Capital Times,* January 8-9, 2005 (re Bush administration's 'propaganda').
Zuckman, Jill, and Silva, Mark, "Medicare drug costs soar," *Chicago Tribune,* Feb. 10, 2005.
Peck, Don, "On the money trail," *The Atlantic Monthly,* April 2004, pp. 46-49 (re contributions to Bush).
Allen, Mike, "White House to cooperate in probe of its leak of CIA agent's ID," *The Capital Times,* September 29, 2003.
McManus, Doyle, and Drogin, Bob, "Speculation on source of leak abounds," *The Capital Times,* Oct. 1, 2003.
Miller, Greg, "Spy leak spins into scandal," *The Capital Times,* September 30, 2003.
Suskind, Ron, *The Price of Loyalty,* Simon and Schuster, New York, 2004.
Crutsinger, Martin, "Book by former aide says Bush detached at meetings," *Chicago Tribune,* January 11, 2004.
Crutsinger, Martin, "O'Neill denies using classified documents," *Wisconsin State Journal,* January 14, 2004.
Bancroft, Colette, "O'Neill author finds controversy 'amazing,'" *The Capital Times,* January 27, 2004.
Clarke, Richard C., *Against All Enemies: Inside America*'s *War on Terror,* Free Press, New York, 2004.

Boorstin, Bob, "The canary in the coalmine," Internet article "Claim vs. fact: administration officials respond to Richard Clarke interview" provided by the Center for American Progress at americanprogress.org, March 22, 2004 (refutes 8 administration claims).
Fireman, Ken, "Clarke hits back hard at hearing," *The Capital Times,* March 25, 2004.
Derby, Samara Kalk, "Robert Kennedy, Jr. rips Bush, press," *The Capital Times,* November 4, 2004.
Trope, Roland L., "Guarding against terrorism -- and liability," *IEEE Spectrum,* January, 2004 (re SAFETY Act and QATT products).
Zaleski, Rob, "No wink as Bush tries to hoodwink," *The Capital Times,* February 3, 2003 (re "Clear skies").
Petit, Charles, "Hazy days in our parks," *Smithsonian,* June, 2005 (re problems with "Clear skies" proposal including negative impact on national parks).
---, "American Jobs Creation Act: a.k.a. the No Lobbyist Left Behind Act," *Time,* January 2005.
Fonda, Daren, "When salmon are 'wild,' and other word games," *Time,* May 10, 2004.
Soros, George, "The bubble of American supremacy," *The Atlantic Monthly,* December, 2003, pp. 63-66.

6) Scandals, frauds, and deceptions...a fair deal

Lowenstein, *When Genius Failed,* Random House, New York, 2000.
Huffington, Arianna, *Pigs at the Trough,* Crown, New York, 2003.
Hays, Kristen, "Enron in free-fall," *The Capital Times,* Nov. 29, 2001.
Maize, Kennedy, "Opening up energy trading," *IEEE Spectrum,* January , 2003, pp. 54-58.
Kurtz, Howard, "Since Sept. 11, other news is hard to come by," *The Capital Times,* Dec. 19, 2001.
Morgan, Dan, and Eilperin, Juliet, "Enron got help from D.C. politicos...ties to GOP started under first President Bush," *The Capital Times,* December 26, 2001.
Hedges, Stephen J., Zeleny, Jeff, and James, Frank, "Enron 'players' worked D.C. ties," *Chicago Tribune,* January 13, 2002 (re Enron contributions to Bush).
Peck, Don, "On the money trail," *The Atlantic Monthly,* April 2004, pp. 46-49 (re contributions to Bush).
Sherman, Mark, "Feds find California power manipulation," Associated Press (via ClariNet), March 26, 2003.
Babineck, Nark, "Enron: What's next?" *The Capital Times,* Feb. 20, 2004.
Hays, Kristen, "Enron transcripts paint sordid picture," *The Capital Times,* June 3, 2004.
Johnson, Gene, "Utility: Enron manipulated market 473 days," *Chicago Tribune,* June 15, 2004.
---, "Lay pleads innocent to 11 felony charges," *Chicago Tribune,* July 11, 2004.
Rawe, Julie, "The case against Ken Lay," *Time,* July 19, 2004.
Johnson, Gene, "Enron scams began years earlier," *The Capital Times,* February 4, 2005.
---, televised report on "Montana Power," *60 Minutes (CBS),* February 9, 2003.
Eriksson, Larry J., *Business Decisions: the impact of corporate mergers and global capitalism on our lives,* Quarter Section Press, Madison, Wisconsin, 2002 (see pp. 115-116, 148 on problems with vaccine production).
---, "Growing list of scandals erodes trust in Corporate America," *Chicago Tribune,* June 30, 2002.
Countryman, Andrew, "False profits lead insiders to riches," *Chicago Tribune,* Sept. 5, 2004.
Chandler, Susan, "Airbus proposes splitting Air Force tanker contract," *Chicago Tribune,* December 4, 2004 (on tanker scandal).
Chandler, Susan, "Rival aims to lower the boom on Boeing," *Chicago Tribune,* May 1, 2005.
Greenhouse, Linda, "Administration says a 'zone of autonomy' justifies its secrecy on energy task force," *The New York Times,* April 25, 2004.

Freese, Barbara, *Coal: A human history,* Perseus, Cambridge, Mass., 2003 (see pp. 193-4 re coal industry and Bush win in West Virginia).
Rohter, Larry, "U.S. waters down global commitment to curb greenhouse gases," *The New York Times,* December 19, 2004.
Hedges, Stephen J., "Halliburton contract questions dog White House," *Chicago Tribune,* February 1, 2004.
Countryman, Andrew, "Halliburton fined for false profit statement," *Chicago Tribune,* August 4, 2004.
O'Harrow, Jr., "FBI broadens probe of Halliburton deal," *The Capital Times,* Oct. 29, 2004.
Zagorin, Adam, and Burger, Timothy J., "Beyond the call of duty," *Time,* November 1, 2004 (re Halliburton whistle-blower).
Orwell, George, *1984,* Plume, Penguin Putnam, New York, 1983 (orig. published in 1949).

7) A state of endless war...the common defense

Longworth, R.C., "A nation alone -- even our friends don't share America's image of itself," *Chicago Tribune,* December 30, 2001.
Madigan, Charles M., "Allies' support is far from solid," *Chicago Tribune,* Dec. 30, 2001.
Knutsen, Kristian, "Corporate-controlled media ignore protests," *The Capital Times,* October 5-6, 2002.
---, "CEO rapped for anti-war donation," *The Capital Times,* November 13, 2002.
---, "Exec apologizes for stir over anti-war gift," *The Capital Times,* November 15, 2002.
Derby, Samara Kalk, "Down to the wire -- marchers rally for peace as war appears imminent: Vigil here for peace is a 'river of candles,'" *The Capital Times,* March 17, 2003.
Mark, Jason, and McConnell, Carolyn, "Opposition to Iraq invasion builds," *YES!,* Winter, 2003.
Neuhaus, Richard John, "Just War and This War," *Wall Street Journal,* Jan. 29, 1991 (re Gulf War in Kuwait and Iraq).
Carter, Jimmy, "Just war ---or a Just War?" *The New York Times,* March 9, 2003 (Internet).
Kiesling, John Brady, "A veteran Foreign Service officer has had enough," *The Capital Times,* March 15-16, 2003.
Lumpkin, John J., "Former CIA officers say Bush slanting case for war," *The Capital Times,* March 15-16, 2003.
le Carré, John, "The United States of America has gone mad," *The Times of London,* January 15, 2003 (on the Internet).
Chittister, Joan, "The global peace initiative of women religious and spiritual leaders," United Nations Conference, Geneva, October 7, 2002.
Longworth, R.C., "Bush has stampeded America into conflict," *Chicago Tribune,* March 23, 2003.
Zaleski, Rob, "Pastor defends crosses," *The Capital Times,* April 25, 2003.
---, "Congregations respond to war," Greene, Debra Illingworth, contributor, *The Lutheran,* June 2003.
Osnos, Evan, and Jervis, Rick, "Fierce fighting rages in Iraq: U.S. military's death toll since invasion last year reaches 1000," *Chicago Tribune,* September 8, 2004.
Trice, Dawn Turner, "Resident offers 1,027 reasons for anti-war rally," *Chicago Tribune,* September 20, 2004.
Trice, Dawn Turner, "Another victim of Iraq war is ability to listen," *Chicago Tribune,* September 22, 2004.
Jacob, Mark, "The extraordinarily long life of the 'dead-enders,'" *Chicago Tribune,* October 3, 2004 (includes timeline of Iraq war and deaths).
Stein, Rob, "Iraq study: 100,000 civilians have died," *The Capital Times,* October 29, 2004.

Ross, Emma, "Death rate in Iraq much higher since invasion," *Wisconsin State Journal,* October 29, 2004.
---, "Iraq: A status report," *Time,* January 31, 2005 (re military casualties in Iraq).
Allen, Mike, "White House to cooperate in probe of its leak of CIA agent's ID," *The Capital Times,* September 29, 2003.
McManus, Doyle, and Drogin, Bob, "Speculation on source of leak abounds," *The Capital Times,* Oct. 1, 2003.
Miller, Greg, "Spy leak spins into scandal," *The Capital Times,* September 30, 2003.
Chapman, Steve, "'Unspecial' prosecutor will do fine," *Chicago Tribune,* January 4, 2004.
Schecter, Danny, *Embedded: Weapons of Mass Deception,* Prometheous Books, New York, 2003.
Moore, Michael, *Hey Dude, Where's My Country?* Warner Books, New York, 2003.
Ivins, Molly, *Bushwacked,* Random House, New York, 2003.
Milbank, Dana, "Weapon fallout grows," *The Capital Times,* February 2, 2004.
Linzer, Dafna, "WMD search in Iraq ended in December," *The Capital Times,* Jan. 12, 2005.
Miller, Greg, "CIA sets Iraq record straight: No big weapons," *The Capital Times,* February 1, 2005.
Fireman, Ken, "Bush rationale for Iraq war changes nearly day by day," *The Capital Times,* July 8, 2003.
Kelley, Matt, "Experts rip Bush claim of Saddam link to al-Qaida," *Wisconsin State Journal,* July 13, 2003.
Ivins, Molly, "Sick and tired of making excuses for 'failuremongers,'" *Chicago Tribune,* September 11, 2003.
Hedges, Stephen J., "9/11 inquiry finding array of deficiencies," *Chicago Tribune,* March 28, 2004.
Hunt, Terence, "9/11 panel undercuts war rationale," *The Capital Times,* June 17, 2004.
Priest, Dana, and Kessler, Glenn, "Cheney maintains connections between 9-11, Iraq," *The Capital Times,* September 29, 2003.
Cooper, Matthew, "The missing link," Time, June 28, 2004 (re no link between 9/11 attacks and Iraq).
Yen, Hope, "9/11 panel reiterates: Iraq/al-Qaida link minor," *The Capital Times,* July 7, 2004.
Cushman, Jr., John H., "Report says Iraq wasn't big threat," *Wisconsin State Journal,* July 11, 2004.
Milbank, Dana, and Pincus, Walter, "Bush claims left in tatters," *The Capital Times,* July 10-11, 2004.
Torriero, E.A., "Ex-inmates allege Guantanamo abuse," *Chicago Tribune,* August 5, 2004.
Lewis, Neil A., "Witnesses say Guantanamo detainees were abused," *Wisconsin State Journal,* October 27, 2004.
Gecker, Jocelyn, "Brit freed from Guantanamo speaks of 'systematic abuse,'" *The Capital Times,* December 18-19, 2004.
Wright, Robin, "Global outrage stuns U.S.," *The Capital Times,* May 4, 2004.
---, "Red Cross asked U.S. to stop abuse," *The Capital Times,* May 6, 2004.
Graham, Bradley, "Rumsfeld said get tough," *The Capital Times*, May 21, 2004.
Tanner, Robert, "Civilians named as suspects in prison abuses...and that raises some thorny issues," *Wisconsin State Journal,* May 23, 2004.
Lumpkin, John J., "White House lawyers say torture is legal," *The Capital Times,* June 8, 2004.
---, "No legal or moral basis for torture," editorial, *The Boston Globe,* June 20, 2004.
Ripley, Amanda, "Redefining torture," *Time,* June 21, 2004.
---, "Bush policy on captives provoked fiery dissent," *The Capital Times,* June 24, 2004.
Wittes, Benjamin, "Enemy Americans," *The Atlantic Monthly,* July/August, 2004 (re endless war, imprisonment).

---, "Runsfeld corrects himself on Iraq prison abuse," *Chicago Tribune,* August 29, 2004.
Blumenfeld, Laura, "Insider rips Bush on terror," *The Capital Times,* June 16, 2003.
Cassel, Doug, "Humiliation: ignorant, inflammatory, undeniable," *Chicago Tribune,* May 9, 2004 (re rights as national value).
Sly, Liz, "U.S. slipping in Afghan war," *Chicago Tribune,* January 11, 2004.
Squitieri, Tom, "Aid workers: Afghanistan in jeopardy," *USA Today,* January 23, 2004.
Munita, Tomas, "GIs chase Taliban in Afghan sanctuary," *The Capital Times,* June 27, 2005.
Fallows, James, "Blind into Baghdad," *The Atlantic Monthly,* January/February, 2004.
Ricks, Thomas E., "Army prof blasts Bush on Iraq," *The Capital Times,* January 12, 2004.
Gonzales, Patrisia, and Rodriguez, Roberto, "Bush tactics in Iraq disquieting, perilous," *The Capital Times,* May 4, 2004.
Hedges, Stephen J., "U.S. adds heavy armor in Iraq," *Chicago Tribune,* April 28, 2004.
Fallows, James, "The hollow army," *The Atlantic Monthly,* March, 2004.
Schodolski, Vincent J., "Ex-general says Iraq war ill-conceived," *Chicago Tribune,* May 29, 2004.
Ricks, Thomas E., "General fears U.S. losing war in Iraq: questions overall success," *The Capital Times,* May 10, 2004.
Priest, Dana, "Report: Iraq is magnet for terrorist training," *The Capital Times,* January 14, 2005.
Hanley, Charles J., "Nuclear weapons treaty in trouble," *Wisconsin State Journal,* May 5, 2005.
Kessler, Glenn, "Clarke's point: Focus on Iraq sidetracked Bush," *The Capital Times,* March 29, 2004.
Byrd, Senator Robert, "A call for an exit door from Iraq," April 8, 2004, on the Internet at http://www.smirkingchimp.com/article.php?sid=686&mode==nested&order==0.
Archibald, Roger, "Six ships that shook the world," *American Heritage of Invention and Technology,* Fall, 1997.
Fuchida, Mitsuo, and Okumiya, Masatake, *Midway: the battle that doomed Japan, the Japanese Navy's story,* Bluejacket Books, Naval Institute Press, Annapolis, MD, 2001 (see p. 95 re Doolittle Raid).
Hoagland, Jim, "Righting the course for Bush: the president's speech lacked the honesty a leader owes his nation in a time of crisis," *Chicago Tribune,* May 28, 2004.
Balz, Dan, and Milbank, Dana, "Bush's credibility is under assault," *Chicago Tribune,* April 8, 2004.
Hook, Janet, "Iraq events strain Bush's leadership," *The Capital Times,* May 7, 2004.
Ivins, Molly, "Regardless of reality in Iraq, Bush refuses to alter course," *The Capital Times,* April 19, 2004.
Dickerson, John F., and Cooper, Matthew, "What happened to Bush's dream team? -- They used to pretend to get along. Now they don't even bother," *Time,* May 17, 2004.
Chapman, Steve, "Iraq looks good through rose-colored glasses," *Chicago Tribune,* July 1, 2004.
Kirkpatrick, David D., "War heats up in the neoconservative fold," *The New York Times,* August 22, 2004.

8) Our immune system under attack...checks and balances

Power, Samantha, "How to kill a country," *The Atlantic Monthly,* December, 2003, pp.86-100.
Vedantam, Shankar, "Shy, sensitive -- and sick?" *The Washington Post National Weekend Edition,* January 5-11, 2004 (re stress and immune system).
---, "Gannett buys Advocate," *Door County Advocate,* July 24-25, 2004.
Lueders, Bill, "Hesselberg is downsized," *Isthmus,* August 13, 2004.
Shepard, Jason "Readers continue to abandon ship," *Isthmus,* June 3, 2005.

Moyers, Bill, "Keynote address to the National Conference on Media Reform," November 8, 2003 (www.mediareform.net or available from *Common Dreams*, November 13, 2003).
Cooper, Mark, *Media Ownership and Democracy in the Digital Information Age*, Center for Internet and Society, Stanford Law School, 2003 (re concentration in media ownership).
Powers, William, "The massless media," *The Atlantic Monthly*, January/February, 2005.
Garvey, Ed, "Money, the media and politics -- a report from the underground," *Our Democracy, Our Airwaves Media Conference*, May 21, 2004, Madison, Wisconsin.
Nichols, John, "Next steps in the media reform movement," *Our Democracy, Our Airwaves Media Conference*, May 21, 2004, Madison, Wisconsin.
Laskin, Tom, "Radio news blues: Local reporting is dying in Madison and across the country," *Isthmus*, June 3, 2005.
---, radio report on China's bookstores, National Public Radio, May 16, 2004.
Skalka, Jennifer, "Not necessarily newscasters at convention," *Chicago Tribune*, Sept. 3, 2004.
Cook, John, "Glimpse at the future looks neither fair nor balanced," *Chicago Tribune*, September 19, 2004.
Feller, Ben, "One-third of high school students say First Amendment goes too far," *The Capital Times*, January 31, 2005.
Yerak, Becky, and Franklin, Stephen, "Wal-Mart target of U.S. probe: Grand Jury looks at allegations of anti-union activity," *Chicago Tribune*, April 23, 2005.
Miller, James P., and Franklin, Stephen, "Lockout weapon," *Chicago Tribune*, Dec. 12, 2004.
---, "Intermet Corp...plans to shut down...plants...," news item in *Briefly, The Capital Times*, December 16, 2004.
Zoll, Rachel, "U.S. shifts away from Protestant majority," *The Capital Times*, July 20, 2004.
Niebuhr, H. Richard, *Christ and Culture*, Harper and Row, New York, 1951.
---, "Bush cuts for family planning draw fire," *The Capital Times*, July 23, 2002.
Kessler, Glenn, and Lynch, Colum, "Sharp UN critic named as next envoy," *Chicago Tribune*, March 8, 2005.
Fournier, Ron, "Bush ad trumpets war in Iraq," *The Capital Times*, November 22-23. 2003.
Nichols, John, "Bush's flag-waving cows progressives," *The Capital Times*, November 6, 2001.
Ivins, Molly, "Democrats are abdicating principled opposition role," *The Capital Times*, April 15, 2002.
Garvey, Ed, "Congress not doing its part to question this war," *The Capital Times*, April 1, 2003.
Dowd, Maureen, "Bush's world of fantasy," *Wisconsin State Journal*, April 25, 2004 (on Bush's absurdities).
---, "Nation's liberals suffering from outrage fatigue," *the Onion*, July 8-14, 2004.
Babington, Charles, "Scorched-earth politics," *The Washington Post National Weekly Edition*, January 5-11, 2004.
---, "Bush-league Lysenkoism," editorial, *Scientific American*, May, 2004.
Ferber, Dan, "Overhaul of CDC panel revives lead safety debate," *Science*, October 25, 2002.
Michaels, David; Bingham, Eula; Boden, Les; Clapp, Richard; Goldman, Lynn R.; Hoppin, Polly; Krimsky, Sheldon; Monforton, Celeste; Ozonoff, David; Robbins, Anthon; "Advice without dissent," editorial, *Science*, October 25, 2002.
---, "Bush axes bioethicists; charges of politics fly," *The Capital Times*, February 28, 2004.
Wakefield, Julie, "Science's Political Bulldog," *Scientific American*, May 2004.
Dawson, Jim, "National Academies Committee sets steps for bringing the best science advice to Washington," *Physics Today*, February, 2005 (re politicization of scientific advice).
Michaels, David, "Doubt is their product: industry groups are fighting government regulation by fomenting scientific uncertainty," *Scientific American*, June, 2005.
Vedantam, Shankar, "EPA left out evidence calling for tighter mercury controls," *The Capital Times*, March 22, 2005.

Nelson, Robert A., "Nuclear bunker busters, mini-nukes, and the U.S. nuclear stockpile," *Physics Today*, November, 2003.
Levi, Michael, "Nuclear bunker buster bombs," *Scientific American*, August, 2004.
Dewar, Helen, and Allen, Mike, "Showdown looms over judicial nominees," *The Capital Times*, December 13, 2004.
Chen, Edwin, "Dems threaten to bring Senate to a halt over rule," *The Capital Times*, March 16, 2005.
---, "Panel OKs Bush's pick for judge; showdown looms," *The Capital Times*, March 18, 2005.
Chapman, Steve, "The Republicans new perspective on the filibuster," *Chicago Tribune*, April 21, 2005 (background on filibuster and judicial nominees.
Zuckman, Jill, "Filibuster fight boils in Senate," *Chicago Tribune*, April 22, 2005.
James, Frank, "Cheney puts filibuster in cross hairs," *Chicago Tribune*, April 23, 2005.
Shepard, Scott, "Frist in 2008 campaign mode," *Chicago Tribune*, April 24, 2005.
Rich, Frank, "A high-tech lynching in prime time," *The New York Times* OP-ED, April 24, 2005 (re "Justice Sunday" telecast criticizing Democratic opposition to judicial nominees).
Stone, Geoffrey R., "A 'nuclear' attack on the Constitution," *Chicago Tribune*, May 1, 2005.
Rosen, Jeffrey, "The Senate nears the point of no return," *The New York Times*, May 22, 2005.
---, "Rehnquist: Recusal up to judge," *The Capital Times*, January 27, 2004.
Holland, Gina, "Dems push Supreme Court to address conflict of interest," *The Capital Times*, January 31-February 1, 2004.
---, "Scalia flew as Cheney's guest on trip," *The Capital Times*, February 5, 2004.
Savage, David G., "Scalia ripped over erasure of press tapes," *The Capital Times*, April 9, 2004.
Lane, Charles, "Scalia's 'charm initiative is seen as bid for top court spot," *The Capital Times*, February 1, 2005.
---, "'Court stripping' -- Congress undermines the power of the judiciary," special report, American Civil Liberties Union, June, 1996 (www.archive.aclu.org/library/ctstrip.html).
Chapman, Steve, "Unforeseen side effect of gay marriage," *Chicago Tribune*, August 1, 2004 (re "court stripping").
Gellman, Barton, "Early alerts about terror faded away," *The Capital Times*, May 17, 2002 (re August, 2001, Bush vacation).
Pinkerton, James P., "Truth about 9/11 will come out," *The Capital Times*, April 12, 2004 (re 9/11 attacks and Bush vacation).
Clarke, Richard C., *Against All Enemies: Inside America's War on Terror*, Free Press, New York, 2004.
---, "Bush opposes more time for 9/11 panel," *The Capital Times*, January 19, 2004.
Yen, Hope, "Sept. 11 commission wants more time for final report," *The Capital Times*, January 27, 2004.
Eggen, Dan, "9/11 panel, White House tensions rise over report," *The Capital Times*, January 29, 2004.
Allen, Mike, and Eggen, Dan, "Bush: Give 9/11 panel more time," *The Capital Times*, February 5, 2004.
Kean, Thomas H., and Hamilton, Lee H, editors, *The 9/11 Report*, produced by the National Commission on Terrorist Attacks Upon the United States ("the 9/11 Commission"), Washington, D.C., 2004 (see also version that includes background on the Commission and coverage on the Report by *The New York Times*, St. Martin's Press, New York, 2004).
O'Shea, James, "Of two minds," *Chicago Tribune*, December 26, 2004 (re 9/11 Commission report and comment attributed to King Hussein).
Schuler, Michael A., "Terror's origins must be discussed," *The Capital Times*, Oct. 23, 2001.
Talbott, John R., "Where America went wrong and how to regain her democratic ideals," *Financial Times Prentice Hall*, Upper Saddle River, New Jersey, 2004.

Beinart, Peter, "Backfire," *The Atlantic Monthly,* March, 2005 (review of *The War for Muslim Minds: Islam and the West* by Gilles Kepel).
Kepel, Gilles *The War for Muslim Minds: Islam and the West,* Harvard, Cambridge, 2005.
Ehrenreich, Barbara, "Their George and ours," *The New York Times,* July 4, 2004.
Murphy, Cullen, "Feudal gestures: why the Middle Ages are something we can still look forward to," *The Atlantic Monthly,* October, 2003.
Winslow, Art, "Culture critic Jane Jacobs warns North Americans of a bleak future," *Chicago Tribune,* June 13, 2004 (review of *Dark Age Ahead* by Jane Jacobs).
Jacobs, Jane, *Dark Age Ahead,* Random House, New York, 2004.
Bothamley, Jennifer, *Dictionary of Theories,* Visible Ink Press, Detroit, 2002 (see p. 481 on separation of powers).
Agel, Jerome, *Words that Make America Great,* Random House, New York, 1997 (see p.15 for The Virginia Declaration of Rights).
Bartlett, John, *Familiar Quotations, 15th ed.,* Beck, Emily Morison, ed., Little, Brown, and Company, Boston, 1980 (see p. 381 for John Adams quote on checks on power).

9) From democracy to oligarchy...all are created equal

Power, Samantha, "How to kill a country," *The Atlantic Monthly,* December, 2003, pp.86-100.
---, "6 months after Florida fiasco voting reforms languish," edit., *USA Today,* May 11, 2001.
Thomas, Ken, "Most states haven't reformed voting process," *The Capital Times,* Nov. 6, 2001.
Grossman, Wendy M., "Ballot breakdown: flaws continue to hamper computerized voting," *Scientific American,* February, 2004.
---, "Florida as the next Florida," editorial, *The New York Times,* March 14, 2004.
Novak, Viveca, "The vexations of voting machines," *Time,* May 3, 2004, pp. 42-44.
Konrad, Rachel, "E-voting debate: can computers ever be fully trusted?" *The Capital Times,* April 24-25, 2004.
---, "Vote-counting machine test results kept secret," *The Capital Times,* August 23, 2004.
McCormick, John, "Bugs make new voting option wild card for Nov. 2 election," *Chicago Tribune,* September 20, 2004.
Powell, Michael, and Slevin, Peter, "Ohio voter: 'You hope it wasn't intentional,'" *The Capital Times,* December 15, 2004.
Drinkard, Jim, "States fall behind on voting-system improvements," *USA Today,* Feb. 14, 2005.
Bendavid, Naftali, "Primary colors," *Chicago Tribune Magazine,* October 24, 2004 (re North Carolina gerrymandering).
Peck, Don, and Casey, Caitlin, "Packing, cracking, and kidnapping," *The Atlantic Monthly,* January/February, 2004.
Gold, Scott, "Financing of GOP takeover of Texas Capitol probed," *The Capital Times,* January 3-4, 2004.
Smith, R. Jeffrey, "Corporate cash helped fund Texas redistricting," *The Capital Times,* July 12, 2004.
Gamboa, Suzanne, "DeLay PAC donated to House ethics members," *Chicago Tribune,* July 16, 2004.
---, "Texas grand jury indicts fundraisers with DeLay ties," *Chicago Tribune,* Sept. 22, 2004.
Lane, Charles, "High court orders review of Texas map," *Chicago Tribune,* October 19, 2004.
Babington, Charles, "DeLay on thin ice over ethics," *The Capital Times,* October 2-3, 2004.
Babington, Charles, "DeLay draws third rebuke on ethics," *The Capital Times,* October 7, 2004.
Shenon, Philip, and Pear, Robert, "DeLay defense fund increases fund raising," *Wisconsin State Journal,* March 13, 2005.
Tumulty, Karen, "DeLay and company," *Time,* March 21, 2005 (re troubles of DeLay and former aide).

Dunn, Bill, "Patriot Games," *The Capital Times,* October 23, 2001.
Lueders, Bill, "Surviving the new McCarthyism," *Isthmus,* October 19, 2001.
Keller, Julia, "Speak your piece," *Chicago Tribune Magazine,* June 29, 2003.
Graham, Renee, "Even big-mouthed celebs have the right to speak their minds," *Chicago Tribune,* April 18, 2003.
Ross, Sonya, "Glover goes from actor to activist," *The Capital Times,* November 28, 2002.
---, "Glover latest star targeted by right," *The Capital Times,* May 19, 2003.
Nichols, John, "The Boss rises to Dixie Chicks' defense," *The Capital Times,* April 24, 2003.
---, "Maines sorry for Bush remark...but no regrets for war censure," *The Capital Times,* April 25, 2003.
---, "Dixie Chicks fans at show outnumber detractors," *The Capital Times,* May 2, 2003.
---, "Ronstadt booted for praising Moore," *The Capital Times,* July 20, 2004.
Boucher, Geoff, and Hilburn, Robert, "Ronstadt won't bow to critics," *The Capital Times,* July 22, 2004.
Foley, Ryan J., "War protest rattles Iowa," *Wisconsin State Journal,* February 8, 2004.
McCarthy, Sheryl, "Right to dissent under fire," *The Capital Times,* April 23, 2003.
---, "Your right to say it...but over there," *Chicago Tribune,* September 28, 2003.
---, "Bush protesters file complaint: allege police carried out violations on GOP's behalf," *The Capital Times,* May 20, 2004.
---, "City apologizes for arresting Bush protesters," *The Capital Times,* July 20, 2004.
---, "Nearly 1,000 arrested: Arnold, first lady praise president," *The Capital Times,* September 1, 2004.
McRoberts, Flynn, and Swanson, Stevenson, "Release protesters, judge says," *Chicago Tribune,* September 3, 2004.
Zucchino, David, "Internet helps cops corral protesters," *Chicago Tribune,* September 4, 2004.
Boyd, Wes, "Republicans trying to gag nonprofits," email message from *MoveOn.org* on proposed new rules to restrict activities of nonprofit organizations, March 30, 2004.
Pariser, Eli, "CBS censors winning ad," email message from *MoveOn.org* on CBS refusal to run a *MoveOn* ad critical of Bush during the Super Bowl, February 5, 2004.
Callender, David, "Feingold: Bush not truthful on 527 ad issue," *The Capital Times,* August 28-29, 2004.
Zinn, Howard, "Opposing the war party," *The Progressive,* May, 2004.
Wilson, Catherine, "1872 law used to charge Greenpeace," *Wisconsin State Journal,* January 25, 2004.
Smith, Lynn, "Crackdown on profanity makes live news risky," *The Capital Times,* May 6, 2004.
Kaner, Cem, "UCITA: A disaster in progress," *IEEE Spectrum,* August, 2002.
Garfinkel, Simson, "The free-software imperative," *Technology Review,* February, 2003 (re illegal software copies and activism).
Feder, Toni, "Publishers sue U.S. Treasury," *Physics Today,* November, 2004 (re right of Office of Foreign Assets Control to require permits to publish).
Feder, Toni, "Publishing restrictions eased, but not rescinded," *Physics Today,* February, 2005.
Donadio, Rachel, "Is there censorship?" *The New York Times Book Review,* Dec. 19, 2004.
Bumiller, Elisabeth, "Bush: Democracy is key in Russia: President urges Europeans to help Iraq," *Wisconsin State Journal,* February 22, 2005.
Rabbit, Jack, "The California recall, part one," DemocraticUnderground.com, July 30, 2003.
Rabbit, Jack, "The California recall, part two," DemocraticUnderground.com, July 31, 2003.
Kershaw, Sarah, "Winner declared in Washington," *Chicago Tribune,* December 31, 2004 (re election of governor of state of Washington).
Postman, David, "Governor's election lawsuit buries parties in debt," *The Seattle Times,* April 22, 2005.

---, "Closest gov race in history is over," *The Capital Times,* June 7, 2005.
Sandalow, Marc, "GOP seeks to steal elections it can't win, Dems charge," *The Capital Times,* September 3, 2003.
Beatty, Jack, "Governing from his biography," *The Atlantic Monthly,* May, 2002, p. 27.
Moyers, Bill, "Our story," *The Progressive,* May, 2004.

Interlude Two - Broken strings

The growth of malignancies...weeds in the garden

Moyers, Bill, "Bill Moyers on Election 2002," *NOW,* broadcast on PBS, November 8, 2002.
Levin, Bernard, *Colorectal Cancer,* American Cancer Society, Villard, New York, 1999.
Nin, Anaïs, and Pollak, Felix, *Arrows of Longing: The Correspondence between Anaïs Nin and Felix Pollak, 1952-1976,* Ohio University Press, Athens, 1998.
DeSimone, Bonnie, "From survivor to titan of Tour," *Chicago Tribune,* July 25, 2004 (re Lance Armstrong and cancer).
Deardorff, Julie, "As Lance knows, cancer can be long, tough race," *Chicago Tribune,* August 15, 2004.
McManus, Doyle, "Bush problem on Iraq: Is team telling truth?" *The Capital Times,* June 27, 2005 (re similarities between decline in public support for Vietnam War and Iraq War).
Kennedy, Jr., Robert F., "Crimes against nature: Bush is sabotaging the laws that have protected America's environment for more than thirty years," (includes FDR quote on fascism; RS 937, December 11, 2003; see www.alternet.org/story/17252/).
Bothamley, Jennifer, *Dictionary of Theories,* Visible Ink Press, Detroit, 2002 (p. 197 re fascism).
Drucker, Peter F., *The End of Economic Man,* Harper and Row, New York, 1969 (publ. 1939).
Ignatieff, Michael, "Lesser evils," *The New York Times Magazine,* May 2, 2004 (re terrorism as cancer).
Bosman, Mary, "Terrorism and cancer," *Door County Advocate,* June 24, 2004.
Power, Samantha, "The original axis of evil," *The New York Times Book Review,* May 2, 2004 (re characteristics of fascism).
Foer, Franklin, "The stealth president," *The New York Times Book Review,* May 2, 2004 (review of *Worse than Watergate* by John Dean, remembered for his Watergate reference to a "cancer growing" on the presidency).
Dean, John, *Worse than Watergate,* Little, Brown and Company, New York, 2004 (re culture of secrecy).
Ryndina, Ella, "Family lines sketched in the portrait of Lev Landau," *Physics Today,* February, 2004 (re oppression).
Rhodes, Richard, *The Making of the Atomic Bomb,* Touchstone, New York, 1988 (see pp. 182-185 re politics and anti-Semitism of Nazis; p. 243 for phrase from Hannah Arendt).
Rubin, Bonnie Miller, and Brachear, Manya A., "CBS and NBC shut door on church ad," *Chicago Tribune,* December 2, 2004.
Williams, Roger, "Moderate Christians must stand up, speak out," *Wisconsin State Journal,* December 19, 2004 (re refusal of UCC ad by networks).
Rich, Frank, "It's all *Newsweek's* fault," *The New York Times,* May 22, 2005.
Riechmann, Deb, "Quran report is headache for Bush: Desecration is downplayed," *Wisconsin State Journal,* June 5, 2005.
Zuckman, Jill, "Durbin tries to quell anger over remarks," *Chicago Tribune,* June 18, 2005.
Zuckman, Jill, and Washburn, Gary, "Durbin yields to onslaught, apologizes in full," *Chicago Tribune,* June 22, 2005.

Page, Clarence, "Can we finally talk?" *Chicago Tribune,* June 22, 2005 (notes similarities between White House backlash against Senator Durbin and Newsweek magazine).
Wineke, Bill, "Rove's remarks only hurt Bush," *Wisconsin State Journal,* June 25, 2005 (re Rove's criticism of Senator Dick Durbin and liberals in general).
Arendt, Hannah, *The Origins of Totalitarianism,* Harcourt, Brace, Jovanovich, New York, 1973.
Perrottet, Tony, "Little Bighorn reborn," *Smithsonian,* April, 2005 (re conflicts between tribes over Battle of Little Bighorn and reservations).
Nafisi, Azar, *Reading Lolita in Tehran,* Random House, New York, 2003 (see p. 268 on need for space).
Eriksson, Larry J., "Reflections on the importance of 'public places,'" Newsletter, Madison Christian Community, April, 2005, Madison, Wisconsin (re comments by Parker Palmer at St. Andrew's Episcopal Church, March 15, 2005).
Kates, William, "45% favor limiting rights of Muslims," *The Capital Times,* December 18-19, 2004 (see Cornell University: www.news.cornell.edu/releases/Dec04/Muslim.Poll.bpf.html and Muslim American Society: www.masnet.org).
---, "Suspicious minds," *The Atlantic Monthly,* April, 2005 (see "Restrictions on Civil Liberties, Views of Islam, and Muslim Americans," Media and Society Research Group, Cornell University).
Ylvisaker, John, *I Was There to Hear Your Borning Cry,* 1985.
Kundera, Milan, *The Unbearable Lightness of Being,* Harper and Row, New York, 1984.

III. Seeking new alternatives...a new birth of freedom

10) Renewing the economy...American ingenuity

Margolis, Jon, "Wal-Marts 'endanger' Vermont group says," *Chicago Tribune,* May 25, 2004.
Davidoff, Judith, "Sam's Club behind East Towne rejected," *The Capital Times,* Nov. 6, 2002.
Laskin, Tom, "Battling the big boxes," *Isthmus,* February 28, 2003.
Laskin, Tom, "Why Wal-Mart has 'em worried," *Isthmus,* January 23, 2004 (re Stoughton).
Milam, Stan, "Wal-Mart's eye roves to Oregon," *The Capital Times,* January 28, 2004.
---, "Wal-Mart downplays defeat in California," *The Capital Times,* April 8, 2004.
Mihalopoulos, Dan, and Rucker, Patrick, "Wal-Mart goes dialing for support," *Chicago Tribune,* May 26, 2004.
Mihalopoulos, Dan, "Wal-Mart gets half a loaf," *Chicago Tribune,* May 27, 2004.
Ivey, Mike, "Neighbors up against the 'Wal,'" *The Capital Times,* December 27, 2004.
Ivey, Mike, "Big box limits make good business sense," *The Capital Times,* February 1, 2005.
Stein, Mark A., "Kinder, gentler? Only to a point," *The New York Times,* May 22, 2005 (re Wal-Mart aggressive opposition to law limiting size of new stores).
Countryman, Andrew, "Shareholders battle corporate 'coronations.'" *Chicago Tribune,* March 30, 2003.
Countryman, Andrew, "Big investors turn to lawsuits to get changes in governance," *Chicago Tribune,* January 18, 2004.
Morgenson, Gretchen, "How to succeed on Wall Street, conflict-free," *The New York Times,* December 19, 2001 (re Glass Lewis and Company, an independent research firm).
Countryman, Andrew, "Deloitte exit puts Molex in a bind," *Chicago Tribune,* Dec. 5, 2004.
Singhania, Lisa, "PBHG founders face fraud charges," *The Capital Times,* November 21, 2003 (re mutual fund trading).
Fonda, Daren, amd Kadlec, Daniel, "The rumble over executive pay," *Time,* May 31, 2004.
Countryman, Andrew, "Give back pay of $100 million, suit tells Grasso," *Chicago Tribune,* May 25, 2004.

Pappu, Sridhar, "The crusader," *The Atlantic Monthly,* October, 2004 (re Eliot Spitzer).
Fonda, Daren, "Spitzer strikes again," *Time,* October 25, 2004.
Beam, Alex, "Books about schnooks," *The Atlantic Monthly,* September, 2004.
Longworth, R.C., "The day that the 3rd world bucked the WTO," *Chicago Tribune,* September 28, 2003.
Goodman, James, "World's farmers stand in solidarity against WTO," *The Capital Times,* October 29, 2003.
Blustein, Paul, "Activists hail weakening of trade pact," *The Capital Times,* Nov. 21, 2003.
Roy, Arundhati, "Do turkeys enjoy thanksgiving?" *The Hindu,* 2003 (see URL: http://www.thehindu.com/2004/01/18/stories/2004011800181400.htm; date:18/01/2004).
Krauss, Clifford, "Argentina's provinces struggle to stay afloat," *The New York Times,* November 18, 2001.
Tobar, Hector, "Rising anger boosts Argentine legislator," *Chicago Tribune,* June 16, 2002.
Faiola, Anthony, "Mob's feeding frenzy tells Argentine woes," *Chicago Tribune,* Aug. 7, 2002.
Jones, Patrice M., "Leadership crisis adds to misery," *Chicago Tribune,* December 1, 2002.
Jones, Patrice M., "Argentina finds beauty in a business model," *Chicago Tribune,* May 25, 2003.
Cox, James, "Argentina strikes a new deal to repay IMF," *USA Today,* September 11, 2003.
Fields, Gregg, "Argentine problem at the fore," *The Capital Times,* February 8, 2004.
Worrall, Simon, "Patagonia: Land of the living wind," *National Geographic,* January, 2004.
Rohter, Larry, "Doomsday prediction wrong; Argentine economy healthy," *Wisconsin State Journal,* December 26, 2004.
Theroux, Paul, *Dark Star Safari,* Houghton Mifflin Company, Boston, 2003 (see p. 322 re furniture).
Fishman, Ted C., "The Chinese century," *The New York Times Magazine,* July 4, 2004.
Friedl-Putnam, Sara, "Saving family farmers," *Luther Alumni Magazine,* Spring, 2004 (re niche markets, coops, CSAs).
Oncken, John, "A little big cheese: Maple Leaf Co-op a benefit for farmers," *The Capital Times,* November 7, 2002.
Connors, Philip, "Holding their ground: How family farmers are joining forces to fend of corporate 'serfdom,'" *Chicago Tribune,* January 26, 2003 (re Pipestone Family Farms and Minnesota Corn Processors).
Jaeger, Richard W., "Bringing the farm to your doorstep," *Wisconsin State Journal,* March 2, 2003.
Weier, Anita, "Health co-ops approved," *The Capital Times,* November 7, 2003.
Martin, Andrew, "Small dairy farmers take on 'Goliath' cooperative," *Chicago Tribune,* September 7, 2004.
Martin, Andrew, "Dairy insider has clout in setting prices," *Chicago Tribune,* Dec. 30, 2004.
Dougherty, Geoff, "Ethanol fueling dispute," *Chicago Tribune,* November 7, 2004 (re sale of Minnesota Corn Processors).
Nijhuis, Michelle, "For sale by owners," *Smithsonian,* October, 2004 (re *The Merc,* a community-owned cooperative store).
Newman, Judy, "Taking on the giants: Independent pharmacies in the area compete against the chains," *Wisconsin State Journal,* October 17, 2004.
Wallmeyer, Andrew, "Cooperating to create cooperatives," *Wisconsin State Journal,* May 22, 2005 (on advantages of cooperatives and UW Center for Cooperatives).
Weier, Anita, " New bill targets municipal cable TV," *The Capital Times,* April 3, 2003.
Bobbe, John, "More evidence that bigger isn't better," *Door County Advocate,* Dec. 10, 2002.
Peck, John, "Small-scale family farms work best, but they face many threats," *The Capital Times,* December 16, 2004.
Onckon, John, "Dairy couple finds success with grazing," *The Capital Times,* Dec. 16, 2004.

Burns, Greg, "Zambia chooses principle over U.S. corn," *Chicago Tribune,* Nov. 24, 2002.
Clendenning, Alan, "Brazilian farmers get rich using illegal soybean seeds," *Wisconsin State Journal,* December 21, 2003.
Charles, Daniel, "Corn that clones itself," *Technology Review,* March, 2003.
Theroux, Paul, *Dark Star Safari,* Houghton Mifflin Company, Boston, 2003 (see p. 331 re hybrid seeds in Africa).
Coates, James, "Jobs' performance, especially on iPod, iTunes, keeps Apple shining," *Chicago Tribune,* May 4, 2003.
Jones, Terril Yue, and Healey, Jon, "Apple's wedding music," *The Capital Times,* October 17, 2003.
Blau, John, "Europe takes bite out of Microsoft," *IEEE Spectrum,* May, 2004.
Stross, Randall, "The fox is in Microsoft's henhouse (and salivating)," *The New York Times,* December 19, 2004
Kaplan, Fred, "D.I.Y. meets N.R.L.(No Record Label)," *The New York Times,* July 4, 2004 (direct online sales by recording artists).
Rose, Barbara, "Midwest pulls out all stops for start-ups," *Chicago Tribune,* July 6, 2003.
---, "Manitowoc Mirro plant has buyer," *The Capital Times,* January 3-4, 2004.
Brinkman, Phil, "Shuttle for shoppers will offer some relief," *Wisconsin State Journal,* March 26, 2005.
Sensenbrenner, Lee, "Good ice cream, good neighbor," *The Capital Times,* July 30, 2003.
Allison, Melissa, "Small banks find room to sprout in Illinois," *Chicago Tribune,* August 18, 2002.
Keilman, John, "Teardown talk has 1 village gearing up," *Chicago Tribune,* July 2, 2002.
Countryman, Andrew, "Sarbanes has firms struggling to comply: companies toil to meet rules on financial controls," *Chicago Tribune,* November 14, 2004.
---, "Do you know where your data are?" editorial, *IEEE Spectrum,* December, 2004 (re Sarbanes-Oxley and threats to privacy due to need for data collection and monitoring of employees).
Koomey, Jonathan G., "Sorry, wrong number," *IEEE Spectrum,* June, 2003.

11) Reforming the government...a more perfect union

Von Drehl, David, "Democratic left re-emerges in time for presidential run," *The Capital Times,* July 10, 2003.
---, "*New York Times* nonfiction best sellers," *Wisconsin State Journal,* April 18, 2004.
---, "Moore's movie worries GOP," *The Capital Times,* July 22, 2004.
Krome, Margaret, "*MoveOn.org* aims to give ordinary people a voice," *The Capital Times,* September 1, 2004.
Gore, Al, "Freedom and security," speech to *MoveOn* supporters, Constitution Hall, Washington, D.C., Nov. 9, 2003.
---, "Crossroads for Bush?" *Time,* May 24, 2004 (Time/CNN poll results).
Lazaroff, Leon, and Dorning, Mike, "Rare admission, then tough scrutiny: Times apology puts focus on news media's prewar role," *Chicago Tribune,* May 27, 2004.
---, "N.Y. Times says no to Moore," *The Capital Times,* September 11-12, 2004 (re request to reprint *Times* self-analysis of its Iraq coverage).
Simpson, Cam, and Pearson, Rick, "Bush to skeptical UN: war rid Iraq of 'outlaw,'" *Chicago Tribune,* September 22, 2004.
Tyler, Patrick E., "European papers hit Bush over UN speech,"
Priest, Dana, and Ricks, Thomas, "Intelligence: Iraq situation dire," *The Capital Times,* September 29, 2004.
Ivins, Molly, "Bush administration knowingly ignores terrible reality in Iraq," *The Capital Times,* September 30, 2004.

Klein, Joe, "Does Bush really get us?" *Time,* May 3, 2004 (re coffins, Bush's cynicism).
Chapman, Steve, "Getting some insight on the president's uncomfortable relationship with reality," *Chicago Tribune,* October 3, 2004.
Fallows, James, "Bush's lost year: How the war on Iraq undermined the war on terror," *The Atlantic Monthly,* October, 2004.
Mazzetti, Mark, "Army Reserve nearly 'broken,' says leader," *The Capital Times,* January 6, 2005.
Burns, Robert, "Grind of insurgency eroding U.S. military," *Chicago Tribune,* January 9, 2005.
Lederer, Edith M., "N. Korea: U.S. forced our hand on nukes," *The Capital Times,* September 28, 2004.
McFeatters, Ann, "Nuclear crises with Iran, N. Korea will shove aside worries over Iraq," *The Capital Times,* September 28, 2004.
Torriero, E.A., and Pearson, Rick, "Kerry: Bush failed in Iraq," *Chicago Tribune,* September 21, 2004.
Barstow, David, "Skewed intelligence data in march to war in Iraq," reported by David Barstow, William J. Broad, and Jeff Gerth, *The New York Times,* October 3, 2004 (re Iraqi aluminum tubes).
Wright, Robin, and Ricks, Thomas E., "First U.S. Iraq leader: we needed more troops," *The Capital Times,* October 5, 2004.
Allen, Mike, and Priest, Dana, "New report: Saddam threat was diminishing," *Chicago Tribune,* October 6, 2004.
Kessler, Glenn, "U.S. reports unravel Bush's war rationale," *The Capital Times,* Oct. 7, 2004.
Strope, Leigh, "Jobs numbers called anemic," *The Capital Times,* October 8, 2004.
Kasindorf, Martin, "Kerry slams Bush over economy," *USA Today,* September 16, 2004.
Stiglitz, Joseph, "The roaring nineties," *The Atlantic Monthly,* October, 2002 (re success of Sweden's modified welfare system).
Grossman, Ron, "A surefire formula? Not quite: Lenin could teach Bush a thing or two about flexibility," *Chicago Tribune,* January 12, 2003.
---, "Report rips feds for withholding Medicare costs," *The Capital Times,* May 5, 2004.
Goldstein, Amy, "Medicare videos with 'reporters' are illegal," *The Capital Times,* May 20, 2004.
Eilperin, Juliet, "House backs GOP shift on overtime," *The Capital Times,* July 11, 2003.
Armour, Stephanie, "Senate votes for overtime as it is," *USA Today,* September 11, 2003.
Dewar, Helen, "Senators snub Bush on overtime pay curbs," *The Capital Times,* May 5, 2004.
---, "Overtime faces new scrutiny," *Wisconsin State Journal,* June 27, 2004.
---, "Gov flouts feds on overtime," *The Capital Times,* August 20-21, 2004.
---, "Edwards rips Bush's new 'hard time' overtime rules," *The Capital Times,* Aug. 23, 2004.
---, "Workers clock in on new overtime," *Chicago Tribune,* September 7, 2004 (re wage losses when salaried and benefit losses when hourly).
Davidson, Paul, "Spending bill settles two key issues," *USA Today,* January 23, 2004.
Silver, Josh, "The FCC rollback hoax," The Free Press Newswire, November 27, 2003 (www.mediareform.net).
---, "Part of Patriot Act called unconstitutional," *The Capital Times*, January 27, 2004.
Neumeister, Larry, "Judge says no to Patriot Act powers," *The Capital Times,* Sept. 30, 2003.
Wallace, C. G., "No right to search protesters, court says," *Wisconsin State Journal,* October 17, 2004.
Holland, Jesse J., "Conservatives, liberals join to push Patriot Act changes," *The Capital Times,* March 23, 2005.
Lane, Charles, "Bush terror tack challenged: court ruling called a 'body blow,'" *The Capital Times,* December 19, 2003.
James, Frank, "Judge orders U.S. to name detainees," *Chicago Tribune,* August 3, 2002.

Graham, Bradley, and White, Josh, "General: 'Ghost detainees' could total up to 100," *The Capital Times,* September 10, 2004.
Bendavid, Naftali, "Justices rule that detainees get day in court," *Chicago Tribune,* June 29, 2004.
Hendren, John, "Judge rules Guantanamo trial proceedings invalid," *The Capital Times,* November 9, 2004.
Zajec, Andrew, "Legal tide turning on detainee issue," *Chicago Tribune,* January 3, 2005 (re growing concern that we follow the 'rule of law').
Schmitt, Richard B. "Seek toughest sentence, Ashcroft says," *The Capital Times,* September 23, 2003.
Holland, Gina, "Ashcroft irks judges on fed sentencing," *The Capital Times,* Sept. 30, 2003.
Harden, Blaine, "U.S. court strikes Ashcroft's order against suicide law," *Chicago Tribune,* May 27, 2004.
Banchero, Stephanie, "Teachers sue over 'No Child' funding," *Chicago Tribune,* April 21, 2005.
Clarke, Sara, "Bush's Border Patrol staffing assailed," *The Capital Times,* March 3, 2005.
Milbank, Dana, and VandeHei, Jim, "Bush's ferocious anti-Kerry ads highly misleading," *The Capital Times,* June 1, 2004.
James, Frank, and Anderson, Lisa, "U.S. warns of new terror plot," *Chicago Tribune,* August 2, 2004.
James, Frank, "Al Qaeda updated pre-9/11 target surveillance in '04," *Chicago Tribune,* August 3, 2004.
James, Frank, "Ridge rebuts critics of notched-up alert," *Chicago Tribune,* August 4, 2004.
Zajac, Andrew, and McCormick, John, "Terror alerts vulnerable to attacks," *Chicago Tribune,* August 8, 2004.
Tackett, Michael, and Jones, Tim, "Some wounds of war have healed -- many others won't go away." *Chicago Tribune,* April 24, 2005.
Gonzalez, John, "Swift boat folks are Kerry's nemeses of old," *Dallas Observer,* posted on Alternet.org, August 11, 2004 (http://www.alternet.org/story/19532/).
Bauder, David, "Two heated TV battles put Chris Mathews in spotlight," *The Capital Times,* September 11-12, 2004.
Dowd, Maureen, "Kerry: slo-mo on Swifties," *The New York Times,* August 22, 2204.
Jones, Terry, "Swift boat skipper: Kerry critics wrong -- Tribune editor breaks long silence on Kerry record; fought in disputed battle," *Chicago Tribune,* August 22, 2004.
Rood, William B., "Swift boat skipper: Kerry critics wrong -- February 28, 1969: on the Dong Cung River -- Anti-Kerry vets not there that day," *Chicago Tribune,* August 22, 2004.
Derby, Samara Derby, "Combat vets rip Swift boat critics," *The Capital Times,* Aug. 23, 2004.
Tumulty, Karen, and Burger, Timothy J., "The vets on a roll," *Time,* September 6, 2004.
Klein, Joe, "What the Swifties cost us," *Time,* September 6, 2004.
Kurtz, Howard, and Ahrens, Frank, "Bush-backing broadcaster slates anti-Kerry film," *The Capital Times,* October 12, 2004.
Kurtz, Howard, "Sinclair show bashes Kerry but gives balance too," *The Capital Times,* October 23-24, 2004.
Alterman, Eric, "Bush not gung-ho in Guard," *The Capital Times,* February 2, 2004.
Ripley, Amanda, "The X files of Lt. Bush," *Time,* September 20, 2004.
Rainey, James, "Memo: Bush failed to meet Guard standards," *The Capital Times,* September 9, 2004.
Dobbs, Michael, "Validity of Guard papers on Bush doubted," *The Capital Times,* September 10, 2004.
Zeleny, Jeff, and Cook, Jeff, "CBS apologizes for Guard story," *Chicago Tribune,* September 21, 2004.

Sniffen, Michael J., "Tight lid clamped on public records," *Wisconsin State Journal,* March 20, 2005.
Ebert, Roger, " 'Going Upriver' documents Kerry's heroism," *The Capital Times,* Oct. 6, 2004.
Zweifel, Dave, "Firings at CBS don't vindicate Bush," *The Capital Times,* January 17, 2005.
---, "Return of the draft?" satirical poll, *the Onion,* October 28-November 3, 2004.
Farhi, Paul, and Vandehei, Jim, "Kerry intensifies criticism of Bush Iraq policy," *The Capital Times,* September 10, 2004.
Zuckman, Jill, "Kerry enlists sharp tongues to attacks Bush," *Chicago Tribune,* Sept. 7, 2004.
Silva, Mark, "Bush assails Kerry in Missouri," *Chicago Tribune,* September 7, 2004.
Jelinek, Pauline, "Where's armor for troops?" *The Capital Times,* December 10, 2004.
Lumpkin, John J., "Army says it is trying to speed up armor production," *The Capital Tımes,* December 11-12, 2004.
Raum, Tom, "Soldiers always grip -- but not like this," *The Capital Times,* Dec. 11-12, 2004.
Thompson, Mark, "How safe are out troops?" *Time,* December 20, 2004.
Berryman, Anne, "Why he popped the question," *Time,* December 27, 2004-January 3, 2005.
Riechmann, Deb, "Bush: winning terror war unlikely," *The Capital Times,* August 30, 2004.
Chen, Edwin, "Bush now says war on terror is winnable," *The Capital Times,* Sept. 1, 2004.
Chapman, Steve, "The flip-flopper running for president," *Chicago Tribune,* March 18, 2004.
---, "U.S. attacks again as it seeks control in Fallujah," *The Capital Times,* September 10, 2004.
Vieth, Warren, "Federal deficit soaring to $442 billion," *Chicago Tribune,* September 8, 2004.
Fram, Alan, "White House numbers show record in red ink for 2005," *The Capital Times,* January 26, 2005.
---, "*Time* poll: The Economy -- Don't pop the corks yet," *Time,* September 13, 2004.
Connolly, Ceci, "Medicare premiums to rise 17 percent in '05," *The Washington Post,* September 4, 2004 (posted on *Chicago Tribune* web site).
La Ganga, Maria, "Medicare hike will affect seniors' votes," *The Capital Times,* Sept. 9, 2004.
Quirk, Barbara, "Rights under attack, policies skewed? Vote!" *The Capital Times,* February 10, 2004.
Dionne, E.J., "Bush's overkill can backfire," *The Capital Times,* September 9, 2004.
Klein, Joe, "Tearing Kerry down," *Time,* September 13, 2004.
West, Paul, "9/11 is key to Bush strategy," *The Capital Times,* September 11-12, 2004.
Green, Joshua, "Karl Rove in a corner," *The Atlantic Monthly,* November, 2004.
---, "Bush's tactics despicable," *The Los Angeles Times* editorial, republished in *The Capital Times,* September 30, 2004.
---, "Deliver us from evil," from Random Samples, Constance Holden, ed., *Science,* December 17, 2004 (re Sheldon Solomon's research).
Trudeau, Garry, "Doonesbury," *The Capital Times,* March 10-14, 2003 (re mad hatter and conservative agenda, up is down).
Tumulty, Karen, "Bush's bounce," *Time,* September 13, 2004.
Milbank, Dana, "Bush's scowls and smirks muddy image," *The Capital Times,* Oct. 2-3, 2004.
Hook, Janet, "Cheney, Edwards both bent the truth," *The Capital Times,* October 6, 2004.
Klein, Joe, "A race is what we've now got," *Time,* October 11, 2004.
Kole, William J., "Explosives looted in Iraq," *The Capital Times,* October 25, 2004.
Mazetti, Mark, "Video shows explosives as U.S. troops break lock," *The Capital Times,* October 29, 2004.
Lumpkin, John J., "Questions unresolved over missing explosives," *The Capital Times,* October 30-31, 2004.
Mazetti, Mark, "Explosives taken in pickup trucks, say U.S. troops," *The Capital Times,* November 4, 2004.
Hundley, Tom, "Bush vs. Kerry has global attention," *Chicago Tribune,* October 19, 2004.

Comer, Gary, "Undecided voters of Wisconsin," personal political statement, *Wisconsin State Journal,* October 29, 2004.
---, "Giuliani compares Bush to Lincoln in Civil War," *The Capital Times,* Oct. 30-31, 2004.

12) The 2004 presidential election...persevering under adversity

---, "Outcome hinges on Ohio," *The Capital Times,* November 3, 2004.
Wineke, Bill, "Why do evangelicals rhapsodize about Bush?" *Wisconsin State Journal,* November 4, 2004.
Rosin, Hanna, "Beyond belief," *The Atlantic Monthly,* January/February, 2005 (see p. 120 for quote regarding God as Republican).
Pitts, Jr., Leonard, "Where is the Christian left now when we need it?" *Wisconsin State Journal,* November 8, 2004.
Phillips, Michael, "Kushner: we're in for some very, very bad times," *Chicago Tribune,* November 7, 2004.
---, "Moderates squeezed out as the Senate moves to the right," *The Capital Times,* November 4, 2004.
---, "GOP drops ethics rule to help DeLay," *The Capital Times,* November 18, 2004.
Espo, David, "Conservatives flex their muscles," *The Capital Times,* November 23, 2004.
Fram, Alan, "Congress increases federal debt limit," *Wisconsin State Journal,* Nov. 19, 2004.
Weisman, Jonathan, "Despite debt, Congress punts," *The Capital Times,* November 19, 2004.
Fram, Alan, "Congress, White House reach agreement on spending bill," *Chicago Tribune,* November 21, 2004.
---, "Abortion rider in vital bill stirs fight," *Chicago Tribune,* November 21, 2004.
---, "Congress OKs spending bill," *Wisconsin State Journal,* November 21, 2004 (notes "raw power" of GOP in Congress).
---, "Bush approves interim bill to fund government," *The Capital Times,* November 22, 2004 (notes delay in final bill due tax provision).
Morgan, Dan, and Dewar, Helen, "Secretive spending bill now GOP embarrassment," *The Capital Times,* November 23, 2004.
---, "Congress argues over tax-return snooping," *The Capital Times,* November 25, 2004.
Fram, Alan, "GOP aide blamed for tax return provision," *Chicago Tribune,* December 5, 2004.
Raum, Tom, "Cabinet naysayers need not apply for second Bush term," *The Capital Times,* November 17, 2004.
Feingold, Russ, "Rice nomination a sign of more gaffes to come," *The Capital Times,* December 11-12, 2004.
Margasak, Larry, "Security pick made $6M off Tasers," *The Capital Times,* December 9, 2004.
Hunt, Terence, "Homeland nominee pulls out," *The Capital Times,* December 11-12, 2004.
---, "Nanny issue was raised," *Wisconsin State Journal,* December 12, 2004.
Carney, James, "Inside Kerik's fall," *Time,* December 20, 2004.
---, "Bush inauguration will see tightest security ever," *The Capital Times,* December 20, 2004.
Babington, Charles, "House GOP won't let Dems participate," *The Capital Times,* November 29, 2004.
Zuckman, Jill, "Bush finds Congress is no pushover," *Chicago Tribune,* May 30, 2005 (re decline in Bush's overall approval rating).
Lester, Will, "Bush ratings drop to new lows," *The Capital Times,* June 10, 2005 (AP-Ipsos).
Havemann, Joel, "'Fear' campaign begins -- Critics: Lies fuel Bush Social Security plan," *The Capital Times,* December 15, 2004.
Ivins, Molly, "Bush plan for Social Security loony, unnecessary and costly," *The Capital Times,* December 16, 2004.
Tumulty, Karen, and Roston, Eric, "Social security: Is there really a crisis?" *Time,* Jan.24, 2005.
Longworth, R.C., "Social Security 'fix' -- the next disaster," *Chicago Tribune,* Jan. 23, 2005.

Heise, Paul, "Social Security crisis: Tax the working the working, untax the rich," *Chicago Tribune,* December 19, 2004.

Arnold, Frederick M., "Bush privatization marks Social Security for death," *The Capital Times,* January 31, 2005.

Alonso-Zaldivar, Ricardo, "Medicare woes on horizon," *The Capital Times,* Dec. 20, 2004.

McNally, Joel, "Privatizing Social Security would help only Wall St." *The Capital Times,* December 25-26, 2004.

Allen, Mike, and VandeHei, Jim, "GOP to begin campaign blitz to sell Social Security changes," *The Capital Times,* January 14-15, 2005.

Ivins, Molly, "AARP attack isn't a joke, but you can't help laughing," *The Capital Times,* March 3, 2005 (re AARP opposition to Bush's Social Security proposals).

Hook, Janet, "Social Security reform a test for Democrats," *The Capital Times,* Dec. 20, 2004.

Allen, Mike, "Semantics huge in Social Security" debate," *The Capital Times,* Jan. 24, 2005.

Simon, Richard, and Reynolds, Maura, "Dems tell Bush no on Social Security," *The Capital Times,* February 3, 2005.

Wallsten, Peter, "Bush wants critics to ease up," *The Capital Times,* March 23, 2005.

Harris, John F., and VandeHei, Jim, "100 days into second term, Bush agenda looks wobbly," *The Capital Times,* May 2, 2005.

Simon, Richard, "House GOP reverses stance on ethics shift," *The Capital Times,* January 4, 2005 (reversing November, 2004, rule change).

Hulse, Carl, "Democrats turn down GOP offer on DeLay," *Chicago Tribune,* April 21, 2005.

---, "Reid and Morgan say Senate DPC will launch series of major oversight and investigation hearings in 109th Congress," *Democratic Policy Committee,* December 13, 2004 (http://democrats.senate.gov/dpc/).

Abrams, Jim, "Senate Dems plan investigatory hearings," *Associated Press,* December 14, 2004 (www.kansas.com, *The Wichita Eagle,* January 6, 2005).

Waller, Douglas, "Bickering heights," *Time,* January 10, 2005 (re divisions between Democrats and Republicans in Congress and role of Bush).

Babington, Charles, "Opposition to Bush picks takes some by surprise," *The Capital Times,* January 27, 2005.

Klein, Joe, "The creative stubbornness of Harry Reid," *Time,* March 28, 2005.

Garvey, Megan, "Californians' stem cell vote sets precedent," *The Capital Times,* Nov. 4, 2004.

Neikirk, William, and Silva, Mark, "Stem cell bill OKd," *Chicago Tribune,* May 25, 2005.

Zuckman, Jill, "Filibuster deal surprises leadership," *Chicago Tribune,* May 24, 2005.

Zeleny, Jeff, "Bitter feud has bittersweet end," *Chicago Tribune,* May 24, 2005.

--- "Clinton to Dems: don't whine; work on image," *The Capital Times,* November 6-7, 2004.

Krugman, Paul, "No surrender," *The New York Times,* November 5, 2004.

Frank, Thomas, *What's the Matter with Kansas?* Metropolitan Books, New York, 2004.

Carney, James, "What happens to the losing team?" *Time,* November 15, 2004.

Herbert, Bob, "O.K. folks: back to work," *The New York Times,* November 5, 2004.

Sullivan, Andrew, "Let's have a truce," *Time,* November 15, 2004.

Krauthammer, Charles, "Why Bush has no fear," *Time,* November 29, 2004.

Lupo, James, "Nominee employs tortured logic," *Chicago Tribune,* Jan. 23, 2005.

---, "Feingold, Kohl vote against Gonzales as attorney general," *The Capital Times,* January 27, 2005.

Tackett, Michael, "Bush sees global mission in 2nd term," *Chicago Tribune,* January 21, 2005.

Silva, Mark, and Hedges, Stephen J., "When vision meets reality," *Chicago Tribune,* January 22, 2005.

Richter, Paul, "White House, Bush soften tone of inaugural address," *The Capital Times,* February 23, 2005.

Sly, Liz, "Shiite with ties to Iran poised to be Iraqi leader," *Chicago Tribune,* January 22, 2005.

Raum, Tom, "Ticking off milestones," *Wisconsin State Journal,* March 4, 2005 (re cost of Iraq War in lives and dollars).
Woodward, Calvin, "Bush didn't tell the whole truth in the State of Union," *The Capital Times,* February 3, 2005.
---, "Russert failed to correct Mehlman's claim that 9-11 Commission, Senate report 'totally discredited' Downing Street Memo," Media Matters for America, June 6, 2005 (from afterdowningstreet.org; see also www.downingstreetmemo.com).
Morley, Jefferson, "The Downing Street Memo story won't die," washingtonpost.com, June 7, 2005 (from afterdowningstreet.org).
Daniszewski, John, "More 2002 memos show U.S. pushing for Iraq War," *The Capital Times,* June 15 2005.
Kurtz, Howard, "Media forced to look at Downing St. memo," *The Capital Times,* June 16, 2005.
Smith, Michael, "War started before Congress gave OK," *The Capital Times,* June 27, 2005 (Downing Street memo and efforts to legally justify war in Iraq).
Silva, Mark, "Bush: Iraq a worthy sacrifice," *Chicago Tribune,* June 29, 2005.
Hedges, Stephen J., "Bush marks clear shift in U.S. mission," *Chicago Tribune,* June 29, 2005.
Easterbrook, Gregg, "There goes the neighborhood," *The New York Times Book Review,* January 30, 2005 (book review of *Collapse* by Jared Diamond).
McLemee, Scott, "Analyzing the interaction of society and environment," *Chicago Tribune,* February 6, 2005 (book review of *Collapse* by Jared Diamond).
Diamond, Jared, *Collapse,* Viking, New York, 2004 (see p. 509 on collapse following success; see p. 498 re sustainability).

Interlude Three - Transformations

Change and personal identity...on letting go

Bartlett, John, *Familiar Quotations, 15th ed.,* Beck, Emily Morison, ed., Little, Brown, and Company, Boston, 1980 (see p. 385 for quote from Barry Goldwater's acceptance speech at the 1964 Republican National Convention).
Fowler, James W., *Stages of Faith,* HarperCollins, New York, 1981 (re helix and life).
Diamond, Jared, *Collapse,* Viking, New York, 2004 (see p. 433 on survival and letting go).
Updike, John, *Towards the End of Time,*Knopf, New York, 1997 (see p. 78 on grandchildren).

IV. Religion, democracy, and the future...liberty and justice for all

13) From exclusivism to pluralism...the blessings of liberty

Bartlett, John, *Familiar Quotations, 15th ed.,* Beck, Emily Morison, ed., Little, Brown, and Company, Boston, 1980 (see p. 264 for use of "a city upon a hill" in a sermon delivered by John Winthrop on board the *Arabella* in 1630; see also Matthew 5:14).
Murphy, Dean E., "God, American history and a fifth-grade class," *The New York Times,* December 5, 2004.
---, "Religious Adherents in the U.S., 1900-2000," *Encyclopedia Britannica Almanac 2003,* pp. 728-729.
Savage, David G., "Commandments in high court," *The Capital Times,* March 3, 2005.
Yen, Hope, "Sharper church-state line," *The Capital Times,* June 27, 2005 (re banning Ten Commandments in courthouses, but allowing displays in neutral settings).

O'Driscoll, Patrick, and Komarow, Steven, "Panel chastises Air Force Academy," *USA Today,* June 23, 2005.
Hunter, Elizabeth, "Chaplain is dismissed from U.S. Air Force Academy," *The Lutheran,* July, 2005
---, "Bishop tells lawmakers how to vote," *The Capital Times,* December 4, 2003.
Williams, Juliet, "Bishop's decree is decried," *The Capital Times,* January 10-11, 2004.
Cooperman, Alan, "Catholic reps warn bishops on tactics," *The Capital Times,* May 20, 2004.
Sullivan, Andrew, "Showdown at the Communion Rail," essay, *Time,* May 24, 2004.
Huffstutter, P.J., "Archbishop links voter's choices to 'grave sin,'" *The Capital Times,* October 7, 2004.
Nichols, John, "Catholic bishops silent on war backers," *The Capital Times,* May 20, 2004.
Powell, Michael, "Green Bay bishop tells how to vote," *The Capital Times,* November 1, 2004.
McClory, Robert, "Absolute, relative, political," *Chicago Tribune,* June 6, 2004.
Rosin, Hanna, "Beyond belief," *The Atlantic Monthly,* January/February, 2005 (see p. 119 regarding religion and voting).
Ostling, Richard N., "Evangelicals see pope as powerful ally," *The Capital Times,* April 25, 2005.
Sullivan, Andrew, "The vicar of orthodoxy," *Time,* May 2, 2005 (re Pope Benedict XVI and authority).
Krauthammer, Charles, "Why lines must be drawn," *Time,* August 23, 2004 (re stem cells).
Ritter, Malcolm, "Surgeons use stem cells from fat to grow bone," *The Capital Times,* December 17, 2004.
Kaplan, Karen, "Setback for stem cell lines: All lines contaminated by mice molecule," *The Capital Times,* January 24, 2005.
Stacey, Mitch, "Schiavo's parents unswayed by finding of brain damage," *The Capital Times,* June 16, 2005
Chapman, Steve, "Who failed Terri Schiavo?" *Chicago Tribune,* June 19, 2005
Page, Clarence, "Even a misdiagnosis from afar doesn't seem to torment the conscience of pundits, pols," *Chicago Tribune,* June 19, 2005
Strauss, Valerie, '80 years after Scopes trial, evolution battle rages on," *The Capital Times,* December 11-12, 2004.
---, "Clergy: Teach evolution," *The Capital Times,* December 17, 2004.
Lemonick, Michael D., "Stealth attack on evolution," *Time,* January 31, 2005.
Anderson, Lisa, "Debate evolves into culture-war front," *Chicago Tribune,* May 22, 2005.
Lilla, Mark, "Church meets state," *The New York Times Book Review,* May 15, 2005.
Bothamley, Jennifer, *Dictionary of Theories,* Visible Ink Press, Detroit, 2002 (p. 310 re liberal democracy).
Kennedy, Donald, "Breakthrough of the year," *Science,* Dec. 17, 2004 (re science and politics).
Mervis, Jeffrey, "Breakdown of the year: The unwritten contract," *Science,* Dec. 17, 2004 (re breakdowns between science and government).
Spong, John Shelby, "Political Pulpit: The Bible as weapon in the culture war," *Chicago Tribune,* May 15, 2005.
Domke, David, "Bush ideology is similar to our worst enemies," *Wis. State J.,* Aug. 29, 2004.
Klein, Joe, "The perils of a righteous President," *Time,* May 17, 2004.
Hulsey, Brett, "Bush and his cohorts would be wise to implement Jesus agenda," *The Capital Times,* December 18-19, 2004.
Silva, Mark, "Bush paints policy with broad brush," *Chicago Tribune,* May 15, 2005 (re Gallup Poll results and Bush rhetoric re democracy).
Chapman, Steve, "More nasty surprises await U.S. troops in Iraq," *Chicago Tribune,* May 15, 2005.

Richter, Paul, and Khalil, Ashraf, "U.S. to up role in running Iraq," *The Capital Times,* May 20, 2005.
Nafisi, Azar, *Reading Lolita in Tehran,* Random House, New York, 2003 (see p. 273 on blurring line between personal and political).
Ford, Peter, "Europe cringes at Bush 'crusade' against terrorists," *The Christian Science Monitor,* September 19, 2001.
Carroll, James, "The Bush Crusade," *The Nation,* September 20, 2004.
Rosin, Hanna, "Beyond belief," *The Atlantic Monthly,* January/February, 2005 (see p. 118 regarding traditionalists and modernists).
Pagels, Elaine, *The Gnostic Gospels,* Vintage Books, New York, 1981.
DiNovella, Elizabeth, "The Gibson God," The Progressive, May, 2004 (reviews *Beyond Belief*).
Pagels, Elaine, *Beyond Belief,* Random House, New York, 2004.
DeWitt, Bryce, "God's rays," *Physics Today,* January , 2005 (comments on Elaine Pagels).
Chittister, Joan, "Discipleship for a priestly people in a priestless period," address at the Women's Ordination Worldworld Conf. in Dublin, June 30, 2001 (re woman and church).
---, "GOP pushing gay marriage as wedge issue," *The Capital Times,* July 9, 2004.
---, Today's quote, *The Capital Times,* September 1, 2004 (re Arnold Schwarzenegger's use "economic girlie-men").
Levitan, Stu, "No girly gov," *The Capital Times,* September 1, 2004 (re Tommy Thompson's use of "girly man").
Rowe, Douglas J., "Full frontal," *Wisconsin State Journal,* March 14, 2004.
Banerjee, Neela, "American ruptures shaking the Episcopal Church," *The New York Times,* October 3, 2004.
Sullivan, Andrew, "If at first you don't succeed...," *Time,* July 26, 2004 (re gay marriage).
Milbank, Dana, "Divided U.S. united in anxiety," *The Capital Times,* November 4, 2004 (re same-sex ban and other moral issues).
Callimachi, Rukmini, "The tide turns for gay couples," *Wisconsin State Journal,* Nov. 8, 2004.
---, "Judge nixes first cousins' request to wed," *The Capital Times,* March 18, 2005.
Chapman, Steve, "Unforeseen side effect of gay marriage," *Chicago Tribune,* August 1, 2004 (re "court stripping").
Dinan, Stephen. "House to debate court stripping," *The Washington Times,* July 22, 2004 (www.washingtontimes.com).
---, "Court-stripping bill on marriage undermines the Bill of Rights," *People for the American Way,* July 21, 2004 (press release: www.pfaw.org/pfaw/general/default.aspx?oid=16519).
---, "Court-stripping: What are the issues? *People for the American Way,* July 21, 2004 (www.pfaw.org/pfaw/general/default.aspx?oid=16522).
---, "'Court stripping' -- Congress undermines the power of the judiciary," special report, American Civil Liberties Union, June, 1996 (www.archive.aclu.org/library/ctstrip.html).
---, "Bush won't push gay marriage amendment," *The Capital Times,* January 17, 2005.
---, "Marriage files axed by Social Security," *The Capital Times,* December 20, 2004.
Belluck, Pam, "Several red states are Splitsville," *Wisconsin State Journal,* Nov. 14, 2004.
Wineke, Bill, "State's hostile attitude toward gays is baffling," *Wisconsin State Journal,* March 20, 2004.
---, "Church people plan opposition to gay marriage amendment," *Wisconsin State Journal,* December 5, 2004 (re proposed marriage amendment in Wisconsin).
Eriksson, Larry J., "The Salt Gone Flat," *Dialog,* vol. 28, no. 1, 58-60, Winter, 1989 (re homosexuality and church).
---, "The varieties of human sexuality: experiences at Advent Lutheran Church," statement by Advent Church Council Study Group, Madison, Wisconsin, June 2, 2004.
Shapiro, Joseph, "Studies on children of gay couple spark controversy," *Morning Edition,* National Public Radio, May 24, 2004.

Crary, David, "Debate flares over teaching gay tolerance," *The Capital Times,* Feb. 3, 2005.
Haslanger, Phil, "SpongeBob gets flak for siding with respect, tolerance, diversity," *The Capital Times,* February 3, 2005.
Eriksson, Larry J., "A Return to the Boundaries," *Dialog,* vol 29, no. 2, 139-140, Spring, 1990 (re "God of the gaps").
Bonhoeffer, Dietrich, *Letters and Papers from Prison: The Enlarged Edition,* Macmillan, New York, 1972 (see pp. 380-383 for book outline).
Brachear, Manya A., "Anglicans ask for Episcopal apology," *Chicago Tribune,* Oct. 19, 2004.
Winik, Jay, *April 1865,* HarperCollins, New York, 2001.
Safire, William, *Lend Me Your Ears: Great Speeches in History,* 2nd edition, Norton, New York, 1992 (see p. 469-471 for Lincoln's Second Inaugural).
Dickerson, John F., "What the President reads," *Time,* January 17, 2005.
Silva, Mark, "Bush draws parallels to Lincoln at Museum," *Chicago Tribune,* April 20, 2005 (re spreading liberty and freeing slaves).
Perlman, Diane, "Misinterpreting Osama's message: erring on the side danger," *Independent Media Institute,* posted on Alternet.org, November 21, 2002 (alternet.org/story/14600/).
McLane, Maureen N., "Critic Terry Eagleton confronts the state of cultural theory," *Chicago Tribune,* August 1, 2004 (review of *After Theory* by Terry Eagleton).
Eagleton, Terry, *After Theory,* Basic Books, New York, 2004.
Le Guin, Ursula K., "A Left-Handed Commencement Address," *Dancing at the Edge of the World,* Grove Press, New York, 1989.
Chittister, Joan, *Heart of Flesh,* William B. Eerdmans Publishing Company, Grand Rapids, Michigan, 1998 (p. 92 re women's losses).
Campbell, Ben Nighthorse, "A long time coming," *Smithsonian,* September, 2004.
Hall, Douglas John, Lecture Series: *Agenda for A Prophetic Faith,* Madison, Wisconsin, February 10, 1991.

14) From conflict to consensus...the new democracy

Fowler, James W., *Stages of Faith,* HarperCollins, New York, 1981.
Eriksson, Karen, "Fowler's faith development model: maintaining the status quo," unpublished article, March 28, 1989.
Erikson, Erik H., *Childhood and Society,* Norton, New York, 1950.
Nagel, Ernest, and Newman, James R., *Gödel's Proof,* New York University Press, New York, 1958.
Brooks, David, "Bitter at the top," from the Internet, *The New York Times,* June 15, 2004 (re civil war between managers and professionals of educated class).
Cowle, Jefferson, "A liberal's heartland lament," *Chicago Tribune,* June 27, 2004 (review of *What's the Matter with Kansas?* by Thomas Frank).
Frank, Thomas, *What's the Matter with Kansas?* Metropolitan Books, New York, 2004.
Rosin, Hanna, "Beyond belief," *The Atlantic Monthly,* January/February, 2005 (see p. 120 regarding Bush and Orthodox Jews).
Chittister, Joan, *Heart of Flesh,* William B. Eerdmans Publishing Company, Grand Rapids, Michigan, 1998 (p. 130 re consensus).
Zuckman, Jill, "Bush finds Congress is no pushover," *Chicago Tribune,* May 30, 2005 (re lack of consensus within Republican-controlled Congress).
Lind, Michael, letter to the editor, *The Atlantic Monthly,* March, 2005, p. 18 (re instant-runoff).
Rhodes, Richard, *The Making of the Atomic Bomb,* Touchstone, New York, 1988 (pp. 34-35 on network of scientists).
Chandler, Susan, "Oregon archdiocese takes a page from corporate playbook," *Chicago Tribune,* August 1, 2004 (re bankruptcy).

Miller, David L., "ELCA bishops meet with sexuality task force," *The Lutheran,* November, 2004 (on debate over same-sex relationships).
---, Report and Recommendations from the Task Force for Evangelical Lutheran Church in America Studies on Sexuality, January 13, 2005 (available on ELCA web site).
Coffee, Melanie, "Lutherans try to find compromise on gay issues," *Wisconsin State Journal,* January 14, 2005.
Buragas, Amelia, "Local Lutherans torn," *The Capital Times,* January 14, 2005.
Wilkinson, Tracy, "Budget wrangling adds to disharmony among EU nations," *Chicago Tribune,* June 18, 2005.
Eriksson, Larry J., *Business Decisions: the impact of corporate mergers and global capitalism on our lives,* Quarter Section Press, Madison, Wisconsin, 2002 (see p. 101 on aircraft carriers and adaptive management).
Pool, Robert, "When failure is not an option," *Technology Review,* July, 1997 (reprinted in *IEEE Engineering Management Review,* 27 (1), Spring, 1999, 27-31; on aircraft carriers).
Foley, Ryan J., "Biz groups challenging pay hike in court," *The Capital Times,* Mar. 31, 2005.
Davidoff, Judith, and Callender, David, "State bill would kill local smoking bans," *The Capital Times,* April 1, 2005.

15) The role of the left...recovering the past, building the future

Reagan, Ronald, "President Ronald Reagan inveighs against the sinfulness of Communism," sermon on March 8, 1983 to National Association of Evangelists, *Lend Me Your Ears: Great Speeches in History,* Safire, William, editor, Norton, New York, 1997 (pp. 492-494).
Reagan, Ronald, "President Ronald Reagan foresees the crisis of communism," address on June 8, 1982 to British combined Houses of Parliament, *Lend Me Your Ears: Great Speeches in History,* Safire, William, editor, Norton, New York, 1997 (pp. 941-947).
Rooney, Andy, "Our darkest days are here," *60 Minutes,* CBS, May 23, 2004.
Wakefield, Julie, "Doom and gloom by 2100," *Scientific American,* July, 2004.
Gutterman, Steve, "Russians relish chance to trumpet WWII role," *Wisconsin State Journal,* May 8, 2005.
Zinn, Howard, *Declarations of Independence,* HarperCollins, New York, 1990 (see summary on p. 268 on communism and the Soviet Union).
Wilson, Edmund, *To The Finland Station,* Farrar, Strauss, and Giroux, New York, 1972 (originally published in 1940).
Heilbroner, Robert L., *The Limits of American Capitalism,* Harper and Row, New York, 1966 (see p. 127 on capitalism as an idea).
Boukreev, Anatoli, *Above the Clouds,* St. Martin's Press, New York, 2001 (see Introduction by Linda Wylie and especially pp. 49, 176-180).
Churchill, Winston, "Winston Churchill warns the West of the Soviet 'Iron Curtain,'" address on March 5, 1946, at Westminster College in Fulton, Missouri, *Lend Me Your Ears: Great Speeches in History,* Safire, William, editor, Norton, New York, 1997 (pp. 864-876; see p. 873 re iron curtain).
Heilbrunn, Jacob, "Winston Churchill, neocon?" *The New York Times Book Review,* February 27, 2005 (re greatness and interventionism).
Hunt, Terrance, "Bush waxes historical on Russia, Roosevelt and postwar Europe," *Wisconsin State Journal,* May 8, 2005 (re Yalta accord).
Kimball, Warren F., *Forged in War,* William Morrow and Company, New York, 1997 (see pp.285-287 on dividing Europe and Far Eastern settlement; pp. 332-333 on open vs. closed spheres; pp. 328-330 on atomic bomb).
Rhodes, Richard, *The Making of the Atomic Bomb,* Touchstone, New York, 1988 (pp. 522-538 re Bohr and Churchill; p. 521 re unconditional surrender).

Rothstein, Edward, "Contemplating Churchill," *Smithsonian,* March 2005 (see p. 96 re Churchill's plentiful ideas; p. 99 on British empire; p. 102 re optimism and decisions).
Jenkins, Roy, *Churchill,* Farrar, Straus and Giroux, New York, 2001 (see pp. 254-276 for Churchill and Gallipoli).
Grimes, William, "London in 1945," *Wisconsin State Journal,* May 8, 2005 (review of *London 1945* by Maureen Waller).
Waller, Maureen, *London 1945,* St. Martin's Press, New York, 2005.
Berry, Todd, "Social capital: missing link in the public school debate," *The Wisconsin Taxpayer,* October, 2002.
Doyle, Rodger, "Civic culture," *Scientific American,* June, 2004.
Beres, Louis Rene, "Have we sold our souls?" *Chicago Tribune,* October 13, 2002.
Silva, Mark, "A kinder, gentler style on display," *Chicago Tribune,* February 23, 2005 (re Bush's comment on Iran).
Hundley, Tom, "Bush to invade Mainz -- for a day," *Chicago Tribune,* February 23, 2005 (re Europe's view of Iran).
DeVoss, David, "Magic kingdom," *Smithsonian,* January 2003 (re Dubrovnik).

Coda: The violin in your closet...finding your path to the future

Konrad, Rachel, "Sleepless in Silicon Valley," *Wisconsin State Journal,* May 22, 2005 (re demands of globalization and growth of labor unions due to speedups in 1920s).
Keillor, Garrison, *The Writer's Almanac,* American Public Media, May 24, 2005.
Bradbury, Ray, "Bringing dreams to reality," *Research and Development,* September 28, 1992.
---, *The First Fifty Years: 1939-1989,* Nelson Industries, Inc., Stoughton, Wisconsin, 1989.
Zoroya, Gregg, "A day in the life of America's plainspoken man of peace," *USA Today,* October 14, 2002 (re Carter).
Rosin, Tori, "They traded badges for Bibles," *Wisconsin State Journal,* December 12, 2004 (re David Couper).
Davidson, Robyn, *Tracks,* Random House, New York, 1980.
Dunn, Bill, "It's time for Americans to support peace instead of war machine," *The Capital Times,* November 25, 2004 (excerpts of interview of Joan Chittister by Bill Moyers).

Appendix I - On strings, violins, and music

The music of the spheres

Hoyle, Fred, *Astronomy,* Crescent Books, New York, 1962.
Gordimer, Nadine, *July's People,* Viking Penguin, New York, 1981.
Hu, Wayne, and White, Martin, "The cosmic symphony," *Scientific American,* February, 2004.
Veneziano, Gabriele, "The myth of the beginning of time," *Scientific American,* May, 2004.
Whittle, Mark, "Big Bang acoustics: Sound in the early universe," *Echoes* (newsletter of the Acoustical Society of America), Fall, 2004 (see also www.astro.virginia.edu/~dmw8f).
Chang, Kenneth, "Vestiges of Big Bang waves are reported," *The New York Times,* January 12, 2005.
Overbye, Dennis, "Songs of the galaxies, and what they mean," *The New York Times,* August 3, 2004 (re tones from black holes).

The violin

Kruckenberg, Sven, *The Symphony Orchestra and Its Instruments,* Crescent Books, Outlet Book Company, Random House, Avenel, New Jersey, 1993.
Wechsberg, Joseph, *The Glory of the Violin,* Viking, New York, 1973.

Shepherd, Steven L., "The mysterious technology of the violin," *American Heritage of Invention and Technology,* Spring, 2000.
Faber, Toby, *Stradivari's Genius,* Random House, New York, 2004.
McKean, James N. (Scott, Heather K., ed.), *Violin Owner's Manual,* String Letter Publishing, San Anselmo, California, 2001.
Pinksterboer, Hugo, *The Rough Guide to Violin and Viola,* Rough Guides, London, 2000.
Benade, Arthur H., *Musical Acoustics,* Dover, New York, 1990.
Levenson, Thomas, *Measure for Measure,* Touchstone, New York, 1994.
Mason, Daniel, *The Piano Tuner,* Vintage, New York, 2002.
Hersey, John, *Antonietta,* Knopf, New York, 1991 (follows fictional life of one violin; see also the movie, *The Red Violin*).
Delbanco, Nicholas, *The Countess of Stanlein,* Verso, New York, 2001 (see pp. 54-57 on *Antonietta* and *The Red Violin*).
Weinberger, Norman, M., "Music and the brain," *Scientific American,* November, 2004.

Appendix II - Numbers and the 2004 presidential results

McChesney, Robert W., "On media and the election," *Free Press,* November 8, 2004 (www.freepress.net).
Cloud, John, "How the wedge issues cut," *Time,* October 25, 2004.
---, "The passions behind social issues," *Time,* October 25, 2004 (*Time* poll on value issues).
D'Arcy, Janice, "Values were key to Bush's election," *The Capital Times,* November 4, 2004.
Madigan, Charles M., "It was the war," *Chicago Tribune,* January 2, 2005.
Brownstein, Ronald, "GOP overwhelms Democrats in south: Analysis reveals erosion of party's former stronghold," *Chicago Tribune,* December 19, 2004.
---, "How Bush pulled it off," Time, November 15, 2004 (see pp. 40-41 for election graphics).
---, "Presidential results by state," *Chicago Tribune,* November 4, 2004 (election data).
---, "2004 in review: Trying times," *Wisconsin State Journal,* December 26, 2004 (re Bush's winning percentages in counties).
Harris, John F., and Muste, Christopher, "Majority now say war a mistake," *The Capital Times,* December 21, 2004.
Silva, Mark, "On the agenda: Bush ambitions, citizen concerns out of sync," *Chicago Tribune,* January 9, 2005.
Zuckman, Jill, "Bush finds Congress is no pushover," *Chicago Tribune,* May 30, 2005 (re decline in Bush's overall approval rating).
Lester, Will, "Bush ratings drop to new lows," *The Capital Times,* June 10, 2005 (AP-Ipsos poll).

♫ ♫ ♫

Index

ORDER FORM

Item	Price		Quantity		Total
Broken Strings, Missing Notes (ISBN 0-9721875-1-0, LCCN 2005905345, sewn softcover, 384 pages, 2005)	$16.95	X	_____	=	_______
Business Decisions (ISBN 0-9721875-0-2, LCCN 2002092680 sewn softcover, 224 pages, 2002)	$15.95	X	_____	=	_______
plus shipping (add $3.00/book)				=	_______
SUB-TOTAL				=	_______
plus sales tax (add 5.5% for Wisconsin orders)				=	_______
TOTAL AMOUNT DUE				=	_______

Name ____

Mailing address ______________________________________

City ____________________ State __________ZIP_________

Phone ___________________ Email ____________________

Please make check payable and mail to:

QUARTER SECTION PRESS
6105 Fairfax Lane
Madison, WI 53718-8262 U.S.A.

608.222.2689 erikssonresearch@execpc.com
www.execpc.com/~erikres www.madisonconsultants.com

Please contact QSP for information on quantity discounts.